NEOCON

NEOCONSERVATISM:

Why We Need It

DOUGLAS MURRAY

Encounter Books

NEW YORK

First edition published in 2006 by Encounter Books,
an activity of Encounter for Culture and Education, Inc.,
a nonprofit, tax exempt corporation.

Encounter Books website address: www.encounterbooks.com

Manufactured in the United States and printed on acid-free paper.
The paper used in this publication meets the minimum requirements of
ANSI/NISO Z39.48-1992 (R 1997) (Permanence of Paper).

FIRST EDITION

LIBRARY OF CONGRESS CATALOGING-IN-PUBLICATION DATA
Murray, Douglas
Neoconservatism: Why We Need It/Douglas Murray
    p.   cm.
ISBN 978-1-59403-147-2
1. Conservatism. 2. Conversatism—United States.
JC573.M87 2006
320.52—dc22
2006012783

10 9 8 7 6 5 4 3

CONTENTS

And so these men then bore themselves after a manner that befits our city;
but you who survive, though you may pray that it be with less hazard,
should resolve that you will have a spirit to meet the foe which is no whit
less courageous; and you must estimate the advantage of such a spirit not
alone by a speaker's words, for he could make a long story in telling you—
what you yourselves know as well as he—all the advantages
that are to be gained by warding off the foe.

PERICLES' FUNERAL ORATION

Thucydides, *Peloponnesian War*

BOOK II, XLIII, TRANS. C. F. SMITH

INTRODUCTION

T HE STATEMENT that "Neoconservatism's time is up," or has at least "passed," has become familiar of late. In the second term of George W. Bush's administration, the "demotion" of Paul Wolfowitz to head the World Bank, or the indictment of "Scooter" Libby have often been used to highlight such opinions. But neoconservatism has been here before—on a regular basis.

The statement is usually voiced not so much with evidence, as with hope. Neoconservatism has numerous enemies, many of whom are identified in this book. But neoconservatism is not a gang or a cabal. It is not a fraternity which sticks together (in fact, as has often been said, neoconservatives are perhaps more than usually likely to disagree with each other whenever two or three gather together). The non-cabal-ishness is part of the reason one can safely predict that neoconservatism will survive the present and any future set-backs which its opponents wish upon it.

Neoconservatism is not a political party, or social set, but a way of looking at the world. It is a deeply rooted and relevant philosophy which only seems to be out of kilter with modern thought because there is so little modern thought.

This book, therefore, is intended to explain honestly something which has often been portrayed dishonestly. Obviously, the ideas explained and defended in this book are ones which I hold true. My hope is that any open-minded reader who reads this book will finish it, if not in agreement, then at least no longer in the dark.

I also hope that, to however limited an extent, this book will encourage and embolden right-thinking American readers. Over the next few years, and certainly by the time of the next presidential election, it is likely that certain policies which neocons have argued for will be increasingly unpopular. That is hardly surprising: America and her allies are engaged in a long and complex war against an enemy who most citizens are fortunate enough not to see. Unfortunately, increasing numbers of people think that because they cannot see the enemy, it is not there. And of course as the toll of Allied combat casualties in Iraq continues to rise, there will emerge more and more people of all parties who look to offload responsibility for war onto a small, indistinct group. Such offloading may even come from those who were once at the forefront of agitation for action.

In his recent ship-jumping exercise, Francis Fukuyama intimated that "the charge will be made with increasing frequency that the Bush administration made a big mistake when it stirred the pot." There are many quibbles to be had with such sentiments, their belatedness being of perhaps least note. Such a claim presumes not only that the "pot" may not have needed stirring, but also that failing to stir the pot would have proved less costly than has stirring it. Fukuyama's belief that "American power and hegemony" aren't going to bring universal human rights, meanwhile, rather leads to the question "What will?"[1] The weak and often malignant powers which currently thrive under the cover of international arrangements show little will, and littler capability to confront the problems of our time. Though the burden of stirring the pot continues to rest with America and her allies, it does remain the only viable game in town, and the only recipe on offer which is not, in truth, inaction. We know that the push for democracy can end up with a party like Hamas in government, but there are ways to deal with that beyond arguing for suffrage to be removed or demeaned. For too many people, the difficult reality of democracy-spread has led them to the cheap mire of democracy-denigration.

The fact that flashes of personal apostasy rather than serious challenges to the neocon position remain the headline-grabbing norm reflects the levity with which many people still treat the current crisis. It is, however, nothing compared with the levity with which many are treating the next crisis. Over the coming years, America and her allies will have to confront a new state terror, even while continuing to mop up stateless terror. The decision over when to deal with Iran's nuclear intent cannot be ignored. If it is ignored, Tehran will get a nuclear bomb: inaction on this matter is, as so often, itself a form and mode of action. Because of the failure to find stockpiles of WMD in Iraq (which by no means undermines the necessity, indeed inevitability, of the Iraq conflict), some commentators and politicians believe neoconservatives cried wolf in that instance. Now the same figures claim the threat emerging from Iran to be just another neoconservative cry of "wolf." Such claims are at best blind and at worst wickedly irresponsible. One sometimes gets the impression that certain people would, nevertheless, like to be proved wrong on this matter precisely so that they can say, "You see what happens." This is in part just a reflection of the descent of politics in the West into petty animosities, a descent which is, sadly, particularly visible in America. But it is a descent which is not only odious, but dangerous. After all, at the end of the story of the boy who cried wolf, there really was a wolf.

The decline of standards in the debate at home now have a practical impact on America's standing abroad, and this is why the causes for which we fight abroad must be fought for just as fervently at home. The origins of these standards lie largely in the philosophy of conservatism, but much of the problem lies in conservatism's recent inability to meet the challenge it has faced. It is my belief that the solution to many, if not all, of our problems lies in neoconservatism—not just because it provides an optimistic and emboldened conservatism, but because neoconservatism provides a conservatism that is specifically attuned, and attractive, to people today.

Conservatism has been for a long time characterized, with some justification, as a force of reaction. It has often seemed not just backward-looking and nostalgic, but unattractive. This unattractive brand of conservatism has both kept conservatism alive and reduced the power of the body as a whole. Conservatism is certainly, in part, about conserving that which is good—preserving the virtues of the past for the future. But it is not, and cannot be, about believing the past to be inevitably superior or desirable. Besides, in this age, with so much changed, what exactly is it that a conservative would wish to conserve?

One of the central dilemmas of conservatism has always centered around the paradox expressed by Giuseppe di Lampedusa in the great conservative novel of the last century, *The Leopard*. "If we want things to stay as they are," Tancredi says to the prince, his uncle, "things will have to change."[2] The reason conservatism is not archaism is because it has always adapted to change. But for conservatives Tancredi's aphorism points down a two-pronged track: one path leads to conservative survival, the other tricks conservatism towards disaster. The crucial thing is to know when you have gone down the wrong path, to realize when you have conceded so much that almost nothing is the same. For many people, this moment of realization is hard or impossible to identify. How can you know whether you are being propelled into something good, or fooled into losing everything? How, most crucially, do you identify the moment when there has been so much change that nothing is the same? And how, if you realize this, do you muster the force to jump paths?

Since the great changes of the Sixties, conservatism has too often taken the wrong path. It has fought long and hard against matters of individual freedom, while too often tying up the public in ever greater levels of state interference. This mixing-up of conservative priorities has often left America's conservatives seeming like people who only look to—or only like—the past. There are aspects of the past which one should certainly look to with longing, but there are also a good many things which it is good to have dropped. The public at large knows enough to feel satisfied that vast swathes of what has been left behind in the last century has been left behind for the good, and conservatives should join them.

But, simultaneously, many changes in American society have had deleterious effects. These are the effects which now most visibly permeate our popular culture and (if there is today any noticeable difference between the two) our culture. The primary reason why the bad effects have been so hard to resist comes down to a philosophical problem. Relativism (including its institutionalized version, political correctness) has left many instinctive conservatives baffled and unprotected. It appears that despite—or perhaps because of—its often innate nature, conservatism was not armed to see off the acrobatics of relativism.

With relativism rampant, and without the armor to see it off, conservatives have been placed in a uniquely unenviable position. Either they must hark back to that which is lost (a position often characterized as "paleoconservatism"), berating with increasing bitterness and in decreasing numbers the slide away from tradition, or they must follow the road of allegedly inevitable socialist "progress," complete with ever-increasing state interference. In this latter situation, they will find themselves defending a status quo that is not their status quo. In other words, they may find themselves defending an unconservative status quo out of something like habit. While the former of these two positions is characterized as predominant by those who hate conservatism, it is, in fact, the latter position which is infinitely more common, with conservatives remaining loyal to institutions and concepts which continually shift and let them down.

In this situation, however, conservatives do have another option: to do it they must do something that is profoundly unconservative. Because the status quo has changed, because the status quo is no longer conservative, conservatives must seek to change the status quo. In so doing they must become new conservatives, radical conservatives—revolutionary conservatives. They should become neoconservatives.

But the door is open to all, not just conservatives. In recent

Introduction

years, a number of prominent politicians and thinkers of the old left have migrated towards neoconservative positions. Such a migration is—as the ensuing chapter will show—very much in the tradition of neoconservatism. Throughout this book I make many attacks on the left-wing view of the world, but other than in those cases where genuine evil intent is displayed, I do not believe left-wingers mean especially ill: often they are very nice people, albeit nice people with strange ideas. There is no reason why, when the realities of the world "mug" them, they should not realize that you can still be a nice person and treat the world as it is. While certainly more liberal in the classical sense of the term, than most conservatives, neoconservatives are also more than usually likely to look at the world with a realpolitik honesty. Though classically liberal-minded, neoconservatives look at the world through realist spectacles, seeing the world as it is, but all the time acting in the world to fashion it as we would like it to be.

*   *   *

Having leapt to public prominence in the lead-up to the 2003 Iraq war, the word "neocon" is now firmly embedded in our language, or at least in our lexicon of political insults. The word is often taken as a synonym for "hawk." Indeed, "neocon" has become a popular catch-all word to identify anything tough or seemingly sinister that emanates from Washington.

That there's a taste for the insult can be seen not only from the anti-war lobby, but across the range of Western media and politics. For the "anti-war" crowd and many on the "left," the term "neocon" now rivals "fascist" as an all-purpose form of abuse. For traditional conservatives, meanwhile, neocons are often treated with either caution or open hostility. Both sides meet in holding neocons guilty not only of war-mongering, but of many associated ambitions, the dark nature of which can often only be hinted at by innuendo. All think they know what they mean when they summon the specter.

Yet ask someone who slings the term around, "What is a neocon?," and you are almost guaranteed an answer that is either thoughtlessly derogatory ("a neocon is a hawk," and so on) or simply startling. As David Brooks noted in 2004, "If you ever read a sentence that starts with 'Neocons believe,' there is a 99.44 percent chance everything else in that sentence will be untrue."[3] Rarely has a term been thrown around so wildly while its meaning remains so popularly elusive.

But it is not just the American public who assume knowledge of neoconservatism while failing to begin to grasp the concept—America's media and politicians have also often failed to engage the issue, too often satisfying themselves with fanciful clichés and grotesque simplifications. This fact can only partly be blamed on the increasing infantilism of American politics and political comment. A more pervasive reason is the fear that often exists today of the grand idea, and a special and perpetual fear—accentuated thanks to political correctness—of rocking the boat. When I say "the grand idea," I do not mean it in the hyperbolic sense used by government when revealing an indiscernible alteration in their healthcare reforms. I mean the kind of big idea that gets people not just voting, but actually proselytizing politics.

There are times when even the most alert citizen can come to the conclusion that there is no particular point in voting at a given election. Many millions of people feel this way semipermanently. Many of these are partly right in thinking that their vote won't make a difference because they sense that there is no big difference left to make—too little, not too much, is at stake. The big ideas often seem either to have been accomplished or else appear tainted beyond use. One might feel justified in such circumstances in declaring America a post-historical state: the grand battles won, with only skirmishes remaining.

But this is not the case—and we should be alert to that fact. When politicians restrict themselves to discussing the small issues, the big issues have a tendency to come creeping silently back. In the wake of the terrorist assaults on America of 2 0 0 1, and the conflicts that have resulted from those assaults, large questions that had long lain dormant surfaced again.

For instance, in the wake of 9/1 1, the presumed consensus on multiculturalism seemed open to question again as it had not been for years. Many eminent people (notably Samuel Huntington in *Who Are We?*) wrote and thought long and hard about what it is that makes America the country it is, and what might make it become something different. The re-deployment of American troops to far-off countries reopened questions thought by some to be long-closed: questions of what America's role in the world should be, and what its duties—if it has any—actually entail. Think-tanks, occasional newspaper columnists and even political representatives, have in the last few years finally been able to raise concerns that they had long had to keep silent on. Questions not of policy detail, but of fundamentals, stood waiting for answers.

It is my contention throughout this book that neoconservatism provides answers to many of the problems facing America and the world today. On all these matters, not just the war on terror, I am aware that not everyone sees that these problems even exist. Among other things, there is always the easy expedient of avoiding a threat by pretending that it is not there. And it is no wonder that for many people, whipped along as they are by the profitable demagoguery of Michael Moore or the BBC's flippant and false show *The Power of Nightmares*, there is *no* continuing terrorist threat, nor any problems of failing states, unstopped genocides, hostile dictatorships or W M D proliferation. With malignant equivalencing abundant, it is no surprise that even the protection of America and her allies in the face of growing W M D threats (in particular those from Iran) is often reduced—when it does arise—to sniggering allegations and satire without humor.

But equally, there are many people who, while they agree on the nature of the threats before us, will not agree with the answers I put forward. If that is the case, then opponents of the neoconservative approach must come up with answers of their own. I say this not as a hollow challenge or taunt, but because of a genuine concern. We must continue to ask—and argue—the big questions, not only because we need answers to current predicaments, but because, if we do not pre-empt the argument and if the big questions are not out in the open, the consensus all too innocently leaves the door open for true extremism. In a free society, nothing should be incapable of being said: the scandal in a society as free as America's is that so much is not even being asked.

From the point of view of neoconservatism, I believe that opponents of its thought will have to meet its arguments head-on at some point. It is a task neoconservatism's opponents have so far failed to even begin, which is why they have instead concentrated on smear, character assassination, and invention to make their points. But the questions which neoconservatism raises, and the answers it suggests, cannot continue to be evaded. In particular they cannot any longer be evaded by pretending, quite simply, that the questions are other than they are. In America, neoconservatism has won whatever audience and influence it has through the simple, honest power and attractiveness of its arguments. I take it as a truth throughout this short book that the receptiveness of the American public to neoconservatism can only grow the freer the public are to understand it as it actually is.

It is, however, worth pausing briefly to deal with a problem in defining not just neoconservatism, but any political belief today. I say this not in order, as a certain philosopher has said, "to become confused by the 'blind scholastic pedantry' that exhausts itself and its audience in the 'clarification of meanings' so that it never meets the nonverbal issues."[4] Whatever else I am accused of in this book, I hope I will not be accused of the obfuscation to which Leo Strauss referred. I raise the issue of broader political definitions because in order to define new creeds one must have some stability in referring to old ones. In this regard we are all in something of a mess at the moment.

To describe something as "right-wing" today is often either to be abusive (when speaking of others) or antagonistically boastful (when talking of oneself). As a British writer put it in 2005, "What is the meaning of 'He is to the right of Attila the Hun'? Was Attila right-wing because he was violent and cruel?"[5] Sadly, the answer commonly given to this question is "Yes." And when not being used to define a propensity to genocidal violence, "right-wing" is too often used simply to denote racism. Ask a political activist who bandies the term "right-wing" around whether one can be racist and a man of the left, and you will either be told "no" or be blessed with a period of silence. Put another way, and as the maker of the Attila point went on, "Lenin was more violent and cruel [than Attila]. Is Lenin to the right of Attila the Hun?" Because of these and similar demonstrations of the term's pitfalls, I shall avoid, wherever possible, referring to the "right."

Concomitantly, I shall try to avoid using the term "left-wing"—a description which, though also carrying pejorative overtones, possesses none that proceed far beyond an implication of woolliness or, at worst, peace-loving idealism. Considering that the idealism of the "left" led in the last century to both Stalinism and National Socialism, the term has got off amazingly and incomparably lightly. Though this is frustrating, it is too prevalent an historical offense to dismantle in a short book on a different subject.

In the end, I believe that the clearest and most basic distinction that can be made in politics today is between those who believe in large amounts of state control and those who believe in as little state control as possible. We would probably be closest to the right path if we could start referring to the former as "socialists," and the latter as "liberals."

But we live in confusing times, and the word "liberal" is now nearly as polluted as "right-wing." In America "liberal" is the term used to describe what people in Britain would call "socialists." They are those with the greatest propensity towards believing the state could make everyone happy if only it was given enough clout to do so. T. S. Eliot described such people in 1 9 3 4, when he wrote of those who spend their days "dream-

ing of systems so perfect that no one will need to be good."[6]
And of course, the matter is not helped by the now omni-
present tendency of conservatives, or those proudly opposed
to the "left," to sneer at "liberals" without using inverted commas. The ironic air quotation marks which should rightly sur-
round any such use of the word "liberal" have long ago been
dropped. It is a problematic and saddening abuse of a great
word. While it may be true that people often intend inverted
commas when they refer to meddlers in their affairs and woolly
thinkers, the result of neglecting to spell out this punctuational detail is that the badge of liberalism has been appropri-
ated, by a group of people with the least right to wear it.

I will, therefore, attempt throughout to use the term "socialist" to describe those people broadly understood as left wing
(or, if you must, "liberal") and "conservative" for those broadly
characterized as "right-wing." I trust that spelling this out at this
stage will save confusion later on, eventually proving head-
clearing rather than head-muddling. In any case I hope that no
reader will now misunderstand the great and noble sense in
which Strauss and others referred to "liberal education." In
particular I hope people will understand that his usage bore
nothing in common with the conglomeration of pseudery,
grudgery and pathological ignorance mistaken as a liberal education on so many campuses today.

The word "conservatism" itself opens up a can of worms,
but I hope that the sense in which I understand and use the
notion becomes clear throughout the ensuing chapters. There
too is a word which has rarely travelled easily, and almost never
with light baggage.

Finally I should clarify what I mean when I refer in this

book to the "West," and "Westerners." I use the term to refer to all those whose cultural heritage comes from that wondrous synthesis of Judeo-Christian religion and Hellenic philosophy. Under this tent I include not only America, Europe, and Australia, but also the State of Israel. Some people will dislike the use of this designation, but I see no better or more appropriate term. Furthermore, it is helpful in order to highlight a central concern of this book, which is that what happens in one corner of the West can perfectly easily happen in another. Thus when I refer to a degradation being suffered today by Europeans or others, I mean American readers to understand that this is a degradation to which they too could be prone, that such examples remind Americans of what they must remain alert to.

As regards the most important definition in this book, it should be stressed from the outset that neoconservatism is not simply "New Conservatism." It is not merely an attempt to reinvigorate conservatism or the natural parties of conservatism, however happy an outcome though that would be. Neoconservatism is a particular creed, and one that I hope will eventually expand the base of conservatism, not only revive the base it already has. There has become an obsession in American politics of late with spin—the branding and rebranding of parties and policies. The effect this has had has often been to turn public off an issue, even an issue of grave importance. The PR approach to politics is, I believe, a mistaken one. Government must present its policies to the people clearly, without playing a perpetual PR game. Once a political party or administration gets involved in spin and counter-spin, the only way out they seem to see is to spin better or more than the other side.

Introduction

Neoconservatism is not about PR. If it were, it should have done a better job of its public image. But the antidote to spin is not more spin, or better spin: the answer to spin is the truth.

Neoconservatism is a philosophy for dealing with the world, a way of looking at the world. It can provide the philosophical and practical solutions to many mature Western political parties, for it provides the moral and practical answers to many aspects of politics, not just conservative politics.

Today, we know that what happens on the other side of the world cannot be divorced from us. A problem on the other side of the globe can easily become our problem, and have an impact on the very streets of our cities. In this world of speeded-up action and reaction, challenges old and new face conservatives, and they must sustain and adapt their principles in the face of this change. To that extent this book argues that in order to adapt to new problems inside and outside our borders there should indeed be a new conservatism, and that the new and revived conservatism should be neoconservatism.

ONE

NEOCONSERVATISM
IN THEORY

F OR THOSE WHO use the terms as insults, "neoconservatism" and "neocons" are merely synonyms for sinister
extremism. For those who are equally aggrieved, hold the
same attitude, but have tried delving deeper, the movement's
intellectual lineage is alternately simplistic and confusing. In
fact, neoconservatism's genesis and progress *is* both simple
and confusing. Neoconservatism does not have a manifesto,
and nor are there any but the broadest tenets on which neocons
could be said to agree. Even if they do agree on certain topics,
there is no guarantee that this makes them neocons. And even
if they are neocons, they may not think of themselves as such,
or thank you for using the N-word to describe them. Neoconservatism is a broad church, embracing many points of view
and directions of thought. And, since it is a type of thought
and not a club or cult, establishing a lineage, never mind for-
mulating a definition, is not a task with obvious beginnings,
middles or ends. Any attempt to pin the matter down, particu-

larly in so short a book, will inevitably lead to some important names being passed over, and others being given idiosyncratic prominence. But in seeking to portray a way of seeing the world, the best one may hope to achieve is a kind of sensory introduction to, or acquaintance with, one of the most misunderstood "isms" of our time.

In the widely disseminated version of events, neoconservatism began in the post-war years, with the philosopher Leo Strauss indoctrinating his students at the University of Chicago. They were then sent out to indoctrinate a further generation of followers, and in this way Strauss's students were able—within a generation—to launch pre-emptive wars against countries of their choosing. Although this calumny is untrue, it does bear *some* relation to reality. Neoconservatism's origins can be traced, if not exclusively to Leo Strauss, then certainly to the period in which he was at his peak. And so Strauss is a useful and necessary point of entry for any investigation of neoconservatism.

But for all the focus he has received in the world press over recent years, anyone reading through Strauss to find reasons for the British and American-led attack on Iraq in 2003 is likely to be baffled and disappointed. Strauss's oeuvre is no invader's handbook.

The Strauss fixation

The present prominent status accorded to Leo Strauss in the States had a suitably shady kick-off. Joshua Muravchik is among those to notice that "the prize for the recent resuscitation of Strauss's name would seem to belong to the crackpot political agitator Lyndon LaRouche."[1] Not entirely coincidentally, LaRouche (a perennial presidential candidate and felon) leads the American field in anti-semitic conspiracy theory. Although he had been making speeches and writing on the matter for some months, it was in March 2003 that LaRouche wrote at greatest length about Strauss, describing him as a "fascist," and cack-handedly talking of his " 'genetically' Nazi-like ideology."[2] *Children of Satan: The Ignoble Liars Behind Bush's No Exit War* was distributed across America throughout 2003 by the "LaRouche 2004" campaign team. In his contribution to this joint work, one Jeffrey Steinberg added that "this cabal of Strauss disciples, along with an equally small circle of allied neo-conservative and Likudnik fellow-travellers" had been waiting thirty years for "the moment of opportunity to launch their not-so-silent coup."[3] All the soon-to-be-popular, or populist, ingredients were there.

By 16 May, Steinberg was boasting in LaRouche's absurdly titled *Executive Intelligence Review* that the LaRouche attack had "drawn blood":

> Just weeks after the LaRouche in 2004 campaign began nationwide circulation of 400,000 copies of the *Children of Satan* dossier, exposing the role of University of Chicago fascist "philosopher" Leo Strauss as the godfather of the neo-conservative war party in and around the Bush Administration, two major establishment publications have joined in the exposé.

The two articles cited (rightly or wrongly) by the author were a piece by James Atlas in *The New York Times* of May 4 (accompanied by a crude caricature of Paul Wolfowitz) and a May 12 *New Yorker* piece by Seymour Hersh. The two articles contained all the hallmarks of conspiracy-theory reportage. Atlas (the author of a biography of Saul Bellow) wrote breathlessly that the Deputy Defense Secretary Paul Wolfowitz "has been identified as a disciple of Strauss," while Hersh revealed that Abram Shulsky, Director of the Pentagon's Office of Special Plans, was not only "a scholarly expert in the works of the political philosopher Leo Strauss," but furthermore, "like Wolfowitz, he was a student of Leo Strauss's, at the University of Chicago." That any or all of this information could have been obtained from an alumnus list did not make the discoveries any less thrilling.

What was definitely less thrilling, and certainly more worrying, was that two of America's premier papers were publishing stories that bore traces suggesting they had been picked up from a document disseminated by LaRouche. It would be a worrying sign indeed if two of America's finest "liberal" papers were finding common cause with a man like that. As Robert Bartley summed it up in *The Wall Street Journal*, "Looking at the striking similarities in these accounts the conspiracy-minded might conclude that *The New York Times* and *The New Yorker* have been reduced to recycling the insights of Lyndon LaRouche. But it's entirely possible that Mr. Atlas and Mr. Hersh have stumbled into the fever swamps all on their own."[4] Encouraged, stumbled or pushed, where the New York papers went the rest followed.

The game of hunt-the-Straussian ran across the entire spectrum of print and news media. Everyone seemed to be asking, as *Foreign Policy in Focus* had it: "Is U.S. foreign policy being run by followers of an obscure German Jewish political philoso-

pher whose views were elitist, amoral, and hostile to democratic government?"[5] For people who had seemingly never
read a word of his writings, Leo Strauss posthumously provided an additional target for the ever cruder anger of those
opposed to the direction of US foreign policy.[6] With Strauss
long dead, it was up to his pupils to absorb the wilder anger of
the anti-neocon lobby. And for those on attacking, rather than
debating, the neoconservative position, sinister motives would
be attributed to almost anyone who had neared Chicago during Strauss's years as a professor there. No one was free from
the taint—unless, of course, like the late Susan Sontag, you
had been a pupil of Strauss, but somehow avoided being nudg-
ingly vilified as "a pupil of Strauss."

Unable to identify quite what was going on, but convinced
there was something afoot, the mainstream press in Britain and
other allied countries also took up the name of Strauss as a by-
word for political nastiness. In January 2004 a column malign-
ing Prime Minister Blair in London's *Daily Telegraph* sneered,
"Perhaps, like Paul Wolfowitz and other neo-conservatives, he
[Blair] is a disciple of the political philosopher Leo Strauss,"
before going on to explain: "Strauss was a champion of the
'noble lie'"—the idea that it is practically a duty to lie to the
masses because only a small elite is intellectually fit to know
the truth."[7] Misinformed Straussian summaries of this kind
became commonplace across the media, culminating in the
BBC's 2004 exercise in immoral equivalencing, *The Power of
Nightmares*. This was the atmosphere surrounding the Iraq war
—a time when conspiracies became commonplace and quacks
became sources. But before any of them had arrived on the

scene, there was already one writer—Shadia Drury—who had attempted to dissect Strauss's teachings, and had done so with notable successes, or at least converts, of her own.

In February 2002, the year before LaRouche's splenetically confused attack the British journalist Will Hutton briefly mentioned Strauss in his *Observer* column, as well as referring in passing (in a new book) to his allegedly "lethal legacy."[8] In the *Observer*, Hutton had launched the wild claim that American conservatives were following Strauss's teachings by uniting "patriotism, unilateralism, the celebration of inequality and the right of a moral élite to rule into a single unifying ideology."[9] By the end of the year, Hutton was describing Strauss as "the high priest of ultra conservatism," and claiming that his American followers intended to use Republican success in the 2002 mid-term elections to penalise and punish the poor and outlaw abortion, a fantasist agenda presented by Hutton as "the most fiercely reactionary programme to have emerged in any Western democracy since the war."[10]

Anyone wondering what had inspired Hutton in these early populist British attempts to grapple with Strauss needed to look no further than his February, *Observer* article. Before revealing that "Paul Wolfowitz . . . is a Straussian," Hutton had written, "As Professor Shadia Drury describes in *Leo Strauss and the American Right*. . . ."[11] It was clear from what followed in that article, as well as his other *Observer* article, that Hutton's understanding of Strauss had certainly been influenced by, if not come wholesale from, Shadia Drury.

Drury is today the most consistently outspoken attacker of Leo Strauss. Currently professor of political theory at the University of Regina in Saskatchewan, her 1998 book *Leo Strauss*

and the American Right had become, post 9/11, a ready-made
guide for Bush-administration critics intent on defaming neoconservatism's most prominent intellectual forebear. The vice-
president of the Hudson Institute, Kenneth Weinstein, is just
one of those who have identified Drury's book as the work
"paraphrased" by LaRouche for his own peculiar screed.[12] It is
no coincidence that the book's misreadings and contradictions
recur in nearly all of the less informed attacks on Strauss.

In the wake of *The New York Times* piece in May 2003, *The
Boston Globe* picked up and stretched the idea *du jour* with a
3,000 word article by Jeet Heer claiming that "we live in a
world increasingly shaped by Leo Strauss," and concluding
that Strauss was a "disguised Machiavelli, a cynical teacher
who encouraged his followers to believe that their intellectual
superiority entitles them to rule over the bulk of humanity by
means of duplicity."[13] *The International Herald Tribune* followed
the Hersh *New Yorker* piece with an article by William Pfaff, in
which he claimed that Strauss teaches that "it has been necessary to tell lies to people about the nature of political reality."
He went on to explain, "An elite recognizes the truth, however,
and keeps it to itself."[14] This is the line that every other hostile
article on Strauss and neoconservatism both inside and outside
the US ran with. In reality, of course, the claim is not just debatable, but wrong. And, as Muravchik was to point out, "neither
Heer nor Pfaff offers a clue as to where in Strauss's corpus one
might find these ideas." We are left, he correctly concludes,
with the impression "that they learned what they know of him
from a polemical book by one Shadia Drury, who holds a chair
in 'social justice' at a Canadian university and who finds Strauss
to be a 'profoundly tribal and fascistic thinker.'"[15]

Neoconservatism

Just as Hersh, Atlas and co. seem to have learnt what they know of Strauss from Drury, so Drury—in a September 2003 article—subsequently used their articles as evidence to support her own contentions. This Drury self-referencing echo chamber allowed her to stretch her earlier conclusions to their inevitable non-scholarly ends. "The trouble with the Straussians is that they are compulsive liars," she wrote in the September 2003 article, going on to compile an imaginative scare-list of the neoconservative "agenda," and concluding, "It is ironic that American neoconservatives have decided to conquer the world in the name of liberty and democracy, when they have so little regard for either."[16]

With any due respect, it should be admitted that Drury's first book on Strauss (*The Political Ideas of Leo Strauss*, 1988) is a useful work, containing interesting and debatable points. Her later book, however—the one that has functioned as a crib sheet for writers from LaRouche to the mainstream newspapers —is a deeply flawed and partisan work, correctly identified by one writer who was a pupil of Strauss as "a snide, careless and inaccurate piece of liberal boilerplate."[17] Whether or not Drury has, as some have it, made it "her life's work"[18] to attack Strauss, she has certainly made a career out of it. Her central accusations are not new, but rather build on older allegations against Strauss, allegations often made by Strauss's contemporaries and rivals, and all of them intent on portraying Strauss as an implacable opponent of American democracy.

In some cases, the misunderstandings of Strauss's writings can be put down to ignorance, in other cases to opportunistic mendacity. But since both groups misrepresent Strauss, it is worth attempting to describe who Strauss was, what impact he had, and why some of that impact can still be felt.

Leo Strauss

Born in the Hessen region of Germany in 1 8 9 9, Strauss was the son of a Jewish small businessman. He received his doctorate at the University of Hamburg in 1 9 2 1, and went on to study with Edmund Husserl and Martin Heidegger postdoctorally. Publishing in various journals throughout the Twenties, his first book, on Spinoza's critique of religion (*Die Religionskritik Spinozas als Grundlage seiner Bibelwissenschaft*) was published in Berlin in 1 9 3 1.

Strauss married in France in 1 9 3 2 and moved to England in 1 9 3 4, where the following year he took a post at Cambridge University. In 1 9 3 7 he moved to New York City, becoming a research fellow in history at Columbia University before moving to the New School. Having left Nazi Germany behind for good, Strauss became an American citizen in 1 9 4 4. In 1 9 4 9 he became professor of political philosophy at the University of Chicago, a post he held for nearly twenty years. It was around this period that his great works were written: *On Tyranny* (1 9 4 8), *Natural Right and History* (1 9 5 3), *Thoughts on Machiavelli* (1 9 5 8), *The City and Man* (1 9 6 4) and *Liberalism Ancient and Modern* (1 9 6 8). From 1 9 6 8 until his death in 1 9 7 3, he taught in California and Maryland, and completed *The Argument and the Action of Plato's Laws* (1 9 7 5).

From this cursory overview of Strauss's career there are perhaps only two things that would stand out to anybody. First, Strauss was an émigré to the United States from Nazi

Germany; second, his area of expertise was classical political philosophy. When taken together, these two facts carry some of the most basic explanations for Strauss's current position of political controversy. The first led, and leads still, to Strauss being considered an outsider. The second either baffles people or sparks instinctive hostility: in the present reductive age, expertise on the classics is characterized as obscurantist or anti-democracratic, while either expertise on, or the merest interest in, Machiavelli is definite evidence of something sinister.

In fact, little of Strauss's impact can be understood from the bare essentials of his life. To begin to understand why he is credited with the influence he has, one must glean from his followers—to those who credit him with their intellectual awakening—something of his essence.

Straussianism

In a 2003 interview, Paul Wolfowitz poured scorn on the rumor that US foreign policy was somehow being dictated by the dead Leo Strauss. "It's a product of fevered minds," he said, "who seem incapable of understanding that September 11th changed a lot of things and changed the way we need to approach the world. Since they refused to confront that, they looked for some kind of conspiracy theory to explain it." Wolfowitz's main point is absolutely right, but it was worth highlighting—as he went on to do—why the *New York Times* caricature of him as Leo Strauss's warrior on earth was flawed. "I mean I took two terrific courses from Leo Strauss as a graduate student," he explained. "One was on Montesquieu's *Spirit of the Laws*, which did help me understand our Constitution better. And one was on Plato's *Laws*. The idea that this has anything to do with U.S. foreign policy is just laughable."[18]

Wolfowitz puts his finger on one of the central confusions of neoconservatism. Many people who are neoconservatives today never encountered Leo Strauss. Among second- and third-generation neoconservatives, it has correctly been said that "few read him today."[20] But Strauss certainly had a great impact on certain thinkers who encountered him—in print and in person—during his lifetime, influencing them in differing, broad, and complex ways.

One of Strauss's most ardent pupils, and one who freely calls himself a "Straussian" is Werner J. Dannhauser. Dannhauser was at Chicago at the same time as perhaps the purest Straussian of them all, Allan Bloom. In 2003 Dannhauser wrote that "it is important to remember, though easy to forget, that he [Strauss] was not the sinister godfather of the Right, nor the pied piper of so-called conservative values."[21] His influence on Dannhauser, Bloom, and many others was quite different, and the star-struck feeling for him is still evident, even today. "Leo Strauss was like a sun around which we thought ourselves privileged to orbit,"[22] Dannhauser recollected. "He was the center of our intellectual and even our moral universe."[23]

The actual father of neoconservatism (as opposed to its suspected godfather)—Irving Kristol—recalls, on first encountering it, that "Strauss's work produced the kind of intellectual shock that is a once-in-a-lifetime experience. He turned one's intellectual universe upside down."[24] But what did that shock consist of? And how did it turn listeners' and readers' minds so completely? The answer begins with an anecdote related by a reluctant Straussian descendant, Anne Norton.

Neoconservatism

Strauss firmly believed that fifth-century Athenian philosophy was capable of assisting—in a practical way—contemporary American democracy. Inevitably, this celebration of ancient thought was paralleled at times by just criticism and condemnation of "The Moderns" and modernity. On occasion Strauss was felt by some to lay this criticism on rather too thick. "But Mr. Strauss," a student asked on one such occasion, "Aren't *we* Moderns?" "Yes," Strauss replied, "but we are not *merely* Moderns."[25]

Strauss's way of looking at the world, and his way of approaching great texts, had a starting point at the opposite end from the modern scholarly norm. His devotion to the text being absolute, his first intention was to attempt to think of it not as a twentieth-century man, but as the thinker himself thought of it, and, furthermore, to understand the thinker as the thinker understood himself. Far from what Strauss's critics claim—that he somehow attempted to limit or reign in his students' thinking, to make them surrender their intellect—from this simple initial process Strauss (as more than one student has testified) sought to awaken the critical instincts of his pupils. "We were not asked to abandon ourselves, but to fulfill ourselves by contact with texts written by minds greater than ours," wrote Dannhauser.[26]

Strauss believed that study of the great ancient philosophical texts was now—and always had been—the principal path to spiritual liberation. But he recognized a problem. Something in the modern age was resistant to the intellectual claims and intellectual revelation of the past. Certain modern philosophical presumptions and deeply questionable assumptions had begun clouding contemporary philosophers' attempts to understand great thinkers of the past. Since we are, by extension and as a result, unwilling to understand the past in its proper manner, Strauss saw that we fast become unable to understand ourselves. Some Straussians have put it more forcefully. Thomas L. Pangle summarized Strauss's attitude by writing that it is as a consequence of its perverse manner of approaching the past that "ours is also an age of spiritual disintegration and intellectual crisis or decay." [27]

But as I mentioned above, the power of Strauss's approach tends to dawn only gradually on the reader. This is true even of Strauss's most provocatively titled books—*On Tyranny*, for example. This—one of Strauss's most accessible works—consists of a superlative commentary on Xenophon's *Hiero* or *Tyrannicus*, a dialogue on the nature of tyrants. From the very outset Strauss maintains that in his own time, "when we were brought face to face with tyranny—with a kind of tyranny that surpassed the boldest imagination of the most powerful thinkers of the past—our political science failed to recognize it." This is one of the clearest allusions in all his published work to the early lessons observed by the philosopher in Weimar Germany. "It is not surprising then," Strauss went on, "that many of our contemporaries, disappointed or repelled by present-day analyses of present-day tyranny, were relieved when they rediscovered the pages in which Plato and other classical thinkers seemed to have interpreted for us the horrors of the twentieth century." [28] Here is a scholarly breath of fresh air, even now, and one whose significance in the academy of Strauss's day cannot be exaggerated. Here is not the modern thinker condescending to interpret the past, but Plato and his contemporaries interpreting us.

Neoconservatism

"Suddenly, one realized that one had been looking at the history of Western political thought through the wrong end of the telescope," wrote Irving Kristol. "Instead of our looking down at them from the high vantage point of our more 'advanced' era, he [Strauss] trained his students to look at modernity through the eyes of the 'ancients' and the pre-moderns, accepting the premise that they were wiser and more insightful than we are."[29] Though perfect common sense to some, the notion that Plato (for instance) was in crucial senses wiser than us discomfits many academics and others for numerous reasons, and not just because it pricks their intellectual arrogance. Critics of the position could, exceedingly coarsely, be divided into two groups. For those of a theistic mindset, Strauss's approach can appear (albeit falsely) to subvert the significance of the position of revealed religion; while for those of an atheistic standpoint, more inclined towards non-theistic theories of historical "progress," Strauss might appear to be negating the much-cherished but little-explained consensus on species betterment. Of the two positions, the latter camp of Strauss critics is by far the more virulent and, naturally, religiously obsessive. That the arrogance needs pricking, even were the approach wrong, was demonstrated with perfect idiocy by Shadia Drury in 2003, when she asserted that "The idea that Strauss was a great defender of liberal democracy is laughable." This accusation was justified with comprehensive incomprehension when she went on to ask: "How could an admirer of Plato and Nietzsche be a liberal democrat?"[30]

But it is not simply Strauss's approach to ancient texts that made his work controversial. On delving into his major works, what becomes clear is that this opening approach is not a scholar's one-off trick. What perplexes many when they first attempt Strauss is that the entire approach seems to continue in a similar vein. Throughout his writing, none of the land on which we "Moderns" believe we safely stand holds fast. Countless presumptions of the modern age are held up to scrutiny and found wanting, or cast aside as unneeded and unhelpful devices. What is more significant is that Strauss clearly believes that, by losing these fundamental presumptions of our situation, we have lost our connection with something far more important—our own souls.

Though this becomes clear from even his simplest texts and commentaries, Strauss never states such a contention explicitly in the manner of a polemicist. It comes across thoroughly, but, to begin with—to the first-time reader—somewhat obliquely. It is in this way, as Pangle observed, that "the initially historical or even pedantic appearance of Strauss's writing reveals itself on closer inspection to be the sign of Strauss's painfully incisive critical stance towards almost every major feature of the contemporary intellectual and political landscape."[31] The small signs, the apparent scholarly idiosyncrasies, reveal beneath their surface a vast and profound feeling of questioning unease about the way in which western society is conducting itself, the direction in which it might be drifting, and the forceless-ness with which it is defending itself. A philosopher himself, it was in philosophy that Strauss made his stand.

Natural Right and History is a monumental book, perfectly fitting Dannhauser's description of Strauss's work as "specializ[ing] in unsettling settled convictions, and usually [doing] so in quiet prose buttressed by formidable scholarship."[32] Assessing the treatment of natural right from the pre-Socratics to the twentieth century, Strauss sets out to demonstrate that there is a natural and true distinction in ethics and politics between right and wrong. Starting with Heraclitus' statement that it is "men [who] have made the supposition that some things are just and others are unjust,"[33] Strauss traces the trend of refutation of natural right, and painstakingly constructs the case for the defense. Not only is the work a profound work of scholarship, it is also Strauss's most comprehensive stand against nihilism, an intention that Strauss outlines in his Introduction.

Nihilism was and is the distinctive enemy of Strauss and his followers. Indeed, in a piece on Allan Bloom in 2000, Christopher Hitchens mentioned—before the current Strauss-fixation began—that "the term 'nihilist' is one of the giveaway words by which one can recognize a member or supporter of the school of Leo Strauss."[34] (It might be noted that in the wake of 9/11, Hitchens was to begin using the term more, as it were, liberally, himself). The identification and use of the term is in no way mere rhetoric, however. Strauss and Straussians recognize how incomparably deep the problem of nihilism has gone in society, and to begin countering it Strauss set out to identify its causes.

For Strauss, in *Natural Right and History*, the cause is clear: "The contemporary rejection of natural right leads to nihilism —nay, it is identical with nihilism."[35] In this, and similar passages, Strauss clearly and repeatedly stands with the American fathers, and against the historical trend that he had seen develop towards relativism once before. It is relativism that is identified by Strauss as the opening that leads to nihilism. Relativism rejects the notion that any principle can be entirely and rationally justified, leaving itself ultimately mute before the excesses of which man is capable: it is the disintegrating component in democracy. "This is not to say," one contemporary Straussian has written, "that all social scientists who deny natural right are consciously nihilists, but only that their rejection of natural right logically leads to nihilism." [36]

Though his successors were to take this stance to attack specific aspects of their culture and society, for Strauss the problem was firstly a problem of erosion within the academy. Equally importantly, the problem was a problem for philosophy itself, and it was in this framework that Strauss set out his argument.

At the very start of his book the philosopher gives examples of "just" and "unjust" laws, and argues forcefully that both are undermined by a rejection of natural right:

> the need for natural right is as evident today as it has been for centuries and even millennia. To reject natural right is tantamount to saying that all right is positive right, and this means that what is right is determined exclusively by the legislators and the courts of the various countries.

But by using the necessary notions of "just" and "unjust laws" —Strauss goes on—we imply:

> that there is a standard of right and wrong independent of positive right and higher than positive right: a standard with reference to which we are able to judge of positive right. Many people today hold the view that the standard in question is in the best case nothing but the ideal adopted by our society or our "civilization" and

embodied in its way of life or its institutions. But, according to the same view, all societies have their ideals, cannibal societies no less than civilized ones.

And here we come to the crux of Strauss's argument:

> If principles are sufficiently justified by the fact that they are accepted by a society, the principles of cannibalism are as defensible or sound as those of civilized life. From this point of view, the former principles can certainly not be rejected as simply bad. And, since the ideal of our society is admittedly changing, nothing except dull and stale habit could prevent us from placidly accepting a change in the direction of cannibalism.[37]

There are two further central points set out early in Strauss's great work that are worth mentioning now, because they are going to recur later. The first is the notion that society had the opportunity to choose the side of natural right, and made the wrong decision.

> [T]here is a tension between the respect for diversity or individuality and the recognition of natural right. When liberals became impatient of the absolute limits to diversity or individuality that are imposed even by the most liberal version of natural right, they had to make a choice between natural right and the uninhibited cultivation of individuality. They chose the latter. Once this step was taken, tolerance appeared as one value or ideal among many, and not intrinsically superior to its opposite. In

other words, intolerance appeared as a value equal in dignity to tolerance.[38]

For followers of Strauss, both conscious and unconscious of the fact, Strauss had, in this passage and this book, set out the ground on which the people eventually to be defined as neo-conservatives were to fight the culture wars. He had illuminated the point that would be popularised by his disciple (for once the term is apt) Allan Bloom, and that would be repeated and extended by others.

Strauss was, *pace* his critics, a passionate believer in liberal education. He saw the situation in what were, for his age, starkly ideological terms. With the ever-present threat of democracy's decline from mass rule to mass culture, Strauss was, like Alexis de Tocqueville before him, alert to the apparently soft "tyranny of the majority." He was also aware, and believed, that a practical and achievable antidote was at hand, both for democracy and for the avoidance of tyrannical conformity: for him it was a simple truth that "liberal education is the counterpoison to mass culture."[39] In terms that Bloom would later extend, Strauss wrote: "liberal education is the ladder by which we try to ascend from mass democracy to democracy as originally meant."[40] Strauss did not believe that liberal education would make all men happy, nor that it would make all men good, but he believed that, if we keep alert to the dangers, and are cognisant of our failings, liberal education enhances, even enables, liberal democracy.

And Strauss was—again *pace* his critics—a great defender of liberal democracy. But his praise came with a caveat. In a phrase that stands greatly to his credit, he wrote in 1968 that,

Neoconservatism

"We are not permitted to be flatterers of democracy precisely because we are friends and allies of liberal democracy."[41] What Strauss knew was that the true friend of democracy and the people is not the fawner and panderer to the people, but the individual who criticizes the people when they deserve to be criticized. This may not allow the true democrat to be regarded with fondness during his own lifetime, "though he may," as Pangle puts it, "win a kind of posthumous respect that is worth much more than popularity."[42]

What Strauss identified, and what he has hardly been thanked for identifying, is that liberal democracy carries within it certain seeds of its own destruction, and that foremost among the seeds are those of relativism. If Strauss's successors stated the case more plainly and antagonistically than he did himself, then it was because they were writing in a period in which relativism had secured a greater hold not just in the academy, but on western democracy as a whole. For Strauss the immediate concern in his writings was for philosophy. He saw that the modern crisis of natural right could become a crisis of philosophy because of the politicization of philosophy. This complaint may, posthumously, seem strong coming from Strauss, but what Strauss was attempting to do was to make philosophy secure from politicization, a process that he considered had been destructive for philosophy ever since it first took hold during the seventeenth century. Since that time, in Strauss's eyes, philosophy had lost its position as "a pure source of humane inspiration and aspiration," and become, instead, "a weapon, and hence an instrument."[43] In part, Strauss's life's work was an attempt to put that right.

When we look at his legacy today, even accepting that he

does not have the impact now that he had when he was alive (and that, alive or dead, he never had the destructive power with which his detractors credit him), it is impossible to deny that Strauss's career left traces. Those traces carried on in thinkers, writers, politicians and philosophers. They carried on in those who learned from Strauss in the classroom and in those who "only" read him. But they also carry on in those who have benefited from neither his books nor his teaching, but who intuit, by the indefinable trickle-down process of ideas, that there were people in the past who thought as they do.

Of the generation of those who directly carried on his legacy, I will focus on two men. In different spheres, and in different ways, they founded a distinctive new ideology, carrying aspects of Strauss and chunks of much else out into the world. They did this in and outside of the academy in a way that Strauss himself had never done, and had arguably never intended to do.

In the realm of politics, the seeds of Strauss's thought were best expanded upon by Irving Kristol. In the realm of the academy the man who stands out is Allan Bloom, a man who continued and extended Strauss's legacy, and who sprang from Chicago passionately advocating the words of Strauss to his class on the occasion of Winston Churchill's death:

> We have no higher duty, and no more pressing duty, than to remind ourselves and our students, of political greatness, human greatness, of the peaks of human excellence.[44]

* * *

Neoconservatism

Allan Bloom

If Strauss had largely kept his criticism within philosophy, Bloom was the person who would take it out into the world. Having studied under him at Chicago, Bloom (who was born in 1930) became Strauss's most celebrated intellectual successor. He can even be glimpsed, acolyte-like, flitting in and out of the philosopher's correspondence with Alexandre Kojève,[45] and once stated that the first occasion he encountered Strauss was the "decisive moment" of his life.[46] After Chicago, and further study and teaching in Paris and Heidelberg, Bloom returned to the States to teach over the following decades at (among other places) Chicago, Yale, and Cornell. His translation of Plato's *Republic* came out in 1968 and his translation of Rousseau's *Emile* a decade later. A much published and revered academic on the campuses on which he taught, Bloom's name may never have become more widely known had it not been for his friendship with Saul Bellow. In the early 1980s Bellow (who was also to become Bloom's biographer in fictional form after Bloom's premature death in 1992[47]) encouraged his friend to collect his wide-ranging thoughts on culture, philosophy, and society into a book, written as much as possible in the manner in which he talked.[48] Working under the title "American Nihilism," Bellow's encouragement eventually paid off in the monumental *Closing of the American Mind*.

If it may now be hard to understand why certain Straussian texts initially had the impact they did, no such confusion could exist over the effects of Bloom's masterpiece. A surprise best-seller when it was published (with an introduction by Saul Bellow) in 1987, *The Closing of the American Mind* is certainly the most widely bought and—they are not always the same thing—probably the most widely read Straussian argument in print.

The book caused a shockwave when it appeared, and Bloom was instantly both vilified and lauded. Its central thesis, that the American mind had become closed by becoming so indiscriminate was, it has been observed, "almost unhinged" by its success, "because the unregarded morbidity of the American soul turned out to be something that millions of Americans wanted to read about."[49] The book was popular not only because it provided a totem of resistance for reactionaries, but because it consisted of the lengthiest, most intellectually solid, and wittily erudite analysis of American education and culture of the decade. It was practical in its appeals and provided crystalline explanations for things that many Americans had been thinking and feeling for a long time.

His friend Bellow began the diagnosis in his superb foreword. Discussing the situation of the artist in contemporary America, he writes: "to put the matter at its baldest, we live in a thought-world, and the thinking has gone very bad indeed."[50] Bloom's ambition in helping to repair this is also stated at the outset. "This essay," as he puts it, is "a meditation on the state of our souls".[52] His own Introduction shows that this is not just a meditation, but a fight for those souls—in particular for the souls of the young.

"There is one thing a professor can be absolutely certain of: almost every student entering the university believes, or says he believes, that truth is relative."[52] Thus the first sentence. The rest of the book is Strauss out of the lecture hall and in the public arena. The students "are unified only in their relativism and in their allegiance to equality. And the two are related in a moral intention. . . . The danger they have been taught to fear from absolutism is not error but intolerance."[53] This attribute of tolerance may seem all very well, or even display a high level of culture and sympathy, but this is not so, says Bloom—worse lies beneath. "The students, of course, cannot defend their opinion. It is something with which they have been indoctrinated. The best they can do is point out all the opinions and cultures there are and have been. What right, they ask, do I or anyone else have to say one is better than the others?"[54] The American mind has not just become open: it has become so open it has become closed. Furthermore, it has become so "open" that it cannot even defend itself from this position in which there is no enemy "other than the man who is not open to everything."[55]

Bloom's theory is set out clearly and fervently: "Cultural relativism destroys both one's own and the good."[56] "Historicism and cultural relativism actually are a means to avoid testing our own prejudices and asking, for example, whether men are really equal or whether that opinion is merely a democratic prejudice."[57]

> It was always known that there were many and conflicting opinions about the good, and nations embodying each of them. Herodotus was at least as aware as we are of the rich diversity of cultures. But he took that observation to be an invitation to investigate all of them to see what was good and bad about each and find out what he could learn about good and bad from them. Modern relativists take that same observation as proof that such

investigation is impossible and that we must be respect-
ful of them all.[58]

Twentieth-century man has set himself up—as though by
nature—as greater than Herodotus.

Where Strauss ventured first, Bloom follows, making—and
this is key—suggestions for where we could go right. In discussing relativism's assassination of free thought and its inability to discern the good from the bad, Bloom argues (not simply
as some have interpreted it, for a "great books" approach to
education) that at the root of *any* meaningful system of learning there must be solidity. He says of his generation that:

> When they talk about heaven and earth, the relations
> between men and women, parents and children, the
> human condition, I hear nothing but clichés, superfi-
> cialities, the material of satire. I am not saying anything
> so trite as that life is fuller when people have myths to
> live by. I mean rather that a life based on the Book is
> closer to the truth, that it provides the material for
> deeper research in and access to the real nature of
> things. Without the great revelations, epics and philoso-
> phies as part of our natural vision, there is nothing to
> see out there, and eventually little left inside. The Bible
> is not the only means to furnish a mind, but without a
> book of similar gravity, read with the gravity of the
> potential believer, it will remain unfurnished.[59]

If the men in Plato's cave[60] are able to discern and ascend
thanks to the light, these "modern" men are starting off (and

remaining) self-inflictedly blind and incapable of movement. Not only, says Bloom, do the young not have any image of the perfect soul—as they do, say, of the perfect body—"they do not even imagine that there is such a thing."[61]

And he does not simply say that this emptiness at the center of the young is tragic. It is also, he recognizes, dangerous. In a land which pretends so completely that everything is open, but in which—as the briefest of glances could show—so much is ignored (a comedy without an *Inferno*[62]), the society and the people who set out to be free in it will become slaves (have perhaps already become so). Tyranny of some kind is looming when, as Saul Bellow put it, "public virtue is a kind of ghost town into which anyone can move and declare himself sheriff."[63]

And what is the tyranny? There are several answers.

One is the tyranny of popular culture, of mass culture, which Bloom believes the people do not in any sense "believe" in. He asks whether, when people talk of "preserving" their culture they really imagine this "artificial notion" can take the place of God or country "for which they once would have been willing to die."[64] Drug-taking has produced people whose "energy has been sapped," for whom "the pleasure they experienced in the beginning was so intense that they no longer look for it at the end, or as the end."[65] In passages of what one critic has described as "extreme dyspepsia,"[66] Bloom consistently attacks the low conformity of rock music—dissected by Bloom with the final analysis that "never was there an art form directed so exclusively to children."[67] In these circumstances the vital objective is not—as this generation has it—"speaking one's own mind," but rather "finding a way to have one's own mind."[68] It is no surprise that the second part of Bloom's book, entitled "Nihilism, American Style," details the crass popular absorption of Continental despair into American culture, with its demeaning end hybrid of "nihilism with a happy ending."[69]

With this form of nihilism rampant, the other main tyranny that Bloom identifies and warns against is the tyranny of "liberalism," or pseudo-liberalism.

Bloom taught at Cornell during the campus upheavals and riots of 1968 and, as one commentator put it, "never recovered from the moment when black students produced guns to amplify their demands."[70] Shocking as some of the violence on campuses was, it was not this that shocked Bloom and fuelled his 1987 book. Rather it was the (not just unwillingness, but) *inability* of his colleagues to defend themselves and liberal education from violence and intimidation that spurred Bloom to make his stand.

Firstly, Bloom saw this fatal weakness as a challenge to the universities. Secondly, it was a challenge for America. Of the universities he wrote that "One cannot say that we must defend academic freedom when there are grave doubts about the principles underlying academic freedom. . . . In order to find out why we have fallen on such hard times, we must recognize that the foundations of the university have become extremely doubtful to the highest intelligences. Our petty tribulations have great causes."[71]

For America, the battle to be fought and re-won was cultural. The cultural battle had been lost in the Sixties—and not, Bloom notes in supremely caustic mode, by people with any especial bravery. These victors did not come to prominence entirely without message or aim, but with ill-thought aims that were tyrannical in their insistence on conformity, so "open" that their thought "pays no attention to natural rights or the historical origins of our regime"[72] (indeed despises them) and so blind that they are led into the worst mass culture of them all—a mass culture into which nihilism has been entirely absorbed as an attitude.

In addition, listing the non-"sacrifices" made by the students in the name of their new-found creed, Bloom makes a pertinent observation on the sheer "coincidence" of it all: "Never in history had there been such a marvelous correspondence between the good and the pleasant."[73] The easy giving-up of cherished principles, the genuflection of elite institutions to barbarism and infantilism, and the resounding sense that a group had been given a victory from a war which, though petulantly fought, had gone un-resisted, informed Bloom's bitterest attack. The ground had been given to people who, having won it, had no idea what they were going to do with it, and who, now in position, were free to wreak their damage.

That damage, Bloom saw, was firstly to the soul. Secondly it was to the institutions which provided the best chances to properly form the soul, but which had been so degraded that they ensured the young have "a long climb just to get back up to the cave,"[74] never mind ascending from there. Thirdly, the damage was to America. At the close of his book, Bloom wrote:

This is the American moment in world history, the one for which we shall forever be judged. Just as in politics the responsibility for the fate of freedom in the world has devolved upon our regime, so the fate of philosophy in the world has devolved upon our universities, and the two are related as they have never been before. The gravity of our given task is great, and it is very much in doubt how the future will judge our stewardship.[75]

In the Preface to his *Philosophy of Right*, Hegel famously wrote that the Owl of Minerva flies at dusk—that philosophy only takes wing when the light is failing. Bloom recalled Hegel's claim midway through his masterpiece.[76] By the book's end it is clear that the "closing" of Bloom's title refers not just to the closing of the American mind and of the American soul, but to the possibility of the closing of America *tout court*, and with it the last best chance, as Strauss too had seen it, for democracy and liberty.

After Allan Bloom died, in 1992, his friend Werner Dannhauser wrote, "The legacy of Strauss lives on, and nobody did more to secure it than Allan Bloom."[77] In his progress from devoted disciple to rightful heir, Bloom's work brought Straussian preoccupations into the mainstream. As many people reading *The Closing of the American Mind* discovered, those preoccupations turned out to be far from just the concerns of academic philosophers. They were the concerns of a large number of those in America and the West who felt that their values were under threat; that they were threatened from within; that the path they were on was not the right one, but that the fight to regain the right path had begun.

Irving Kristol once wrote that "It is the self-imposed assignment of neoconservatism to explain to the American people why they are right, and to the intellectuals why they are wrong."[78] With Kristol—the next Straussian on the horizon

—this concern became overtly political. Becoming political involved many things Strauss would never have intended, and many things with which he would have disagreed. But Strauss himself was no longer the center. As the political movement began, it was Straussianism that became absorbed into neoconservatism.

Irving Kristol

Irving Kristol is commonly referred to as the father, grandfather, or godfather of neoconservatism. Born in 1920, and thus, with the likes of Norman Podhoretz, among the first generation of those to be identified as a "neoconservative," no individual has done more to define, explain and argue the neoconservative point of view. Married to the social commentator and historian Gertrude Himmelfarb, and the father of William Kristol (editor of *The Weekly Standard* and chairman of the Project for the New American Century), Kristol is, like Podhoretz, head of a neoconservative family as well as movement. Having edited, among other publications, *Commentary* and (with Stephen Spender) *Encounter*, and having co-founded *The National Interest* and *The Public Interest*, Kristol has been central in encouraging other neoconservative thinkers, as well as in leading the way in his own articles and books. He is best defined, as one admirer has put it, as simply "the central figure in neoconservatism."[79]

Having started his life as a Trotskyite, Kristol found the two great formative influences of his mature years to be, in the 1940s, the literary and social critic Lionel Trilling, and in the 1950s, Leo Strauss (acquaintance with whose thought provided Kristol with the intellectual revelation quoted earlier).

Trilling was a skeptical liberal, whose gifts to future neoconservatism included the phrase "adversary culture," identifying the paradox at the heart of contemporary American cultural life. From very different schools and disciplines, and with widely differing aims, what Trilling and Strauss had in common, as Kristol noted half a century later, was that "their skepticism went to the very roots of modern liberalism and modern conservatism, respectively."[80] Apart from the influence of their ideas, one result of Kristol's discovery of these two thinkers was that from the very outset of his career he understood that almost all the presumptions of modern American society were open to question. Kristol was to spend his career ensuring that they were not merely questioned, but interrogated forcefully and repeatedly in order to expose cant, false ideology, and lies. The first big target Kristol aimed at was communism.

From the beginnings of his career as a writer and journalist in the late 1 9 4 0 s, Kristol had become a forceful and lucid anticommunist. At this point anti-communism was itself a defining political stand, and one that could by no means be taken for granted. But even by the Sixties, anti-communism was retrospectively seen by many in the West as some kind of an "elaborate con game on behalf of the power structure."[81] Later generations—often urged on by no more than an acquaintance with Arthur Miller's most famous work—have been prone to regard McCarthyism as something as medieval and fruitless as the witch trials. But the truth is that the problem existed, was growing, had nuclear weaponry, and possessed a great many supporters in the heart of America. For those like Kristol, living through the period and seeking to retain traditional liberal Americanism while utterly opposing communism, Senator McCarthy was still an unappealing figure, described by Kristol in one essay as a "vulgar demagogue." As, however, Kristol wrote in the same essay, " 'Civil Liberties,' 1952—A Study in Confusion": "there is one thing that the American people know about Senator McCarthy: he, like them, is unequivocally anti-Communist. About the spokesmen for American liberalism, they feel they know no such thing. And with some justification."[82]

Kristol led the way in smoking out those whose real sympathies were far from American and far from liberal. "It is a fact that Communism today rules one-third of the human race, and may soon rule more," he wrote in 1954. "It is the most powerful existing institution which opposes such changes and reforms as liberalism proposes. Why, then, should not liberals, and liberals especially, fear and hate it?"[83]

But with time it was not just its inconsistencies, but the fundamental assumptions of liberalism that became questionable to Kristol. As the "culture wars" of the 1960s began, Kristol noticed that the liberal ethos was fast moving leftward. "My liberal credentials became tattered, in my own eyes as well as in the eyes of others," he wrote.[84] The blame for this lay principally with the counterculture that emerged after 1965, engulfing the universities, and overwhelming popular culture. It was during this period, wrote Kristol, that "we discovered that traditional 'bourgeois' values were what we had believed in all along, had indeed simply taken for granted."[85]

What Bloom had witnessed on the campus, Kristol, Podhoretz, and others noticed in society at large: that the values and presumptions which had successfully underpinned society in America from its beginnings were being openly and popularly attacked—and furthermore, this assault was taking place at all levels of society. Even though they had initially regarded themselves as liberals, living through a period of terrible societal change (and, for instance, recognizing innate flaws in the Great Society initiatives of Lyndon B. Johnson) Kristol and his fellow thinkers came to believe not just that liberalism was not up to the job—that there were unbridgeable flaws in the liberal program—but that the whole liberal world-view was faulty. It wasn't that liberalism didn't feel nice, or didn't look nice; the problem was that it was wrong.

By its consistent refusal to adequately condemn Nazism's single moral equivalent in Russia, liberalism had shown that it possessed none of the attributes its name suggested. By undermining the society that was defending true liberal values from the threat of communist tyranny, it had shown its flaws and its deceits.

It was in this climate that neoconservatism was born. The first appearances of the word itself are debatable, though it is commonly thought to have been used first by Michael Harrington and *Dissent* magazine. Though it was initially intended as a term of insult, Kristol was one of the few among his contemporaries to happily embrace the new and still indistinct moniker, content simply to be free of the "liberal" label if liberals themselves were going to retain their presumptuous use of the term. Many others who were identified as neoconservatives held out against the term, unwilling to have it thrust upon them, but Kristol accepted it readily "perhaps because," he joked, "having been named Irving, I am relatively indifferent to baptismal caprice."[86] Becoming a neoconservative did not require any great leap in itself—to become a neoconservative in the

Neoconservatism

1960s, Kristol later remarked, "all you had to do was stand in place."[87] It was the ground itself that was slipping: neoconservatives were not going to totter with it. In defiance of both conservatism and liberalism, Kristol best defined his movement at an unattributable moment: "A neoconservative," he said, "is a liberal who has been mugged by reality."

Kristol found that embracing the new identity provided "an experience of moral, intellectual, and spiritual liberation."[88] He said later, "It usually makes no sense ... to argue over nomenclature. If you can, you take what people call you and run with it."[89] Abandoning the increasingly narrowing position of "anti-communist liberal" in favor of "neoconservative" allowed Kristol to confess to something he had long suspected:

> I no longer had to pretend to believe—what in my heart
> I could no longer believe—that liberals were wrong
> because they subscribe to this or that erroneous opinion
> on this or that topic. No—liberals were wrong, liberals
> are wrong, because they are liberals. What is wrong with
> liberalism is liberalism—a metaphysics and a mythology
> that is woefully blind to human and political reality.[90]

That blindness was increasingly demonstrating itself in American society. Kristol recognized that what he termed "the rot and decadence" within American society was not just a consequence of the liberal agenda, but the actual aim of it. This "liberalism" was simultaneously aiming for "political and social collectivism on the one hand, and moral anarchy on the other."[91] In order to stand against this threat, Kristol and other first-generation neoconservatives had not just to call for reversals in the progress of the agenda of socialism, anarchy, and nihilism, they had to explain how and why an end should be made of it. Liberalism had failed. To replace it, neoconservatives had to adopt a better stance: not only one that was practical, humane, and truly liberal, but also one that expressed the politics of reality, not the perpetually dangerous politics of fantasy. It required, as Philip Selznick put it, "moral realism."[92]

Assisting him in that objective was Kristol's study of the theologian Reinhold Niebuhr, which pointed him—as he put it—"beyond liberalism,"[93] helping him to read, among other things, the Book of Genesis with new insight. Michael Novak wrote of the effect of Niebuhr on neoconservative thought in a 1972 *Commentary* piece, and Mark Gerson rightly cites the significance of one particular line of Niebuhr's (from *The Children of Light and the Children of Darkness*): "It is man's capacity for justice that makes democracy possible, but it is his tendency to injustice that makes it necessary."[94] From time spent on the liberal-left and as anti-communists, neoconservatives were convinced that, flawed though it may be in places, liberal democracy provided the best possible means by which man's natural tendency towards evil could be contained. As they read through the past for its insights on their own time, and contemplated the present, neoconservatives found it increasingly remarkable that liberals were able to sustain the attitudes they did on the fundamentals of human nature.

To get right down to it (as Leon R. Kass says and does at the very opening of his commentary on the Cain and Abel episode in Genesis—an essay in honor of Kristol), when it comes to tracing the source of human troubles and misery, liberals are inclined to blame external causes—for example, poverty, soci-

Neoconservatism

etal prejudice, misfortunes in upbringing, and so on—while conservatives are inclined to blame "causes lurking naturally within the souls of men," such as greed, pride, vanity and so forth.[95] Kristol realised that the drift since the 1950s, and certainly during the 1960s, had been towards an unalloyed vision of human perfectibility—a vision that was socialist inspired, even when the end aim was not knowingly socialism. He realized the terrible dangers of this drift of vision. Drawing on a wealth of philosophical ancestry, not least Strauss, Kristol came to the conclusion that, although we can improve our condition, governments cannot make it immeasurably better, or unrecognizably better. Though our conditions may be improved, the basic, flawed mold cannot be altered. Though many of neoconservatism's critics have complained that such analyses make neoconservatives pessimists or worse, the result, both in Kristol's thought and in the thoughts of those who have come after him, is, on the contrary, optimistic and encouraging. It recognizes the limits of our ambition, and aims for the achievement of that which can be achieved—not in the best of all possible worlds, or in a different world, but in this world, now.

Of all the consensus attitudes that stood at the opposite end from this achievable and encouraging aim of Kristol and co., none was more glaring than the increasing cult of unending "welfarism": a thing whose grand end aims were often so impossible, its attempted explanations so tortuous, that the whole edifice was in need of a drastic overhaul. Having studied —through his wife's writings—the successes of charity in areas of Victorian society, Kristol accepted none of the common modern perceptions.

Compassion organized into a political movement is a very dangerous thing and, I think, a wicked thing. If you want to be compassionate, go out and be compassionate to people. If you want to give money, give people money. If you want to work with poor people, go out and work with poor people. I have great respect for people who do that. But when people start becoming bureaucrats of compassion and start making careers out of compassion—whether political, journalistic or public entertainment careers—then I must say I suspect their good faith.[96]

Welfarism was not, as it stood, the answer—it was a problem, and it had become a problem because a piece of false or bad logic had been taken for granted, and then acted upon. The same thing was happening elsewhere.

At the root of many of these assumptions, on race, welfare, employment and other issues, lay the most mistaken rallying-cry of liberals: "equality":

I know the question of equality is something that many religious people are quite obsessed with. Here, I will simply plead my Jewishness and say, equality has never been a Jewish thing. Rich men are fine, poor men are fine, so long as they are decent human beings. I do not like equality. I do not like it in sports, in the arts, or in economics. I just don't like it in this world.[97]

Kristol pioneered robust attacks on every aspect of liberalism, but this did not mean that his position—or that of neocon-

Neoconservatism

servatives as a whole—was traditionally 'conservative'. From their very beginning neoconservatives were different from traditional American conservatives. And it wasn't always merely a matter of outlook. For a start, most of the first neoconservatives were from lower-middle or working-class backgrounds. Veterans of the Second World War, they had also seen the process from triumph against one totalitarian regime to hostile peace with the other, and they were disillusioned with conservatism's weak response.

What was needed was not, as a conservative might have it, the turning back of the clock: neoconservatives did not want to see society return to the 1930s, 1920s, or even a Victorian heyday. Neoconservatives saw that society had made, not least economically, significant progress. But socially, economically, and philosophically they represented something very different from conservatism—they represented revolutionary conservatism. Richard Perle said in a 2004 interview, "We're closer to being revolutionaries than conservatives,"[98] and the title "revolutionary conservatives" certainly fits the movement well, when from its very outset the differences were plain in policy and outlook.

The work of Kristol's that permanently separated him from traditional conservatism, and that supplied neoconservatism with a distinct stand on economics (an area into which neocons had not previously strayed), was the result of a sabbatical year from teaching at New York University during 1976–77. By this point a supporter of the Republican party, Kristol recognized that Republicans would have to be able to do more than book-balance if they were ever again to become a dynamic political force and return to power. Following the period in the

Seventies of simultaneous inflation and depression that had destroyed his faith in Keynesian economics, Kristol decided "with the greatest reluctance that 'neoconservatism' could not blandly leave the economy to the economists." He decided he had to become "economically literate" himself.[99]

Taking his lead from E. M. Forster (on whom Lionel Trilling had been an authority) and his *Two Cheers for Democracy*, Kristol wrote his 1978 book *Two Cheers for Capitalism*. In it Kristol performs the difficult task of securing the humane ground in the successful capitalist state. It is, as Michael Novak wrote in *Commentary* "a liberal critique of both corporate capitalism and socialism."[100] In E. M. Forster's argument on democracy, two cheers were permissible because they allow for criticism —a third is undeserved. For Kristol a similar equation is at play. Market capitalism cannot be given unanimously good reviews because it neglects man's need for the moral authority that can only come with tradition. Economists cannot fulfil all the needs of men, they can only make economic sense of the world, "and the world does not move by economic sense alone."[101] "On the whole," Kristol confessed, "being a humanist rather than an economist, I think this is a good thing."[102]

His second major complaint (argued against later by the neoconservative economist Irwin Stelzer in his essay "A Third Cheer for Capitalism"[103]) is that the capitalist free market, though allowing the people to have nearly limitless choice over what they can buy, brings with it profound non-economic questions. Only libertarians would argue that people should have anything they like. Kristol argues (in an essay in *Two Cheers* entitled "Capitalism, Socialism and Nihilism") that there are repercussions for society beyond those conceived of by economists, and though they are "quite obvious and easily comprehensible," they "are terribly difficult to explain to economists."[104] So as the economy only makes up a part of our lives, it must not be allowed to take over and entirely dictate to our society. In a spirit of mature acceptance of that which is largely good, Kristol argues that a third all-praising cheer for capitalism would destabilize this necessary balance. Capitalism should not be allowed to tread on, let alone dictate, ground on which it has no business. Warning capitalism to stay within its respectable confines, it is in the end simply "safer" to give it "only two cheers."[105]

Aside from being a comment on the position in society of economics, Kristol's argument was also, of course, a sustained and lengthy explanation to those in government of the rightful limits of their power. Just as there were areas in which economists would cause damage if they ventured, so government should avoid the trap of thinking that ever increasing interference, indeed comprehensive interference, would either endear it to the people, or make the people happier.

In his writings over a fifty-year career, Irving Kristol set out, in thoughts on morality, politics, and economics, the first comprehensive vision of a new approach to politics. Profoundly disenchanted with the liberal slide to decay, neoconservatives were happy to join the fray on behalf of traditions for which conservatism *per se* seemed to have lost its voice. And that they were a new breed was made eminently clear by Kristol. Even the optimistic manner of neoconservatives differed from their conservative colleagues. "The trouble with traditional American conservatism," Kristol once explained, "is that it lacks a naturally cheerful, optimistic disposition. Not only does it lack one, it regards signs of one as evidence of unsoundness [and] irresponsibility." [106] It is not "tradition" that made American conservatism morose and unappealing, however, but "nostalgia." And as Kristol wrote in 1964, "nostalgia is one of the legitimate, and certainly one of the most enduring of human emotions; but the politics of nostalgia is at best distracting, at worst pernicious." [107]

Despite having seen much of their culture degraded, and much of their conservative instinct on liberty trampled upon, neoconservatives refrained from gloomy nostalgia because they knew that they had two things on their side. Firstly, their arguments were broadly in tune with the American public, who had felt similarly adrift stuck between the nihilistic world of the counterculture and unrestrained capitalism. Secondly, neoconservatives knew that their ideas had persuasiveness on their side, and that their attack on the status quo of socialist-inspired "liberalism" in particular had only just begun. In the battle to come, neoconservatives knew that everything was to play for, that they were on the right side of America, and the right side of history.

TWO

NEOCONSERVATISM
IN PRACTICE

T HE LINE OF descent from Leo Strauss is the most notorious as well as the clearest of the neoconservative lineages, but it is not exclusive. Neoconservatism could have sprung up without Strauss, or indeed any single one of its forebears, because it is the result of specific cultural and social circumstances, created by a vacuum in society and political life. And it is worth remembering what Kenneth Weinstein pointed out: that Strauss's writings are philosophic inquiries with "nothing of the dogma of a political movement."[1] Today Strauss gives neoconservatives an intellectual pillar, and remains a monumental forebear, but the history of neoconservatism is replete with examples of people who owe no conscious debt to him. What I have aimed to show by tracing the thought of Strauss, Bloom, and Kristol is that, during the peace that followed the Second World War, conservatism—and indeed society—shifted in such a way that certain observers saw a fault line open up. Strauss and his followers identified the chasm, because it had opened up on their ground, on ground they had thought was secure: liberal democracy.

A set of major objections to the status quo of post-war politics had arisen. Individual thinkers identified their objections, felt their own concerns being voiced, and were emboldened to make their own diagnoses and stands. There was never any question, when the issue at stake was the future of liberal democracy, but that neoconservatives aimed to affect things in practical ways. They did not intend to grumble while the world slid by. They wanted to act for the good, and that meant taking the concerns of academia out into the mainstream. Kristol saw the shift in clear terms. In his analysis, Strauss's own students produced a generation of students who relocated to Washington, in part because the academic political science community had by then become antagonistic towards Strauss and his school.[2] It remains a pleasing and common taunt to hostile academics that their objections to Straussians having a say in the running of the universities led to the same people instead having a prominent say in running the country.[3]

Identifying neocons

In relating neoconservatism's progress from theory into practice, several considerations should be borne in mind. Firstly, a matter of nomenclature: a great many people who are broadly or selectively neoconservative utterly reject any identification as such. For instance, Tony Blair is, like Paul Wolfowitz, almost perfectly neoconservative on foreign policy, yet he would certainly reject the label; Wolfowitz himself shuns it in preference to being described as a "Scoop Jackson Republican."[4] If we are to get anywhere in identifying neoconservative trends and achievements, we will have to accept that many have been carried out, and will continue to be carried out, by people who would hesitate at being described as a neocon. Of course, much of this has to do with the term's presently less-than-happy connotations. Few serving politicians can afford the uninformed opprobrium that the label now brings; even certain journalists and writers, whose careers would—were the neocon label used—be less affected than that of a serving politician, steer clear of an explicit link. But just because someone doesn't call himself a neoconservative does not mean that his ideas, outlook, and actions are not neoconservative or neoconservative-inspired.

Which brings us to another caution: neoconservatives are not a homogeneous group (let alone a cabal), and, as will become clear, there is no party-like manifesto to which they adhere. Indeed, in America it was by no means even inevitable that neoconservatism would end up finding its party-political home among the Republicans. "There is," Irwin Stelzer has stated plainly, "no such thing as a neoconservative 'movement.'"[5] By "movement," Stelzer means the word in the sense of a group of persons with the same object, and in this sense he is right: indeed many neoconservatives have played up intellectual feuding among themselves precisely in order to demonstrate this.

To assist in defining the phenomenon, Norman Podhoretz has described what he calls a "neoconservative tendency";[6] Kristol has termed it a "persuasion";[7] while James Q. Wilson has described it as more of "a mood, not an ideology."[8] All are far closer to the truth than those who talk of cabals and organized coups. Since many people have neoconservative instincts without knowingly ever having met a neoconservative or read one of their books, we should suspect neoconservatism of being a propensity or outlook much like liberalism or any other political bias: a peculiarly relevant modern political frame of mind. That it is a modern phenomenon cannot be doubted, but it is so because it has been necessitated by modern problems. Its central tenets, however, are timeless. Since neoconservatives have, from the outset, been united only by their broadest beliefs, and since it is these beliefs that most clearly define them to the outside world, it is worth summarizing, however briefly, what those common beliefs are.

In domestic policy, neoconservatives are united by specific and general objections to the post-Sixties western status quo, to increasing secularism, to illiberalism masquerading as liberalism, and to the destructive effects of the counterculture. Implacably opposed to relativism, they invariably differ in what they believe the specific foundations of contemporary culture should be, but not in the belief that American society was better off and more itself when the common values of organized religion formed its bedrock. Although neoconservative domestic beliefs can most often be summarized by identifying what they oppose, on foreign policy neoconservatives are demonstrably less reactive.

Spurred on by Professor Donald Kagan (father of Robert and Frederick Kagan, and, for a time, a colleague of Allan Bloom at Cornell) as well as by Strauss, neoconservatives drew, and continue to draw, inspiration for their attitudes to conflict from the ancients, in particular from Thucydides. It is important to stress that they do not read his *History of the Peloponnesian War* in order to learn how to act in the world, but rather regard it as a text that supports their instinctive beliefs on foreign policy. These instincts may be summarized, as they were by Kristol in 2003,[9] to include three basic notions: that patriotism is a good and natural thing; that world government is to be rejected because of the likelihood of its leading to tyranny; and that leaders should distinguish clearly between friends and enemies. On the face of it, none—except possibly the second —of these proposals would ordinarily seem controversial. But they are, and this is at the root of the problem as neoconservatives see it. An age which regards moral clarity as suspect, extraordinary, or dangerous, is a world in which one has to be newly armed, for clearly none of the old assumptions work here. This is the sinew that connects neoconservative thought: the world is adrift, but for our safety it needs to be moored.

Conservatism has failed because it will not proselytize for its instincts, nor defend its just causes. It has failed because it did not stand up against the arrival and ingraining of attitudes to which conservatism should be instinctively opposed. And since conservatism would not take up the mantle on behalf of its own causes and the causes of liberty, a new form of conservatism and liberalism is required. This is neoconservatism, revolutionary conservatism—conservatism that refuses to sit back, but steps forward, because someone has to, and because it is the right thing to do.

Moral clarity

The moral clarity that was such a defining aspect of Kristol's career and writings runs through the foreign policy decisions and approaches that best exemplify the neoconservative worldview. An early and palpable such event took place in 1975 at the United Nations, when Daniel Patrick Moynihan spoke against an infamous motion proposed by Idi Amin.

Attending university in New York in the 1940s, Moynihan had been a contemporary of Daniel Bell, Irving Kristol, and many other first-generation neoconservatives. He was a scholar as well as a politician. His 1963 book *Beyond the Melting Pot* (co-written with fellow neocon Nathan Glazer) was an enormously influential look at the situations of the various racial groups in New York, arguing for the immovable significance of ethnicity in a person's identity. As the authors wrote in their preface, the very concept of integration had to be rethought because "the point about the melting pot ... is that it did not happen."[10] In 1965 (the same year Kristol and Daniel Bell founded *The Public Interest*), Moynihan's office at the Department of Labor issued what became known as the Moynihan Report, a scholarly, influential, and deeply humane study of the problems confronting black families within American society. But the report was widely misinterpreted in the press when it was leaked, and, faced with misinformed and outrageous accusations of racism, Moynihan and his fellow neoconservatives could not but notice that the liberal and academic communities, which should have been loudest in their defense, not only failed to support him, but abandoned him entirely.[11]

With experience in a range of cabinet and sub-cabinet positions under Presidents Kennedy, Johnson, Nixon, and Ford, Moynihan was appointed US Ambassador to the United Nations in 1975, in the wake of an article he had published in Norman Podhoretz's *Commentary* ("The United States in Opposition"[12]) which was well received by both President

Neoconservatism

Ford and Secretary of State Henry Kissinger. Among other things, Moynihan's article attacked those liberals within the US who had proved so incapable of defending liberalism in the face of communist and Arab hostility. Though Moynihan was to end his career serving almost twenty-five distinguished years as a Democrat Senator, for neoconservatives his finest hour came on the floor of the UN in 1975.

Moynihan's moment came as the result of the 10 November passing (by seventy-two votes to thirty-five, with thirty-two abstentions) of Resolution 3379, which stated that "Zionism is a form of racism and racial discrimination," and is furthermore "a threat to world peace." The motion was led by Idi Amin—Ugandan President, genocidal wife-eater, and Hitler and Holocaust supporter—and supported by the Muslim countries and a swathe of African nations. In his speech to the UN, Amin declared that the United States had been "colonized" by Zionists, and claimed that these Zionists were controlling the country. He then called for the "extinction" of Israel. When he finished his speech, Amin received a standing ovation. The following night, UN Secretary-General Kurt Waldheim, previously Oberleutnant Waldheim of the SA and an implicated Nazi war criminal, threw a party in Idi Amin's honor.[13]

The Amin resolution was, naturally, condemned by Israel and her allies, but it was Moynihan's reaction, speaking on behalf of the United States, that had the greatest impact. Known for his occasional bluntness,[14] Moynihan entirely abandoned the diplomatic niceties that would have been so inappropriate under the circumstances, and, in a speech partly written with Norman Podhoretz, he made the case plain:

Neoconservatism in Practice

The United States rises to declare before the General
Assembly of the United Nations, and before the world,
that it does not acknowledge, it will not abide by, it will
never acquiesce in this infamous act.

Noting that the resolution had given international sanction to
anti-Semitism, and reiterating painstakingly why the idea that
Jews are a race "was invented not by Jews, but by those who
hated Jews," Moynihan stated baldly that historians alone might
see what damage had been done to the UN by the passing of
this resolution. Americans and the world would have cause to
reflect, he noted, "that if there were no General Assembly, this
could never have happened." The resolution "is a lie. But as it
is a lie which the United Nations has now declared to be a
truth, the truth must be restated," he said. And Moynihan proceeded to do just that.

The seriousness of the act committed by the UN was plain.
It had, among other things, Moynihan said, granted "symbolic
amnesty—and more—to the murderers of the six million
European Jews." For this, and for many other reasons that he
gave, the lie would have repercussions. There were prophetic
words:

The terrible lie that has been told here today will have
terrible consequences ... people [will] begin to say,
indeed they have already begun to say, that the United
Nations is a place where lies are told.

Moynihan explained that the motion that had been passed
threatened not only the security and legitimacy of the State of

Neoconservatism

Israel, but also the legitimacy and standing of all nations of the UN. The motion harmed the fight against racism, by stripping the term of any meaning and potentially damaging the security of all nations, for if "racism" could be so drained of meaning today, then so, tomorrow, could "national self-determination" or "national honor." Finally, the resolution damaged the idea and language of human rights. By assaulting a word, assaulting language, assaulting the truth and telling lies, the United Nations had done something that the United States "does not acknowledge [and] will not abide by." Moynihan stated in conclusion that the United States "will never acquiesce in this infamous act."[15]

Moynihan's speech before the UN was a pivotal moment, and one of the earliest opportunities for a neoconservative in a position of influence to make a stand for neoconservative values. But what were the aspects of the matter that were specifically neoconservative?

Firstly, the occasion had only arisen because of the existence of the pseudo-world government of the UN. Under any other system, such an opinion from a man like Amin would have been deemed morally and politically negligible. Under a system that accurately reflected and upheld the cause of liberty and free peoples, as opposed to a system that gave equal power and voice to countries led by homicidal hate-mongers, Amin's voice would have been drowned out. Resolution 3379 provided the neoconservatives with evidence of the long-felt truth: world government was a dangerous and potentially tyrannical concept, giving, as it did, equal significance to freedom and tyranny, equivalent significance to right and wrong.

Secondly, Moynihan's response to Resolution 3379 bucked

the accepted trend of diplomatic discourse. The acclaimed master of realpolitik, Henry Kissinger, disapproved of what Moynihan did (and of Moynihan's description of Amin as a "racist murderer"[16]), but to neoconservatives this simply demonstrated a flaw in conventional conservative thought and practice. If conservatism was epitomized by the retention of diplomatic nicety, and the honoring of the status quo over the defense of right and the support of allies, then conservatism had shown itself—like liberalism—to be incapable of discerning right from wrong, truth from lies, and friend from foe.

Finally, the Moynihan speech was important because it expressed in clear terms the neoconservative attitude towards Israel.

During the 1970s, and especially in the wake of the 1973 Yom Kippur War, neoconservatives noticed not just a rise in hostility towards the state of Israel, but an increasing unwillingness to defend Israel on the part of many countries that had, like the UN, previously acknowledged her right to exist. And this was occurring during a period in which Israel had been under continuous aggressive attack, in which her physical survival was at stake. Neoconservatives felt that Israel—militarily invaded by all her neighbors—deserved more than lukewarm support, and deserved it for many good reasons. These reasons are far from the libel of dual loyalties that is levelled at neoconservatives by those whose anti-Semitism is ever more thinly veiled behind "anti-Zionism." Neoconservatives who are Jewish, and neoconservatives who are not, have always supported Israel's rights to exist and defend herself because Israel has, for a long time, been the only democratic nation in a region of squalid dictatorships. Neoconservatives believe

Neoconservatism

that Israel, assailed as it is by tyrannies from all sides, needs and deserves the support of free people, not simply because it is Jewish, but because those who enjoy democracy and freedom should always defend their own against despots and tyrannies.

Zionism was also, it may be said, itself a precursor to neoconservative thinking. When Theodor Herzl envisioned the Jewish state he did so because there existed a problem (a problem *for* the Jews, not *of* the Jews). The comprehensive solution Herzl envisaged was, like much neoconservative thinking, intended to start the solution to the problem, not tinker with the failing status quo. When Herzl wrote in 1895 that "the Christian bourgeoisie would not be unwilling to cast us as a sacrifice to Socialism,"[17] he did not know how absolutely his prediction would be demonstrated. But after that knowledge was learned, neoconservatives, like all those inclined towards the defense of liberal principles, backed the beginning of the answer to the problem. With all the other problems that have undeniably issued from that first step, it is a basic neoconservative intuition that a state for the Jewish people in their historical homeland was the inevitable and just positioning of the answer onto the right track.

But there is a more philosophical cause for neoconservatism's stance on Israel, which has nothing to do with race or specific politics. For in the episode typified by Resolution 3379, neoconservatives saw a moral inversion taking place. In the reasoning quagmire induced by relativism and countercultural equivalence, vast swathes of the West's populations, as well as their representatives, were proving incapable of telling truth from lies. Warnings, explicated in theoretical terms by Strauss and others, were physically demonstrated at the UN in

Neoconservatism in Practice

1975. Israel, a democratic country whose existence had been approved at the UN, was being assailed by totalitarian enemies seeking her total annihilation. In these circumstances, not only did vast numbers of people and countries not support Israel in her fight to exist, but they also allowed the moral situation to be inverted. In an inversion that was to persist, Israel's Arab enemies equivalenced their way around their offenses, and relativized away any condemnation to portray themselves as the injured party. Wars that Israel had mercifully won were turned against them, with the Arab aggressors now *themselves* posing as the victims of aggression. Were this a pose that persuaded nobody, the matter could have been dismissed. But the pose became the norm, indeed the agreed-upon version in much of the West. The neoconservatives were fuelled in their realization that the West was slouching to decay. At a time when lies could become truths, then aggressors could masquerade as victims.

The Evil Empire

The effect on neocons of the UN's Zionism vote paved the way for louder moral clarity on a range of issues. Moynihan's UN legacy was most obviously continued when, five years later, the same post was given to another neoconservative who was also a Democrat, Jeane Kirkpatrick. As happened earlier with Moynihan, an article in *Commentary* brought Kirkpatrick to the attention of a president (or at least a president-to-be), in this case Ronald Reagan. Her article, "Dictatorships and Double Standards," appeared in Podhoretz's magazine in November 1979, and was passed to the presidential hopeful by his National Security Adviser, Richard V. Allen.[18] Summing up many of the neoconservatives' widest-ranging feelings on

Neoconservatism

foreign policy, the piece dissected President Carter's policy of not engaging with the leaders of countries like El Salvador and Iran, while continuing to trade, negotiate, and remain opaque on the natures of communist dictatorships like the Soviet Union. Kirkpatrick believed this policy of Nixon's and Carter's towards the communist countries displayed not only a glaring double standard, but also terrible naiveté. Apart from anything else, the possibility of a communist tyranny in any of the countries whose regimes America hoped to see fall would, Kirkpatrick argued, be far worse for America's interests and the interests of the countries themselves. Marxist uprisings that succeeded led inexorably to only one thing—totalitarian tyranny. "However incomprehensible it may be to some, Marxist revolutionaries are not contemporary embodiments of the Americans who wrote the Declaration of Independence," she wrote, "and they will not be content with establishing a broad-based coalition in which they have only one voice among many."[19]

Like many of her neoconservative contemporaries, Kirkpatrick saw that the problem at the root of recent American governments' attitudes to the Soviet Union and other communist dictatorships came, in part, from the counterculture's misunderstanding of political ideology—a misunderstanding that fundamentally failed to grasp the threat posed by socialism:

> Because socialism of the Soviet/Chinese/Cuban variety is an ideology rooted in a version of the same values that sparked the Enlightenment and the democratic revolutions of the eighteenth century; because it is modern and not traditional; because it postulates goals that appeal to Christian as well as to secular values (brother-

hood of man, elimination of power as a mode of human relations), it is highly congenial to many Americans at the symbolic level. Marxist revolutionaries speak the language of a hopeful future while traditional autocrats speak the language of an unattractive past. Because left-wing revolutionaries invoke the symbols and values of democracy—emphasizing egalitarianism rather than hierarchy and privilege, liberty rather than order, activity rather than passivity—they are again and again accepted as partisans in the cause of freedom and democracy.[20]

The intellectual rigor and moral clarity which Kirkpatrick's article brought to the debate on foreign policy greatly impressed Reagan, and his appointment of her to the UN position when he came to office in 1 9 8 1 was a great advance for neoconservatives. Indeed James Mann, in his superb, if unfortunately titled, book *Rise of the Vulcans: The History of Bush's War Cabinet* describes the appointment of Kirkpatrick as "the beginning of an epochal shift."[21] Having earlier often backed Democrat leaders like Henry "Scoop" Jackson and Hubert Humphrey (especially the former during his quests for the presidential nomination in 1 9 7 2 and 1 9 7 6), neoconservatives by the time of the Reagan campaign were nearly all firmly behind the Republicans.

Years later, Kirkpatrick confessed that her switch to the Republicans came at a time when foreign policy dominated her political thinking absolutely.[22] In part, that transition reflected a broader trend in American society, in which, since Vietnam, a person's position on foreign affairs strongly suggested their wider societal impulses. Carter's administration had drifted far enough to lose the loyalty of a number of older Democrats, and when in the 1980 race for the Democratic candidacy Carter's leading challenger, Edward Kennedy, campaigned even further from the middle ground, a break was inevitable. But for Kirkpatrick, as with many others, the break had been coming since before the Vietnam War.

Kirkpatrick later wrote that, though it was generally believed it was the resistance to the war that had sparked the counterculture, she believed that, in truth, "the ideological assault on authority symbols and structures preceded the anti-war movement and made it possible." She explained that "the central aspect of the anti-war movement was less its rejection of the Vietnam War than its rejection of the United States. The argument was less that the war was unwise or unnecessary than that the United States was immoral—a 'sick society' guilty of racism, materialism, imperialism, and murder of Third World people in Vietnam." The anti-war movement "constituted a wholesale assault on the legitimacy of American society." And Kirkpatrick echoed the feelings of Kristol and many others when she asserted, "I believe this assault became the foundation of the opposing neoconservative position."[23]

If the Kirkpatrick diagnosis of the effect of Vietnam seems high-pitched today, it should be remembered at what a pitch the debate was run in the Sixties. It was a time, as Kirkpatrick remembers, when *The New York Times* could run columns stating that "The United States is the most dangerous and destructive power in the world," and during which a prominent cleric declared that Lieutenant Calley (who had been sentenced to life imprisonment for his part in the My Lai massacre) "is all of us. He is every single citizen in our graceless land."[24] And, of course, it was a time when political discourse monotonously equated America's state to that of Nazi Germany. Kirkpatrick remembers the president of a leading university claiming that "We conquered Hitler but we have come to embrace Hitlerism."[25] Remembering his own similar experiences, Allan Bloom summarized: "So refined had the capacity for moral discrimination become, it followed that the elected American officials and the duly approved federal, state and local laws had no more authority than did Hitler."[25] Kirkpatrick deplored the tendency "to blame America first and most, and to extend to others 'understanding' and tolerance denied the United States," and she summed up the feelings of all neoconservatives when she wrote, "We did not doubt that American society could be improved but we believed it first had to be preserved."[27]

To preserve American society, America had at least to have the right stance for dealing with her enemies. But Kirkpatrick urged—in opinions that (like her suspicion on the viabilities of transplanting democracy) were by no means unanimously held by other neoconservatives—that America should vary the way it dealt with countries of whose regime it disapproved. After all, as she later observed, "morally responsible people recognize that there are degrees of evil."[28]

But it was partly as a result of Kirkpatrick and other neoconservative influences that Reagan was to make one of his most morally uncompromising and famous pronouncements —a pronouncement that was to gratify, and become an example for, all neoconservatives. Writing in *Commentary*, Norman Podhoretz had spelled out in 1981 why the communist empire was so incomparable and un-nuanced a threat to America and the West. The Soviet system was unambiguous not just because it was evil, but because it seemed so uniquely appealing to intellectuals in the West. And it was partly as a result of moral ambiguity on the issue of the Soviet Union from the US government that the views of such people were allowed to seem acceptable or legitimate. For Podhoretz and other neoconservatives, the situation was clear: the "conflict between the United States and the Soviet Union is a clash between two civilizations. More accurately, it is a clash between civilization and barbarianism." [29] This was the language that Reagan adopted two years later.

The "evil empire" speech was given on March 8, 1983 at the National Association of Evangelicals. It constituted one of the acts of "truth telling about the Soviets" which David Frum and other next-generation neoconservatives clearly see as having "accelerated the delegitimization of Soviet rule." [30] At the event in Orlando, at a time when the calls for a cessation of the arms build-up were growing, Reagan called on his listeners to avoid the temptation

> to declare yourselves above it all and label both sides equally at fault, to ignore the facts of history and the aggressive impulses of an evil empire, to simply call the arms race a giant misunderstanding and thereby remove yourself from the struggle between right and wrong, good and evil. [31]

As Allan Bloom noted sarcastically: "right-thinking people joined in an angry chorus of protest against such provocative rhetoric ... [at] the presumption that he [Reagan], and America, know what is good." [32] Such opposition to Reagan's rhetoric had been explained by Leo Strauss thirty-five years earlier when he had written that "Our political science is haunted by the belief that 'value judgments' are inadmissible in scientific considerations, and to call a regime tyrannical clearly amounts to pronouncing a 'value judgment.'"[33]

Reagan's speech was the absolute antithesis of the orthodoxy complained of by Strauss. The speech constituted a stand —a stand that neoconservatives encouraged and wanted repeated: clarification on democratic opposition to tyranny, and support for absolutes, in particular, and, unapologetically, the necessity and incomparability of freedom. Moving beyond a purely "anti-communist" stand, neoconservatives began arguing for the encouragement and kindling of democracy across the globe. Those who still suspected that this espousal of democracy was merely an anti-communist stance were surprised at the scope of the ambition, expressed, for instance, in the pressure beginning to be applied from State Department to the governments of countries like Chile. In part, the policy shift represented a moral decision to stand firm against tyranny, but it also spelt simple good sense. The new moral clarity on the Soviet Union (reiterated in Reagan's 1987 call to "tear down" the Berlin Wall) proved to be "both morally satisfying *and* politically prudent"[34]: morally satisfying in the short term, and politically prudent in the long term, because, as Kirkpatrick said (though she was not the first neoconservative to observe), "democratic nations don't start wars."[35]

By the year of the "evil empire" speech, other neoconservatives were doing well in the administration. Kirkpatrick was at the UN, Paul Wolfowitz had been made Assistant Secretary of State for East Asian and Pacific Affairs, and Caspar Wein-

Neoconservatism

berger had brought in Richard Perle as Assistant Secretary of Defense, responsible for dealing with the Soviet Union and Europe. Perle, who had been a staffer to Wolfowitz's hero, "Scoop" Jackson, during the previous decade, was among those profoundly opposed to the status quo "détente" with the Soviet Union, and one of those in the administration urging a rethink. The Kissinger school of diplomacy was fading from prominence, and those of a neoconservative persuasion were happy to see it go.

At the UN, meanwhile, recognizable diplomacy of any kind was deserting the neoconservatives. Kirkpatrick was not alone in having become disenchanted with the entire institution. To her eye, there was a fundamental contradiction in the UN's Charter: it assumed that the member states would embody democracy, yet the Soviet bloc and its comrades had never posited any democratic pretense whatsoever. The UN was founded on—and was living—a lie. That democratic nations of the free world should be deemed within the UN to have moral parity with dictatorships—communist dictatorships at that—displayed the futility of the enterprise.[36] The failure of the UN was inherent from its very origins. Like the League of Nations, its case had been laid out in part in Immanuel Kant's *Perpetual Peace* and *An Idea for a Universal History*. Yet Kant's precepts, though aped, had been ignored—in particular the First and Second Definitive Articles, which make it plain that, for a system of perpetual peace, every constituent nation must be "republican" (that is a liberal democracy) and "the law of nations should be founded on a federation of *free* states."[37]

Official American expressions of distaste for the UN reached a high point in 1983 when the deputy chief to the UN mission, Charles Lichtenstein, said in response to a proposal to move the UN from New York, "We will put no impediment in your way, and we will be down at the dock bidding you a fond farewell as you sail off into the sunset." Irving Kristol— who lauded Kirkpatrick in an article the same year[38]—sent Lichtenstein a congratulatory telegram. For neoconservatives, the UN was fundamentally compromised by the equivalence with which it treated democratic and totalitarian regimes. Outright opposition to, or simple ignoring of, the UN became commonplace, summed up with characteristic force by Irving Kristol at the American Enterprise Institute in 1987, when he declared, "I just want to go on record as saying that I thoroughly deplore in this serious conversation on foreign policy, any mention of the UN Charter."[39]

The new generation

Within months of the Reagan administration's arrival in office, Wolfowitz had brought in an almost entirely new set of policy planning staff. Many came from the same schools as he did: a number were fellow former pupils of the nuclear theorist Albert Wohlstetter, whose direct impact on Wolfowitz had been far greater than that of any other professor, including Strauss. But Straussian descendants were also brought in, prominent among them Francis Fukuyama, who had studied under Bloom at Cornell. Later Irving Kristol's son—William Kristol—moved to Washington to act (from 1985) as an aide to Secretary of Education William Bennett. Though neoconservatives, let alone pure Straussians, never had the grasp over the Reagan administration that some commentators have credited them with, there were enough of them to make an

Neoconservatism

impact, and also to give a flavor of the kind of opposition they were going to face during the George W. Bush presidency. Even a touch of the later misrepresentations can be felt in the 1987 *Newsweek* article entitled "The Cult of Leo Strauss," which asked in conspiratorial tones, "Why are so many Straussians in the Reagan administration?" The writer, Jacob Weisberg, even went so far as to say, "Some of their critics suggest that the brotherhood [*sic*] is committed to no less than halting the drift of modern democracy."[40]

Yet what Straussians and neoconservatives were actually committed to doing during the Reagan administration was defending and reinvigorating democracy: first by altering the unsatisfactory status quo of détente with hostile ideologies, and second by preventing the United States' humiliation before supranational bodies. In advocating massive increases in spending in areas such as defense, neoconservatives were going by one of their basic political rules, expressed succinctly by Irving Kristol: "[W]e should figure out what we want before we calculate what we can afford, not the reverse, which is the normal conservative predisposition."[41] Although many convincing economic arguments for avoiding the Reagan-era arms race were put forward, for neoconservatives the issue of prime importance was that America should hold overwhelming military superiority over the Soviet bloc. Although some neoconservatives have not so much overemphasized the significance of the arms build-up as underplayed the importance of the cracks already emerging in Soviet society, the Reagan doctrine, by any analysis, increased pressure on the Soviet authorities, and at the very least greatly assisted the collapse of the communist empire.

Neoconservatism in Practice

That collapse—in the last year of Reagan's presidency—
spelt for neoconservatives both a victory and a period of
deliberation, for the victory over communism saw the end of
the struggle in which neoconservatism had been rooted. It left
some first-generation neoconservatives, such as Norman Podhoretz, vindicated, but it also left them temporarily redundant.
Some, including Irving Kristol, saw the collapse of the mono-
lith that had defined aspects of their neoconservatism as an
opportunity for America to stand back from the world for a
period. But among the younger generation, neoconservative
preoccupations proved more than relevant and adaptable to
the new post-1989 environment. In a 1986 *Commentary* article,
Brigitte and Peter Berger had written, "We believe that the most
important political and moral challenge of our time is the
struggle for the survival of freedom. In the international context this struggle has its focus in the resistance to the spread of
Soviet-style totalitarianism."[42] For the younger generation
of neoconservatives, such as Charles Krauthammer, Joshua
Muravchik, and William Kristol, it was always clear that the survival of freedom was a fight and goal that would long survive
the collapse of the communist enemy. During that momen-
tous year, the central themes of this debate came right out into
the open in an article by Bloom's pupil Francis Fukuyama.

"The End of History?" was published in the Summer 1989
issue of *The National Interest*. Although written before Fukuyama joined the policy planning staff of the State Department
as, by his own admission, "a relatively junior official with little
impact on policy,"[43] Fukuyama's fifteen-page article caused a
stir equalled only by Samuel Huntington's 1993 essay "The
Clash of Civilizations?" Easily understandable and at the same

time easily able to be misunderstood, in both cases the simple central theses were bolstered by formidable scholarship as well as popular appeal.

By the end of the Nineties, the work of Fukuyama and Huntington (both of whose articles were extended into books) held incontestable sway over political discourse, albeit a sway that could occasionally fall into the irritating "binary simplicity"[44] which too often proved misinformed or glib.[45] Huntington's thesis (which gained many more admirers after events in 2001) broadly attracted "realists" of the school associated with Huntington's Harvard contemporary Henry Kissinger, whereas Fukuyama's thesis—while by no means introducing a neoconservative consensus—provided a version of world history deeply appealing to those of a neoconservative persuasion. Apart from anything else, the theory displayed (especially in its book version) a number of Straussian preoccupations—though Strauss himself is nowhere cited. In his book, Fukuyama charts some of the inherent flaws of the liberal democratic state, both the apparently harmless and the specifically destructive. Among the latter, Fukuyama notably highlights the problem of relativism in democracies where "we are fundamentally adverse [*sic*] to saying that a certain person, or way of life, or activity, is better and more worthwhile than another."[46] It is not the specifics, however, but the general sweep of Fukuyama's argument that is important and most debated.

There was, and remains, much misunderstanding of the nature of that argument. This arises largely from a misunderstanding of the sense in which Fukuyama used the word "history" (Fukuyama was using the term not in its sense of "the end of worldly events," but in the Hegelian sense of "the end of the evolution of human thought about ... first principles"[47]). What Fukuyama suggested to his readers was that "we may be witnessing not just the end of the Cold War, or the passing of a particular period of postwar history, but the end of history as such: that is, the endpoint of mankind's ideological evolution and the universalization of Western liberal democracy as the final form of human government."[48] Or, as he summarized in his book's Introduction, "there would be no further progress in the development of underlying principles and institutions, because all of the really big questions had been settled."[49]

Many neoconservatives agreed with Fukuyama's theory, and all agreed with aspects of it. But Fukuyama never intended his article as the last word on the matter. In a set of responses to Fukuyama, published in the same magazine issue as the original article, a number of people, including Gertrude Himmelfarb, Daniel Patrick Moynihan, and Irving Kristol, wrote reactions to the piece. Of perhaps greatest interest was Allan Bloom's response. It had been thanks to Bloom and Nathan Tarcov (both of the Olin Center for Inquiry into the Theory and Practice of Democracy) that Fukuyama had been invited to Chicago to deliver the lecture on which his subsequent article and book were based. In responding to his former pupil's thesis, and expressing his concern at this juncture for all the "faithful defenders of the Western Alliance," Bloom noted:

> Now that it appears that we have won ... what are we to do? This glorious victory, if victory it really is, is the noblest achievement of democracy, a miracle of steadfastness on the part of an alliance of popular governments, with divided authorities and changing leaderships,

Neoconservatism

over a fifty year period. What is more, this victory is the victory of justice, of freedom over tyranny, the rallying of all good and reasonable men and women. Never has theory so dominated practice in the history of human affairs, relieving the monotony of the meaningless rise and fall of great powers. As Fukuyama underlines, it is the ideas of freedom and equality that have animated the West and have won by convincing almost all nations that they are true, by destroying the intellectual and political foundations of alternative understandings of justice.[50]

But a new problem now confronted western man, one that Irving Kristol (who disagreed with Fukuyama's thesis for Aristotelian reasons) picked up on in the same issue. It was Kristol who acknowledged, with characteristic succinctness, that though it is nice to have won the Cold War—indeed "more than nice, it's wonderful"—it does mean "that now the enemy is us, not them."[51]

Opposition to communism had provided western man, as well as neoconservatives, with a clear ideological enemy. It also, as Bloom saw it:

> protect[ed] us from too much depressing reflection on ourselves. The global nature of the conflicts we were engaged in imposed an unprecedented uniformity on the world. It has been liberalism—or else. The practical disaster of the anti-liberal Right and Left has in general been taken to be a refutation of the theories which supported or justified them. Now, however, all bets are off.

The glance back towards ourselves, as Fukuyama indicates, is likely to be not entirely satisfying.[52]

What is more, liberalism may have won, says Bloom, but not necessarily forever. It is a claim to which Fukuyama was alert, but which he ultimately rejected. In his sheer optimism, apart from anything else, Fukuyama shares more with his own generation of neoconservatives than he does with their predecessors. While the pessimism of many people regarding the process of history may be understandable, he writes, "it is contradicted by the empirical flow of events in the second half of the twentieth century. We need to ask whether our pessimism is not becoming something of a pose, adopted as lightly as was the optimism of the nineteenth century."[53]

Attacks on Fukuyama's theory have been persistent, and gained credibility throughout the 1990s. Most recently, attacks on Fukuyama have ranged from Francis Wheen's questioning of his method and motive,[54] to Philip Bobbitt's debatable accusation that Fukuyama had "missed [out] the resurgence of nationalism" from his thesis, and the specifically erroneous suggestion that he had also "missed Islamic fundamentalism."[55] Though events of the 1990s were evidence to many people that Fukuyama's theory was wrong, most such objections had been either considered or answered in the course of *The End of History*. Aware of democracy's imperfections, the author remains alert to the threats which face it from outside. Perhaps he underestimated the extent and speed at which the post-Soviet world changed, but the central claim, that liberal democracy was the rightful endpoint of human achievement

Neoconservatism

continued to have a resonance beyond the walls of *The National Interest* or the University of Chicago. What Fukuyama gave impetus to, and a further ideological justification to, was a view of history which had become part of the neoconservative DNA—that democracy is the desirable endpoint of all human societies, and that, though democracy could not alone make people good, it is the surest means of preventing nation-states waging war on each other.

The challenges of the 1990s

Samuel Huntington later wrote, with a realist's grim satisfaction: "the moment of euphoria at the end of the Cold War generated an illusion of harmony, which was soon revealed to be exactly that. The world became different in the early 1990s, but not necessarily more peaceful. Change was inevitable; progress was not."[56] In distinction to Huntington, neoconservatives continued throughout the decade not only to increase their belief in, and rationalization for, democratic progress, but to argue harder to see their dream achieved. If Fukuyama's position was, as Huntington later characterized it, "the expectation of harmony"[57] then—in the wake of the Cold War—it was an expectation that many people shared, and, for a variety of reasons, fought to achieve.

But two distinct challenges arose during the decade that threatened both the security of America and her allies, and also—the two being intertwined—the advance of freedom. The first was the emergence of the familiar border-crossing dictator in the form of Saddam Hussein. The second was the fracturing of a nation-state in Yugoslavia, and the country's descent—under the supervision of Slobodan Milosevic—into

inter-ethnic conflict. Both developed into humanitarian catastrophes, and appeared to show for a time the "return" of history to the post-Cold War world. But neoconservatives had
other explanations for the resurgent problem. Bloom had
written in response to Fukuyama:

> Liberalism has won, but it may be decisively unsatisfac-
> tory. Communism was a mad extension of liberal ration-
> alism, and everyone has seen that it neither works nor is
> desirable. And, although fascism was defeated on the
> battlefield, its dark possibilities were not seen through
> to the end. If an alternative is sought there is nowhere
> else to seek it. I would suggest that fascism has a future,
> if not the future. Much that Fukuyama says points in
> that direction. The facts do too.[58]

Communism was a spent force, its return in a recognizable
guise made impossible by its comprehensive ideological and
physical destruction. But fascism presented a different problem, and Fukuyama acknowledged his old teacher's point of
view when he wrote in his book that "Fascism was not around
long enough to suffer an internal crisis of legitimacy."[59] The
1990s presented—especially in the continental version of
Milosevic—a freakish coda of that creed. For those of a neoconservative mind-set, the task of dealing with such aberra-
tions was viewed not just as a mopping-up exercise, but as a
challenge to be dealt with effectively and comprehensively, in
order to send the twentieth century's twin evil ideologies con-
clusively back into history.

When Saddam Hussein's forces crossed the border into

Neoconservatism

Kuwait on August 2, 1990, a new international problem came to the fore and remained there for thirteen years. In the run-up to the 2003 war in Iraq, it was often misleadingly stated that there had been a consensus for removing Hussein's troops by force the first time round. This was not the case. In 1990, opposition to American intervention came from both right and left, and, as in 2003, many characteristics united the opposing ends of the political spectrum. Both their rhetoric and the direction of their finger-pointing were to become familiar. For instance, to the eyes of Pat Buchanan, the only supporters of the war in Iraq were the "Israeli Defense Forces and its Amen corner in the United States," into which category he grouped A. M. Rosenthal, Richard Perle, Charles Krauthammer, and Henry Kissinger. Of course, all those fingered as being "for" the war were Jewish.[60] As in 2003, individuals on right and left were encouraging people to draw very particular conclusions.

The Bush administration, however, ignored the opposition and honored its obligations. Iraqi forces were expelled from Kuwait after a ground war lasting less than a hundred hours. The fact that the Allied military did not, as Margaret Thatcher urged (she was then no longer British Prime Minister), use this momentum to go on to Baghdad and remove Saddam Hussein from power, split many neoconservatives and stored up regrets for many others. But the appetite for regime change was simply not there; the notion of a link between insecurity at home and hostile dictatorships abroad was not yet solid. Even Paul Wolfowitz was not advocating the toppling of the Iraqi menace.[61] But the missed opportunity was summed up later by Robert Kagan and William Kristol when they wrote of the episode: "if the United States is prepared to summon the forces necessary to carry out a Desert Storm, and to take the risks associated with expelling the world's fourth-largest army from Kuwait, it is absurd, and in the event self-defeating, not to complete the job." [62]

Though he may not have been in favor of regime change, Wolfowitz was certainly one of those in the first Bush administration for whom Iraq's propulsion to the foreground of the international agenda did not come as a surprise. In the late Seventies he had worked on both the Pentagon's Team B intelligence review and its Limited Contingency Study, focusing on the likelihood of a new instability arising in the Persian Gulf. At that time, the threat had centered around the Soviet client states in the region. But by 1990 it was clear that, though no longer a Soviet client, Iraq could be a problem all on its very own. As Margaret Thatcher said, "When Soviet power broke down, so did the control it exercised, however fitfully and irresponsibly, over rogue states like Syria, Iraq, and Gadaffi's Libya." In effect, these states were "released to commit whatever mischief they wish without bothering to check with their arms supplier and bank manager." [63] In the 1979 Pentagon Limited Contingency Study, Wolfowitz and his colleagues had specifically considered the likelihood of an invasion of Kuwait by Iraqi forces intent on seizing her oil fields. The Pentagon study had also cited admiringly the "timely" British military intervention when Iraqi troops had threatened Kuwaiti sovereignty in 1961. [64] Yet, though the right precedents were cited, the impetus for a newer type of solution was just not yet there.

In a new era and an unclear global situation, America and her allies responded to the 1990 invasion of Kuwait in a way

Neoconservatism

that was reflex-like in its reliance on old-style realpolitik. The Iraqi army had been driven back to within its own borders, and the regional status quo restored. No great shake-up in the region was contemplated or even deemed particularly desirable. Paul Wolfowitz wrote in 1994 that "nothing could have insured Saddam Hussein's removal from power short of a full-scale occupation of Iraq ... even if easy initially, it is unclear how or when it would have ended."[65] Old-school realism approached this threat in the way it did because the threat seemed familiar. It would soon re-emerge as a challenge that was quite new.

The other great challenge that preoccupied neoconservatives and the international conscience throughout the Nineties also cropped up before the Republicans were out of the White House. Reactions to the break-up of Yugoslavia factionalized all political parties and persuasions. Neoconservatives were no different; nonetheless, throughout the decade their voice became increasingly unified, coherent, and admirable. Unfortunately, this was a decade when they were arguing from outside the government, not within it.

Out of power, and with the collapse of its defining foe having robbed it of its most salient antithesis, neoconservatism began to be seen by many as a spent force. As the US–Soviet relationship warmed, Jay Winik wrote in the pages of *Foreign Policy* that "America is witnessing the end not just of the Reagan era, but perhaps of the neo-conservatives as well."[66] Such premature obituaries for neoconservatism continued throughout the Nineties, even as the phenomenon was redefining itself. Even some inside the fold thought they were observing neoconservatism's passing—though for different reasons. In

Neoconservatism in Practice

1995 Irving Kristol wrote that "it is clear that what can fairly be described as the neoconservative impulse ... was a generational phenomenon, and has now been pretty much absorbed into a larger, more comprehensive conservatism."[67] In other words, neoconservatives were now un-prefixed conservatives. Kristol saw Newt Gingrich and the 1994 congressional elections as exemplifying the change, in which neoconservatism had become "an integral part of the new language of conservative politics."[68] The other grand old man of neoconservatism, Norman Podhoretz, concurred, writing an essay entitled "Neoconservatism: A Eulogy,"[69] and suggesting with characteristic boldness in a speech to the American Enterprise Institute that "neoconservatism is dead."[70] Of course, neoconservatism was not dead, but rather—as Podhoretz also posited in his speech—temporarily "missing."[71] For while older neoconservatives were looking for direction, a younger faction had already found theirs.

Figures like Joshua Muravchik and Charles Krauthammer recognized that the basic mission of America remained the same, on either side of the Cold War. "Communism may be dead, but the work of democracy is never done," wrote Krauthammer. "With the decline of communism, the advancement of democracy should become the touchstone of a new ideological American foreign policy."[72] Krauthammer, Muravchik, and many of the other younger-generation neoconservatives understood that corollaries of erasing tyrannies and spreading democracy were interventionism, nation-building, and many of the other difficulties that had long concerned traditional conservatives. The choice, they recognized, was difficult but inevitable. After all, as Krauthammer wrote, "If America wants stability, it will have to create it ... the alternative to such a robust and difficult interventionism ... is chaos."[73] The Balkans dilemma highlighted the disparities between old conservatives and neoconservatives, but what was clear was that the neoconservative tendency still existed, treading a path that remained distinct both from traditional conservatism and from most of the Clinton White House.

Yet it was because of the Balkans that a small number of neoconservatives had earlier switched parties and backed Clinton's presidential bid. From the outset of the Balkans crisis, many were disenchanted with the first Bush administration's inertia or lack of interest in the growing humanitarian catastrophe. Richard Perle later described Secretary of State James Baker's initial comment that the US "has no dog in this fight" as "one of the most appalling statements from somebody who claims to be a leader."[74] The administration's torpor in the face of the break-up of the Yugoslav state during its last months in office struck some in the neoconservative camp as typical, just another part of a wider pattern of dithering on major issues. Joshua Muravchik even contributed to a 1992 *New Republic* feature, "Conservatives for Clinton," in which he traced a sequence of foreign policy misjudgments that had propelled him into supporting the Democratic candidate in 1992. "When Chinese students demonstrated for democracy in 1989, Bush was inert," he said. "When Communist regimes fell, Bush did not rush to shore up new democracies." And, of course, "Bush kept democracy off Desert Storm's agenda."[75] To this list of grievances was added the Balkans.

Those neoconservatives who did swing towards Clinton were unanimously driven by his criticism of Bush's inaction in those situations where human rights violations were taking place. Though all came to feel let down by the perpetual disparity between what Clinton said and what he did, neocons who supported him at least felt that Clinton couldn't do less in these areas than Bush. "On what I care about—human rights and promoting democracy, keeping some sense of ideals in our foreign policy—Clinton is more amenable than Bush," declared Muravchik.[76] But neocons who swung to Clinton turned out to be bitterly disappointed by the lack of moral clarity and the hesitancy over the Balkans in the administration, and ended up finding solace only in the op-ed pages and Washington think-tanks. From there they wrote of how American policy ought to be operated, for the falling-out with Clinton was lasting and mutual. A dejected Muravchik wrote of this disenchantment when he stated that he had come to the conclusion that "Clinton turned out to care not a whit more about Bosnia than had the elder Bush."[77]

But the wars in Yugoslavia demonstrated to neoconservatives not just the inactions of the Democratic administration, but also the iniquities of many of the international systems that were meant to be in place to deal with precisely this sort of event. When the Luxemburg Foreign Minister Jacques Poos declared at the start of the Yugoslav crisis that this was "the hour of Europe," many neocons, like many conservatives across the board, were happy, as Richard Perle put it, "to let the Europeans have a go."[78] But the Europeans proved hopelessly incapable of containing, let alone dealing with, the situation.

Within a year of election in 1992, the President and the highest officials in his administration were repeatedly calling for multilateralism, and specifically UN-directed peacekeeping

Neoconservatism

operations. An open letter to the President in *The Wall Street Journal* of September 2, 1993 attacked Clinton for failing to act in Bosnia, and criticised the UN's efforts at peacekeeping. Signatories included Wolfowitz, Kirkpatrick, Perle, and Daniel Bell.[79] The distrust neoconservatives felt towards the UN, and in particular its ability to co-ordinate any such operation, may be said to have been vindicated by events in the ensuing years. The massacre, under the UN's eyes, in Srebrenica in July 1995 was just the worst of many dates in the Yugoslav disaster, which fulfilled their gloomiest predictions.

Throughout the period, once again facing ethnic cleansing and genocide in Europe and government inaction at home, neoconservatives kept up what pressure they could from outside government. Paul Wolfowitz, for instance, was at the forefront of the Balkan Action Council, a pressure group that called for military intervention on the side of the Bosnians. Even their opponents acknowledge that it was genuine moral outrage at what was occurring that fuelled neocons in the policy fray over the Balkans.[80] In an already complex situation, multiple misunderstandings (largely the result of making sloppy moral equivalences between sides) allowed neoconservatives to inject much-needed moral clarity into the situation. In petitions, letters to the newspapers, speeches, and articles, Wolfowitz, Perle, and Jeane Kirkpatrick were among neoconservatives who consistently lobbied for armed intervention to halt the progress of ethnic cleansing and slaughter. "After seven years of aggression and genocide in the Balkans, the removal of Milosevic provides the only genuine possibility of a durable peace," they wrote in a 1998 letter to President Clinton.[81] It was a stand dictated by morality, and though many people subsequently lambasted the same neoconservatives during this and subsequent interventions aimed at saving Muslim lives, there were some who took notice. The British-born writer Christopher Hitchens was among them:

> That war in the early 1990s changed a lot for me. I never thought I would see, in Europe, a full-dress reprise of internment camps, the mass murder of civilians, the reinstitution of torture and rape as acts of policy. And I didn't expect so many of my comrades to be indifferent —or even take the side of the fascists.
>
> It was a time when many people on the left were saying "Don't intervene, we'll only make things worse" or, "Don't intervene, it might destabilize the region.". . . And I thought—destabilization of fascist regimes is a good thing. Why should the left care about the stability of undemocratic regimes?. . .
>
> It was a time when the left was mostly taking the conservative, status quo position—leave the Balkans alone, leave Milosevic alone, do nothing. . . .
>
> That's when I began to first find myself on the same side as the neocons. I was signing petitions in favor of action in Bosnia, and I would look down the list of names and I kept finding, there's Richard Perle. There's Paul Wolfowitz. That seemed interesting to me. These people were saying that we had to act.[82]

The Kosovo campaign allied the neoconservatives with many liberal and humanitarian interventionists: all believed in the moral imperative to act to prevent the ethnic cleansing being committed by Serb forces. Ad hoc moral, as well as military, coalitions became common, and neocons were surprised when they found no ground whatsoever separating them and Clinton's Secretary of State, Madeleine Albright (whose own family history gave her something of Strauss's understanding of—and distaste for—tyranny). Indeed, so apparently similar had the instincts of some liberal interventionists and neoconservatives become by the time of Kosovo that Norman Podhoretz was at pains to stress, in *Commentary*, the importance of what separated them—in particular the emphasis placed by neoconservatives on "interests as well as values."[83] There is some truth in this distinction, for although neoconservatives were driven by humanitarian instincts, they remained certain that it was also in the interests of American security that such interventions were carried out.

Neocons advocated intervention from anyone willing and able to do the job, but they advocated quasi-unilateral intervention only when they observed that Europe was not equal to the challenge before it. "The hour of Europe" boast, in Robert Kagan's words, "proved hollow when it became clear that Europe could not act even in Bosnia without the United States."[84] The problem was not simply that Europe was suffering a bureaucratic failing, but that its bureaucratic failing was partly a result of—and not just coincidental with—its military failing. Europe had taken the opportunity, in the wake of the Soviet Union's collapse, to "cash in on a sizeable peace dividend," and take "a holiday from strategy,"[85] spending the money it saved on welfare programs and the like. As European defense spending continued to lag behind that of America, Europe found that it depended on America's military assistance even when it did not want it. Many neocons used the crisis over the Balkans to lambaste Europe *en masse,* citing the military debacle as part of a pattern of continental stubbornness, fuelled by a refusal to boost defense spending, and an unwillingness to "take the other necessary steps to establish an independent foreign policy."[86]

The disparity in defense spending between the two continents could not have been better highlighted than it was in the defining intervention of the Nineties. When a coalition of nations, without UN approval, launched air strikes on Slobodan Milosevic's regime to halt the Serb army's atrocities in Kosovo, the reliance on American military technology became appallingly apparent. Not only did American planes fly the majority of missions, but almost all of the precision-guided weaponry used was American made, and American technology provided 99 percent of proposed targets. As Kagan cites in his analysis, the UK—one of the few countries internationally that had kept anywhere near America's technological lead—provided only 4 percent of the planes, and the same percentage of bombs dropped.[87] Other countries in the coalition, though useful on paper, often proved a hindrance. Not only did mainland Europe's legal teams sometimes seem larger than their military, but also certain allies, while bringing nothing special to the table, cost the mission significantly in effectiveness and secrecy. In short, some allies were more of a liability than a boon.[88]

Yet American military spending and technology actually saved lives in the conflict. The precision-guided munitions used in the conflict had been honed for years. During the Seventies, the process often referred to as R M A (the Revolution in

Military Affairs) had proved the key to finding a strategic route out of nuclear deadlock, with the development of conventional weaponry providing a peaceful way out of nuclear stand-off. As Michael Ignatieff put it, "The beauty of such weapons was that, unlike the nuclear arsenal, they could be used."[89] Munitions like the cruise-missile enhanced the opportunities and possibilities of wars like Kosovo which targeted the regime, while causing minimal risk to the lives of the civilian population. The clumsier technologies of the majority of European air forces were just not up to this new job.

But if European capabilities had dictated much of the argument away from home, within America the use (or non-use) of ground troops to assist in solving the Kosovo crisis proved to be the recurrent domestic dilemma. Clinton's opposition to sending in ground troops was highly controversial. It only reinforced an emerging international view that America was keen to engage in regime change only if it could do so from 15,000 feet. Hostile regimes could well draw the lesson that, though America might be willing to kill for its values, it was not willing to die for them.[90] Belligerent Hussein-style tyrannies could only be emboldened by such a lesson. If American forces were taking care to minimize civilian casualties, despots, by contrast, could learn to use collateral damage as a weapon against America and her allies. Clinton's pre-emptive certainty seemed to be not only a moral, but also a military blunder. One of those hoping to take over the President's job expressed his feelings on hearing that Clinton had stated that ground troops would not, under any plan, be used in Kosovo. "I think it said, 'We're coming to fight you with one hand,'" said Governor George W. Bush. "I happen to think it's important for Milosevic to hear one voice, and that we're serious. . . . We need to have one objective in mind and that is to achieve the goals and to do so ferociously."[91]

The lessons taken away from the Kosovan conflict were varied and complex. Neoconservatives learned a number of practical lessons. A relatively swift war, using massive, technologically advanced power could prevent a humanitarian catastrophe and eventually topple a regime. This was the ideal postmodern war. Humanitarian aims, mixed with massive contemporary military technology, allowed America to target a regime without waging war on the people who suffered under that regime. Humanitarian intervention to alleviate suffering —which had hitherto so often been desirable—was proved to be practical and possible. It was a landmark in warfare: as Prime Minister Blair said, "Twenty years ago we would not have been fighting in Kosovo. We would have turned our backs on it."[92] But turning one's back would no longer be considered an option. And it was no surprise that those who, like the historian Brendan Simms, took most notice of the Balkans debacle and observed neoconservative participation in the debate often came out of that conflict at the very least "sympathetic" to neoconservatism.[93]

But flaws and hindrances to the campaign had registered. As Robert Kagan wrote in his masterly new-generation neoconservative tract *Paradise and Power*, "by the end of the 1990s the disparity of power was subtly rending the fabric of the transatlantic relationship. The Americans were unhappy and impatient about constraints imposed by European allies who brought so little to a war but whose concern for 'legal issues' prevented the war's effective prosecution."[94] This second issue in particular was to arise again: neoconservatives were insistent that a Europe that wouldn't act should not hold back an America that could.

By this time America was gearing up for another election, and the neoconservatives had become a revitalised force. The period in governmental exile had seen the succession of a new generation of young neocons. The Project for the New American Century (PNAC), founded in 1997 by William Kristol (also the founder of the neoconservative *Weekly Standard*) epitomized the distance neoconservatism had travelled in exile. Situated in Washington, in the same building as the American Enterprise Institute (which had many neoconservatives in its ranks), the PNAC invigorated and led much of the post-Kosovo discussion on major issues. It also symbolized a neoconservatism that was almost exclusively foreign-policy inspired. It was not that the neoconservative attitudes to domestic affairs did not continue, but in an era of global crises, it was on foreign policy that neoconservatives made their most distinctive and impassioned mark.

"American foreign and defense policy is adrift," the PNAC declared in its founding Statement of Principles. Citing the "incoherence" of the Clinton administration's policies, the PNAC set out how a conservative (un-prefixed) foreign policy should look. The signatories declared that the use of American power had been repeatedly shown over the previous century to be a force for good. For the next century America needed, among other thing, to: increase its defense spending to enable it to carry out its global responsibilities; strengthen ties with its democratic allies; challenge regimes hostile to American interests and values; and 'promote the cause of political and eco-

nomic freedom abroad.'" The Statement finished by declaring:
"Such a Reaganite policy of military strength and moral clarity
may not be fashionable today. But it is necessary if the United
States is to build on the successes of this past century and to
ensure our security and our greatness in the next." [95]

What is striking about this now famous statement is the
political scope of the signatories. Among them were a number
of usual neocon suspects, Norman Podhoretz and his wife
Midge Decter, Paul Wolfowitz, Donald Kagan, and Francis
Fukuyama. But also adding their names were older, non-neo
conservatives—Jeb Bush, Dick Cheney, and Donald Rumsfeld.
The PNAC solidified an alliance, molding together surprisingly
disparate types of conservatives, many of whom were going
to be neocon-tagged even if they only had a few broad views
in common with signed-up neoconservatives.

Some of the PNAC foreign policy stances that were going
to define the post-Clinton era were clearly expressed in a 2000
book edited by William Kristol and Robert Kagan. *Present Dangers:
Crisis and Opportunity in American Foreign and Defense Policy*
laid out the neocon case for the new century. Kagan and Kristol
set out to show that what they and their colleagues were pro-
posing was not a mere "tinkering around the edges" of American policy: "What is needed today is not better management of
the status quo, but a fundamental change in the way our leaders
and the public think about America's role in the world." [96] The
authors took it for granted that, even if America had, for
instance, never intervened in Kosovo or expressed disapproval
of China's record on human rights, it "would still find itself the
target of jealousy, resentment and in some cases fear." [97] What
was important was not a public relations exercise, but a sus-

tained American attempt to spread freedom and democracy ("with democratic change sweeping the world at an unprecedented rate over these last thirty years, is it 'realistic' to insist that no further victories can be won?"[98]) and, for security's sake, the deterrence that comes from sending the message to America's foes, "Don't even think about it."[99] The editors also famously stated that "we will occasionally have to intervene abroad even when we cannot prove that a narrowly construed 'vital interest' of the United States is at stake."[100]

Elsewhere in the book, Richard Perle wrote of the threat posed by Saddam Hussein, and demonstrated how Clinton's "flailing, ineffectual policy" on Iraq had merely postponed an inevitable confrontation, one which now left "a heavy burden for the next American President."[101] Inaction on Iraq had remained a major neocon preoccupation since Desert Storm, and, as Saddam Hussein's non-compliance with weapons inspections, arms control, and sanctions became more and more flagrant, neoconservatives were among the few to realize that Saddam Hussein was not a problem that was going to go away, but a problem that would have to be taken away. This was exactly what Rumsfeld, Wolfowitz, and the other signatories of a 1998 open letter from the PNAC to President Clinton had called for. There were indeed strikes, and talk of regime change, but the Iraqi President remained in place, to flaunt his position and pose further problems at a later date. The signatories of the PNAC letter recognized that Hussein's continuing presence was not only threatening to the US and disastrous for the Iraqi people, but also destabilizing for the entire region. The old "big idea"—containment—was not working. Another way had to be considered.[102] The signatories were calling for not merely a specific answer to a specific problem, but a new and different type of statecraft. In what turned out to be perhaps the most important contribution to *Present Dangers*, Paul Wolfowitz provided a lengthy blue-print for such a policy—"Statesmanship in the New Century."

Wolfowitz's prescriptions and solutions were and are in the distinctive tradition of neoconservatism. He even quoted aptly from George Orwell (writing in 1942): "One effect of the ghastly history of the last twenty years has been to make a great deal of ancient literature seem much more modern. . . . Tamerlane and Genghis Khan seem credible figures now, and Machiavelli seems a serious thinker, as they didn't in 1910. We have got out of a backwater and back into history."[103] The piece sets itself against a trend of traditional conservative foreign policy debate by acknowledging that the global situation had changed and that America must change to cope with it. Wolfowitz lambastes old-school Buchananite conservatives, who seem "willing to let almost any hostile superpower dominate Europe or Asia if the alternative is risking major war."[104]

The United States, is not Switzerland (nor, for that matter, is it the United States of George Washington's or John Quincy Adams's time), which can afford to isolate itself from a world over which it has little control and focus simply on how to make money and enjoy its life in peace. With so great a capacity to influence events comes a requirement to figure out how best to use that capacity to shape the future.[105]

Neoconservatism

The nature of that shaping centers, he writes, around the spreading of liberal democracy, for which "there are no visible philosophical contenders."[106] Discussing events in Iran and Korea, Wolfowitz comments that it is impressive "how often promoting democracy has actually advanced other American interests."

Wolfowitz recommends clear practice in treating with difficult regimes, agreeing with Kissinger that Harold Macmillan's exploration of "pragmatic" concessions at the time of the Berlin crisis only emboldened Kruschev. Advocating firmness, he states that any "signalling" of the use of force "should not be done without a careful calculation of what might come next."[107] In contrast to some other neocons, he praises America's history of coalition-building, and explains its practical benefits. This is realism—moral and strategic realism. At times Wolfowitz may be mistaken for a typical "hawk" or "vulcan." For example, America must deal effectively with rogue states, he says. And for practical as well as moral reasons:

> A country determined to mount a major attack on the status quo would find in a country like Iraq a willing ally and a source of leverage against the U.S. and its allies. The Clinton administration's tendency to temporize rather than go for the jugular, although understandable in many circumstances, has had the effect of piling up future problems.[108]

But Wolfowitz's break with traditional "hawks" is that he believes that democracy is the surest way to defend American interests against the forces of aggression. The same realism that dictated his judgment in 1991 remains, however. Wolfowitz is practical, not Panglossian, on the possibilities of global democracy. "We cannot ignore the uncomfortable fact," he admits, "that economic and social conditions may better prepare some countries for democracy than others."[109] One of the countries that was seen as ripe for democracy was Iraq, and on that neocons and their friends in Washington began to agree.

This was not just a neoconservative vision, but a neoconservative vision with which many traditional conservatives could agree. So when George W. Bush won the 2000 presidential election, it was unsurprising that Wolfowitz, Perle, John Bolton, and others of a neoconservative persuasion received government appointments. After the Clinton years and multiple claims of an early death, neoconservatism arrived, with the younger Bush, at its strategically strongest point to date.

But those who thought neoconservatives had taken over the government hadn't done much thinking. Among the top level of officials in the administration, not one could be described as a neoconservative. Cheney, Rumsfeld, Powell: all were various categories of the Republican species, but none was a neocon. The popular confusion came about with events later in 2001, demonstrated perhaps by the progress of National Security Adviser Condoleezza Rice. Rice—who had been trained and had risen as an expert on Soviet affairs, unparalleled in her field on issues like détente—shared her boss's early concern for neoconservative watchwords like "nation-building" and "democracy spread." But her stance, like George W. Bush's, was to change because events changed. The Rice of the campaign season was not the same Rice who began to emerge even before the catastrophe of 2001, conceding to William Kristol, when she called him to the White House for a talk before 9/11, that she was coming round to the idea of democracy spread, and believing a little less in pure realpolitik.[110]

The first months of the Bush administration were unpromising, quiet, and, not only in retrospect, over-hung with an air of near somnolence. But neoconservatives knew what to expect from quiet moments on the world stage, and were familiar with the way in which the savageries of the past re-emerge. In the opening pages of *The End of History*, Fukuyama acknowledged the pitfalls and presumptions of prejudging history, citing two famous examples of pre-First World War misjudgment. There was the famous eleventh edition of the *Encyclopædia Britannica* (1910–11) which had written of torture that "the whole subject is one of only historical interest as far as Europe is concerned," and the claim by Norman Angell in his popular and esteemed 1910 book, *The Great Illusion*, that free trade had made war in Europe irrational and obsolete.[111] Kagan and Kristol also pondered the lessons history taught, when they reflected, in 2000, that in 1788 Louis XVI was on the throne of France, with philosophers proclaiming the age of peace, yet ten years later the King had been executed, and Napoleon was "rampaging across Europe."[112] They were right to expect and fear the return of historical turmoil. Though neoconservatives could not have expected the horror of September 11, they were ready with some of the answers. Neoconservatives did not "take over" the Bush administration, nor did they—as some critics have offensively put it—"hijack"[113] it.

Neoconservatism in Practice

But what happened that day brought home a threat that was new to America, though long considered by neoconservatives. Since the neoconservatives had a head-start in the thinking, and since their philosophy alone adequately covered the enormity of the problem, it is hardly surprising that figures like Rice and Bush seemed to "come over" all neocon. The actual neocons were not among Bush's senior appointees: Wolfowitz was a deputy, Perle was chair of the advisory Defense Policy Board. That was as high as the neoconservatives had got, but the influence of their ideas and the significance of their combined thought at this period could not be overestimated, even if their personal influence could be. What neoconservative ideology did was help define George Bush's escape not just from the shadows of his father's style of politics, but from the whole oppressive philosophy of status-quo American conservatism.

A veteran intelligence official told James Mann eighteen months after 9/11, "I've been schooled for thirty years that things go back to normal within six weeks or two months or so after a crisis. But these people aren't changing. There's a clear commitment on their part to make a difference. They refuse to go back to business-as-usual."[114] The seismic shift happened from the day itself. What neoconservatives had been saying for years—that America's security was inseparable from global security—became startlingly clear that day. A barbarous regime on the other side of the globe, if left to fester, could erupt, not in a far-off place, but on the streets of New York and Washington, and over the skies of Pennsylvania. Richard Armitage, Powell's deputy (and himself no neocon) summed up the new mood in a meeting on the day itself. Armitage cut off a run of diplomatic platitudes on historical complexity from Pakistan's Ambassador and its head of Intelligence Services with the simple and curt statement, "History starts today."[115] And so it did.

After 9/11

"America did not change on September 11," wrote Robert Kagan. "It only became more itself."[116] That process was epitomized in the country's President. Having given off many signals on the campaign trail and since arriving in office that he pretty much followed in his father's footsteps, President Bush underwent a change. September 11 made him, as Norman Podhoretz put it, "politically born again as a passionate democratic idealist."[117] Bush had always believed in the concepts that became his mantras after 9/11, but the events of that day clarified and reinforced them. If America was to stay free, then it had to work to make other people free. But in order to support and help spread democracy, America must first comprehensively wage war on the forces of anti-democratic reaction —the forces of terror. Before a month was out, America had launched its military against the aspirant-medieval tyranny of the Taliban, and Defense Secretary Rumsfeld was declaring that "these strikes in Afghanistan are part of a much larger effort, one that will be sustained for a period of years, not weeks or months. This campaign will be much like the Cold War. We'll use every resource at our command. We will not stop until the terrorist networks are destroyed."[118] There was to be none of the short-termist, Clinton-era approach, which had—at best —just stored up problems that America would have to deal with another day. The new impetus given by the September outrages meant the whole pitch could be changed.

Neoconservatism in Practice

At his coming-of-age speech to a joint session of Congress on September 20, with Tony Blair looking on, George Bush declared:

> This country will define our times, not be defined by them. As long as the United States of America is determined and strong, this will not be an age of terror; this will be an age of liberty, here and across the world. Great harm has been done to us. We have suffered great loss. And in our grief and anger we have found our mission and our moment. Freedom and fear are at war. The advance of human freedom—the great achievement of our time, and the great hope of every time—now depends on us.

The world, not just America, had been transformed. Among world leaders, none grasped this faster than George Bush and Tony Blair. Both realized the new threat: not just terrorist cells, but the threat of terrorism combined with the threat originating from the proliferation of weapons of mass destruction. A new nightmare scenario was suggested by the possibility that a non-state terror organization could acquire weapons, wreak devastation worse than 9/11, and yet—unlike in the Cold War—provide no target for response. This new threat required new strategies. George Bush said at a speech at West Point on 1 June 2002:

> For much of the last century, America's defense relied on the Cold War doctrines of deterrence and containment. In some cases, those strategies still apply. But

new threats also require new thinking. Deterrence—the promise of massive retaliation against nations—means nothing against shadowy terrorist networks with no nation or citizens to defend. Containment is not possible when unbalanced dictators with weapons of mass destruction can deliver those weapons on missiles or secretly provide them to terrorist allies.

America had two jobs to do, and they went hand in hand: the elimination of hostile terrorist groups and the toppling of governments that harbored them. The two goals were indistinguishable from one another: it was failed, rogue states that had allowed the terrorist menace to fester and to train within their borders; it was these states that gave the threat sanctuary.

One of the things that the President grasped when the Twin Towers fell was that this was not a crime. It was not a case to be treated, as the 1993 World Trade Center bombing had been, as an FBI crime-scene investigation. What had occurred was an act of war—a monumental assault on the peoples and government of the world's supreme superpower and defender of freedom. This was so not because of the enormity of the attacks or the number of innocent people targeted and killed in the attacks. It was so because governments had harbored the people who had done this deed, governments that overtly and covertly applauded those deeds, and indeed would like to see the same thing done on an even grander scale. Foremost among those to welcome the attacks was the regime of Saddam Hussein.

In such a situation, Bush did not take the Clinton route—what the former CIA Director James Woolsey referred to as the "PR-driven" approach to terrorism: "Do something to show you're concerned. Launch a few missiles in the desert, bop them on the head, arrest a few people. But just keep kicking the ball down the field."[119] Bush's practical view was that for the terrorist swamp to be eradicated it would have to be drained. Draining the swamp meant removing those regimes that entertained terrorists within their borders. The only countries that did this were tyrannies. Democracies were not just nice; they were America's only natural allies.

Bush's view on this, and on America's duty, upheld and acted precisely on the theories Fukuyama had suggested in *The End of History*. The great battles, Bush saw, were over—the right ideology had fought and won. As he said at West Point:

The twentieth century ended with a single surviving model of human progress, based on non-negotiable demands of human dignity, the rule of law, limits on the power of the state, respect for women and private property and free speech and equal justice and religious tolerance.

Over the following years, America's commitment to those principles was going to be tested, but not altered. Also tested were American alliances—alliances America had thought it could rely on. For 9/11 had opened up a gulf between America and Europe—one straddled by Britain. When Donald Rumsfeld was asked by a soldier in December 2001, after the toppling of the Taliban, "What's next?" in the war on terror, Rumsfeld replied: "the answer is that the president and the government will be considering that in the period ahead. Your

job certainly is not over. There are a number of countries that
are known as being on the terrorist list. There are a number of
terrorist networks that exist around the world."[120]

Reaction to 9/11 briefly brought expressions of consola-
tion and support from many allies of America, summed up by
Le Monde's famous headline, "We are all Americans now." But
such sympathies were short-lived. Allies which America might
have expected to be secure turned on America, if not from the
start, then over a remarkably short space of time. The stomach
for a prolonged conflict did not exist in Europe. Part of this had
to do with Europe's inability to sustain a prolonged and costly
modern war: as Robert Kagan observed (adapting the Rums-
feldian toolbox-approach metaphor to military matters[121]),
"When you don't have a hammer, you don't want anything to
look like a nail."[122] But Europe's unwillingness was also non-
practical, part of its somnolent belief in an inevitable progress
towards "post-historical" paradise. Iraq was the point of depar-
ture, the signal that a colossal philosophical, as well as military,
breach had evolved between old allies. For Europe, war was the
past, part of history and—as it had been for Norman Angell in
1910—a pointless and irrational thing in the modern world.

Much of the population and political class of Europe tried
to cover over the philosophical chasm by claiming it was actually
a linguistic chasm, as though one did not stem from the other.
It was President Bush's rhetoric that was the problem, they said.
From the very outset they seemed to be under the impression
that this was not a real war, but a PR war. Distaste and outrage
were expressed at Bush's simplicity—even backwardness—of
rhetoric and vision, outrage expressed in language and imagery
wearyingly similar to the kind that had been used to denigrate

Neoconservatism in Practice

President Reagan in his day. Bush was aware that he made enemies by his use of certain terms, but equally he understood that anyone who was incapable of grasping the nature of the threat, or who thought the threat could be reduced by semantics and the employment of the language of equivalence, was not likely to be a useful ally. Allies who was willing to back out of the war because they didn't like his vocabulary could hardly be surprised when they were not missed. In his West Point speech, Bush said:

> Some worry that it is somehow undiplomatic or impolite to speak the language of right and wrong. I disagree. Different circumstances require different methods, but not different moralities. Moral truth is the same in every culture, in every time, and in every place. . . . We are in a conflict between good and evil, and America will call evil by its name.

The pillars of the Bush doctrine were built, as Norman Podhoretz wrote, "on a repudiation of moral relativism and an entirely unapologetic assertion of the need for and the possibility of moral judgment in the realm of world affairs."[123] Just as Reagan had had the "evil empire" to deal with, so now Bush had the "axis of evil."

But this was simply not the language of the new Europe. A continent, whose Brussels leaders were speaking proudly of Europe's "post-Christian" era, reacted with cynicism and not a little superiority when Bush stated, for instance, "I believe [that] freedom is not America's gift to the world; it is the almighty God's gift to every man and woman in this world."[124]

Neoconservatism

Over the four years since 9/11, two major conflicts have been fought in the new war: in Afghanistan and Iraq. The first of those conflicts was fought with much raucous and serious opposition. The second was almost universally unpopular outside the United States. Neoconservatives were suddenly sprung into the limelight. Figures who had been famous in Washington think-tanks for years suddenly achieved notoriety in popular papers and street demonstrations, and became (albeit not in a flattering sense) household names. Paul Wolfowitz was a particular favorite for attack, largely by people with no idea of his superb and humanitarian record. All they knew, as Mark Steyn put it, was that his name "started with a scary animal and ended Jewishly." [125] Even the German *Financial Times* joined in the barely concealed anti-Semitic slurs and echoes of the blood libel when it warned darkly that "Wolfowitz still has appetite." [126] Cartoonists in even the most esteemed papers portrayed Paul Wolfowitz, Richard Perle, and others of the hated and much misunderstood neocons in the most libelous and familiar terms, as bloodthirsty, even blood-drinking, monsters. In demonstrations on the streets of Europe and in the US, lists of neocons were trotted out as the hate figures *par excellence*. "Neocon" became an ill-defined term of insult, something that could be replaced by—or conflated with— "warmonger" and worse.

Journalists led or followed suit—it became impossible to discern who led whom—as comment in the lead-up to and then after the Iraq war plummeted lower and lower. When the British journalist Robert Fisk wrote in the run-up to the Iraq war that figures like Ken Adelman and Eliot Cohen (both members of the Defense Policy Board, the significance of which has been much misunderstood and exaggerated) were leading America into a war against Islam, the inferences he wanted his readers to draw were clear. Fisk accused both men of singling out "militant Islam" as the enemy of America. Why did he select these two over the more significant Donald Rumsfeld or Richard Armitage, for instance? The answer harked back to libels that had followed certain neocons from the very beginning. Fisk followed Pat Buchanan's lead of a decade earlier when he snidely described Adelman and Cohen as men who "have not vouchsafed their own religion." [127] In using his investigative skills to reveal that Eliot Cohen was a Jew, Fisk was simply stepping in line with the anti-Semitic, conspiracy theory-ridden attitudes of the anti-war movements on the streets.

But the level to which commentary on neoconservatism sank was not just a result of anger at the war in Iraq, or shorthand for expressions of distaste for the non-neocon Republican administration. It was a sign, in part, of desperation. Neoconservatives had put forward, and were in the process of putting into practice, a vision of the world that was vastly at odds with prevailing "liberal" orthodoxies in the West. Yet it was answering the very questions with which that orthodoxy had been trying, unsuccessfully, to grapple. Neoconservatives had provided the only coherent policies for dealing with the dilemmas of the day: genocide, dictatorships, and human rights abuses. To all of these increasingly fashionable dilemmas, neocons had answers and suggestions for action, and "liberals" had none, other than a vague reliance on international institutions whose record in such areas was, to say the least, unimpressive. The actions and beliefs of the Bush team drove the left to distraction, because it exposed—as Michael Gove put it

Neoconservatism

—"the bankruptcy of [the left's] international vision."[128] That neoconservative vision may seem, to its more reputable detractors, "a new political animal born of an unlikely mating of humanitarian liberalism and brute force,"[129] and to its lowest haters as some kind of vampiric conspiracy. But neoconservative attitudes cannot be dismissed easily. It is an ideology that is not only desirable, but necessary, even vital. It is also—that rarest of things—achievable.

And American conservatism and neoconservatism are, as a result, in a successful and powerful position, with opposition to American policy now almost entirely reactive. The narrative of meaningful global progress is at present largely in America's hands. In March 2005, Condoleezza Rice announced that President Bush was nominating John Bolton as UN Ambassador, and said something that only heightened the pleasure of hearing of that appointment. "Through history," said Rice, "some of our best ambassadors have been those with the strongest voices, ambassadors like Jeane Kirkpatrick and Daniel Patrick Moynihan."[130] It seemed that the second Bush administration not only had all the right people, but all the right predecessors as well.

THREE

RELATIVISM AND
THE IRAQ WAR

THE PROBLEM WHICH neoconservatism addresses, and which society as a whole must address, begins not with deeds but with thoughts. We live, as the passage quoted from Saul Bellow in Chapter 1 puts it, in a thought-culture, but the thought has gone bad. Justifications, actions, and presumptions have been allowed to persist within society despite demonstrably affecting policy and detrimentally influencing people's lives. The impetus is not simply bad reasoning, but rotten reasoning. There is one predominant thought-disease, a disease that links, and is carried by, all bad aspects of unhealthy contemporary thought. That disease is relativism, together with its practical demonstration in the technique of "equivalence."

In his homily to the College of Cardinals before he was elected Pope, Cardinal Ratzinger fingered the rot at the core of western thought when he identified the "dictatorship of relativism," a theory and a mode of thought that "recognizes nothing definite and leaves only one's own ego and one's own desires as the final measure."[1] Francis Fukuyama describes relativism as "not a weapon that can be aimed selectively at the enemies one chooses. It fires indiscriminately, shooting out the legs of not only the 'absolutisms,' dogmas, and certainties of the Western tradition, but that tradition's emphasis on tolerance, diversity, and freedom of thought as well."[2] It is the expression of the rejection of natural right, of a comprehensive objection to the notion of fixed truth.

How this perverse mode of thought became so all-pervasive in the West that it can indeed be described as a mode of mental, if not actual, "dictatorship" is a story that bears out the most basic Straussian warnings. While taking Isaiah Berlin to task in the 1960s, Strauss highlighted "the crisis of liberalism" as having come about "due to the fact that liberalism has abandoned its absolutist basis and is trying to become entirely relativistic."[3] By the end of the Sixties, society as a whole was lurching the same way. Societies physically and morally shattered by great conflict were, unsurprisingly, vulnerable to the attractions of a system that appeared at first to offer no value judgments. But its widespread adoption has had devastating effects, permitting the adoption into the nation's heart of a nihilism which should never have flourished in a democracy. That nihilism may not be deeply felt, and it may indeed largely be an attitude. But it is an attitude that is destructive, and conservatism must eradicate it. What it decays is not just the family, the Church, and other foundations of society, but society itself. Like Strauss, we should recall that, although ours is the surest and noblest means by which man can be free, it is not a system without flaws. Only if we remain aware of those flaws and alert to their danger can we avoid tumbling into their trap.

Relativism and the Iraq War

Today, the crisis originates in the fact that swathes of our people and leadership find it all but impossible to draw lines in the sand or speak in absolutes— even in defense of their own existence. The supposed advance of rationalism since the nineteenth century has led not to greater understanding, but to greater confusion. It is a confusion from which western nations seem unable to extricate themselves. This ever-growing sector of opinion can find no reason to protect its national beliefs. Like its European allies, America today finds herself with (as Bloom and Fukuyama have pointed out) fewer and fewer logical reasons not to let limitless numbers of refugees across its borders.[4] It is this "rationalism" that makes it so hard to find a reason why an individual or group that desires, or even encourages, the downfall of our society should not remain a part of it—a "rationalism" that produces examples of greater and greater irrationality every day. These examples arrive under the guise of the same phenomena—equivalence, relativism, and their most workable everyday expression in the mini, petty tyranny of political correctness. All rely on the technique of preventing something, or condemning something, because the same rule does not apply equally to all peoples, places, and cultures across the globe. The result is a "liberal" inability to defend tradition, national identity, and even, in its worst case, the nation's security. The original impetus was, perhaps, often meant to be fairness to all, but the results are enough to at least provoke a rethink on whether they are really "fair" to anybody.

In the case of the defense of faith, for instance, it has become the accepted trope that any special privilege or priority given to one faith must be levelled by the same privileges and advantages being given to others. Even ignoring the fact that

Neoconservatism

America has a fundamental and established faith that should enjoy just such special privileges, the educationalists of the twenty-first century are often at a loss to explain why equal opportunity in life should not be joined by equal competition in the marketplace of faith. Thus children are commonly informed of the virtues and teachings of each of the major faiths, with no faith in particular taught—let alone the traditional faith of the nation and its founders. Faced with even a single complaint that a Muslim or Sikh or atheist child should not be introduced to Christian teachings, the authorities consistently crumple. No "rational," "logical" answer to rampant equivalence appears to exist in our advanced twenty-first-century society.

The fact is that, though this equality does no discernible good, it does do a definite amount of harm to the intellectual and spiritual welfare of children. For what we are asking them to do—or rather presuming that they can do—is to recognize the validities of all beliefs, and to choose between them like cars in a showroom (of course all the time with the message that opt-out is just as valid as any choice). If we set children out on this road in life, we can hardly be surprised when they grow up to believe the gospel of relativism. For since their very earliest thoughts, they have been shown faith and truth only as a variety of tools with which they might, if they so chose, tackle life. In her superlative *All Must Have Prizes* (a *Closing of the American Mind* for the 1990s), Melanie Phillips quotes Marianne Talbot of Oxford University, who has written of the effects of relativism on the young:

> Many of the young have been taught to think their opinion is no better than anyone else's, that there is no

truth, only truth-for-me . . . to question it amounts in the eyes of the young, to the belief that it is permissible to impose *your* views on others.

The young have been taught, or so it seems, that they should never think of the views of others as false, but only as *different*. They have been taught that to suggest someone else is wrong is at best rude and at worst immoral: the truth that one should always be alive to the possibility that one is wrong has become the falsehood that one should never be so arrogant as to believe that one is right.[5]

As more and more individuals are produced by a system that extols this anti-ethic, so increasing numbers of individuals expect ever greater demonstrations of relativism to be practiced on institutions, communities, and people. Non-relativists, meanwhile, become increasingly helpless in the face of relativism's charms.

Every week brings in more examples of how the apparently benign form of relativist tyranny takes over. One week an elementary school in Skokie, Illinois decides to cancel its traditional Thanksgiving celebrations in order to welcome, instead, a member of the local Oglala Lakota tribe—horse-riding buffalo hunters from the Plains who have no connection whatever to the Wampanoag fishermen and farmers in Massachusetts who celebrated Thanksgiving with the European settlers almost four hundred years ago. Another week the story is of the Jefferson School in Berkeley, where pressure groups fight to take Jefferson's name off the school because the founding father owned slaves. Yet another week, the triumph of relativism is seen in the incapability of a courthouse in Alabama to keep the Ten Commandments stationed in its midst.[6]

In all these cases there are cases to be made, and arguments to be had, but relativism curiously denies this, attacking what it sees as tyranny while—in the process—replacing the tyranny itself. Once relativism has coated itself over a subject and populace, even being a founding father isn't enough to let you off.

And of course it might be observed from these and other examples of relativism's workings that it tends to work one way. As Arthur Schlesinger, Jr., argued in 1992 with the "ethnic upsurge," what began as "a gesture of protest against the Anglocentric culture," has become "a cult, and today it threatens to become a counter-revolution against the original theory of America as "one people," a common culture, a single nation."[7] There are of course always people to argue a particular corner, but what relativism does is to elevate whatever is against the status quo, or against the norm into something at least equal to the status quo and equal to the norm. From there it becomes more than equal, because it is new, and its merits previously unconsidered. Slowly that which was accepted is not merely challenged and undermined, but incapable of being upheld.

There are answers to this, but most of the populace do not want to—and should not have to—fight for their inherited culture and faith against persistent assault. It is, however, in the realm of the personal that relativistic arguments are succeeding in the West, thanks to the tirelessness with which individual feelings and beliefs are held up as equal to, and—by being singled out—uniquely worthy of, attention. The current undermining of American and Western traditions and beliefs often begins, for instance, in the presumption that people who have come into the country have as much right to have their beliefs reflected in the country as people already there. A Muslim immigrant into the United States who claims the same rights as those enjoyed by an American whose family have lived in the country for generations presents an even greater challenge to America's philosophy than it does to Europe's. Because of its greater history of toleration and acceptance, relativism has a route into the heart of America potentially swifter even than its route into Europe.

The demands of those hostile to America and her traditions often win through because of a benign acceptance of a new and sometimes attractive creed. Most often, there is no anger, no stand, no railing against sacrilege or desecration when this new creed has its way, only a benign acceptance that before the juggernaut of relativism and its practical destructions there is no adequate reason not to bow.

The feelings behind this will be familiar to many working people in America and across the West. The impetus, as often as not, comes not from "ethnic" people, or people of non-Christian faiths. The impetus commonly comes from people with simply no idea of what they are talking about or what it is that they are getting involved in. They just know that there is a status quo on acceptance and niceness, and that they must follow it. What we should see in such events however is not some new, highly developed, and universally applied critical faculty, but rather a self-lacerating votary, dedicated to misunderstanding the difference between cultural defense and cultural aggression. This problem covers the West.

In the UK, the Samaritans, a charity staffed largely by unpaid

Neoconservatism

volunteer counselors, is a service available to anybody who calls them. Yet in February 2005, a grant application from the Samaritans to the National Lottery was turned down because the handsomely remunerated lottery organizers decided that the Samaritans were not doing enough to target, among others, ethnic minority communities and asylum seekers.[8] Quite how the lottery felt the Samaritans could better advertise their charitable service to asylum seekers was not explained, but the message was clear: charities, like churches, can no longer expect to be treated with either deference or respect by those practicing relativism. In other words nothing is "sacred." A month after the decision on the Samaritans, a Christian refuge for the homeless in Norfolk was told that it would have its local council funding withdrawn unless it ceased the practice of saying grace before meals, and unless all alienating mentions of Christianity were removed from the Christian shelter.[9]

What is destructive about this is not just that such a force targets those things that are precious and established, but that it speaks to them as though it has control over them. In fairness, it should be said that often it speaks as though it has control of them because it does. In Britain or America, an order from a school board, grants board, judge, or other authority may sound from a distance like an edict which can be ignored, but the tyranny of relativism isolates those who do not follow its edicts and often leaves them with the feeling that they are fighting alone. This happens because independent and superannuated government busybodies are learning to wield a new and entirely uncertain form of moral judgment.

When people follow these relativistic routes they are not simply being idiotic though: they are revealing an agenda. That agenda follows the "liberal"-socialist fallacy of uniformity, conformity and spiritual agreement in the name of undefined political and moral "inevitability." No such inevitability exists, but political correctness implies and lies to people that it does, saying that the end of all human endeavors is their view of the world, a world in which everyone will be happy because they will be treated in the same way. But this is not merely vanity and folly. What the perpetrators of this absurd and ill-thinking new "system" cannot see—and this is why they must be removed from their positions of influence—is that their actions, carried out under a misguided creed of doing good by making people equal, loses sight of reason, and gives little to the few while plundering much from the many.

These petty tribulations have great repercussions. In *The End of History* Fukuyama described how relativism as a mode of thought could create "no barriers to a future nihilistic war against liberal democracy on the part of those brought up in its bosom," that, indeed, it destroys the possibility of raising such barriers.[10] This defenselessness caused by relativism might end up, he posited, not only undermining, but eventually destroying democracy and the tolerant values that come with it. A decade later, the prediction began to be vindicated.

When relativism became a serious problem

The period since 9/11 has afforded us unique opportunities to study the state of our society's soul, its well-being, and its durability in the face of a new threat. What we learn from the story so far should make us worried.

At present, wars fought by our country are not waged by civilians. Though people commonly talk grandiloquently about why "we" went to war or why "we" are at war, most people's participation in these conflicts is not so much limited as non-existent. They do not participate in the events, and there is not even any requirement to demonstrate support for those who do. For the vast majority of people, the war against Islamic fundamentalist terror has taken place (and their part in it has occurred) only in the worlds of thought and emotion. This is why we can learn so much about our present state from what has been written and said since 9/11. For these have not been the emotions of those under fire, thrown out in the rage of battle. They are the reflections, thoughts, and beliefs of people who are generally safe, more than provided for, and yet consistently and often wilfully wrong. Those judgments, recollected in tranquility, have demonstrated more about the intellectual and moral crisis of our time than their authors intended, precisely because they were writing from a position of comfort. The opponents and disbelievers, rather than critics, of the new world crisis are uniquely privileged by their life in the West, yet they are involved in a process which first undermines and then threatens the very fabric of that society. They are doing this at a moment of great importance, for events from 2001 to the present have brought back into focus a problem that fits Strauss's identification of "the crisis of our time, the crisis of the West."[11] If we cannot find ways to protect our society from jobsworths and busy-bodies from local schools of relativism, how will we fare when faced with proponents of an ideology that seeks our absolute subjugation or annihilation? What begins as a local crisis of morality and philosophy eventually becomes a crisis of something much larger—our will to survive. With the Church often sidelined, and political leaders ever more distrusted, "leadership" often comes from the mass media. But this is something that follows the mass culture, at the same time as it tries to lead it. This is the root of our popular degradation: the media and culture have become the same beast—one that is chasing its own tail. The rot both starts and finds its fruition here.

On any single day, civilians can see examples of equivalence. These examples range from the lazy and ill-informed to the grotesque and wicked. Events in American foreign policy in the years since 9/11 have made commentators, journalists and opinion-formers dust off their skills in the techniques of moral and historical equivalence, but the result has been intensely monotonous, universally unhelpful, but nonetheless simultaneously revealing.

From the moment the Twin Towers in New York were hit, people both near and far from government began to consider what response America and her allies might make. On the home front in America, many sources first of all incessantly warned the American people of the need for tolerance: the White House bent over backwards to portray Islam as a religion of peace, and did its utmost to ensure, as Mark Steyn put it with indignant irony, "that the American people should resist their natural appetite for pogroms and refrain from brutalizing Muslims."[12] That is, before any reaction was possible, the familiar knee-jerk reaction of much of government and the media was one of anticipatory self-blame. Common first questions were "What did we do?" and then "How can we stop our people from behaving brutally?" That is—even in the US—from the outset, significant portions of the media and the public tried to find reasons in the wrong place for why the attacks had occurred. Self-absorption found its inevitable end point, as observers pretended they could locate the cause of the conflict inside themselves. And of course no fundamentalists would have to be sorted out if the attacks simply led to prolonged periods of self-reflection. Such reactions have been repeated: the specific presumption that the public must be prevented from a bout of Muslim-lynching (a thing which is both without precedent and likelihood) was repeated by UK authorities after the first bomb attacks on London. These are ways to avoid the real issue, not deal with it, so it is fortunate that at least some people in the US government understood from the outset that what the attacks meant was war.

When attention focused on Afghanistan, where the perpetrators of the atrocities resided courtesy of the Taliban regime, those who offered opinion, to large or small publics, had to find out fast about a regime and country of which most knew little. Many waited for colleagues to say something that they could then repeat, which is why so many atrociously bad predictions about the Afghan conflict were echoed in such a short space of time—the "Afghan graveyard," for instance, or the lethal "Afghan winter" line. All foretold the hubristic undoing of the American army. But this was largely poorly disguised antagonism to American and Allied efforts. What was far more subtly disguised, and far more widespread, were new lines and depths in ignorant equivalence.

The line that became most useful to dig up was the charge that soldiers among the murderous al-Qaeda forces had been provided, two decades earlier, with tactical assistance from the United States. This weaponry had been supplied to expel the Soviet menace when it had invaded Afghanistan. But by 2001 the world of "my enemy's enemy" was a very long way behind. A deposed Serb leader was facing trial in The Hague, and supranational bodies were having a greater and greater say in how a new era of global harmony could be brought about. During the post-communist era, many learned people had become carried away with what this all meant. Professor Amy Gutmann of Princeton University declared that it was "repugnant" that American students should learn to be "above all, citizens of the United States." Their "primary allegiance," she argued, "should not be to the United States or to some other politically sovereign community," but rather to "democratic humanism."[13] Such opinions may never have had much currency on America's streets, but among its university and media elites, such theories had become commonplace and often sacrosanct.

Because for people of all opinions, the central events of the Cold War began to seem—by 2001—so far in the past that the iniquity and comprehensiveness of the Soviet threat often seemed entirely forgotten. For some on the left, old fellow travelers, this was both convenient and satisfying; for others (especially the young) it was a simple result of historical ignorance. And so, with the nature of the original link derided, the "clever" charge to make became the charge of American hypocrisy. The "facts" as they stood were that America was seeking to destroy a group it had armed. Under such circumstances, what right did America have to act?

The Soviet-era al-Qaeda link gave the people who wanted it two things. Firstly, it gave them the opportunity to say that the world was not black and white— that even after such a clear outrage as 9/11, no one group could be absolutely blamed or

condemned. The second thing it gave them was the intellectually narcissistic opportunity to imply that they were, and
always had been, informed on the intricacies of Afghan politics. In other words the "America armed al-Qaeda" line was
useful because it implied a degree of historical, as well as moral,
sophistication—an ideal mixture for contemporary poseurs
(and of course as such extraordinarily appealing to students and
the young). It relieved individuals from making serious moral
decisions, an abnegation that is by no means brave or interesting when you're so far outside government that an opt-out
from moral or strategic involvement is neither a real act nor
any sacrifice. But this process of diminishing the assault and
spreading the blame around a little was popular across the
West, and proved the beginning of relativism's journey towards
nihilism, and eventually to genocide-protection and the excusing of terror.

The old Marxist Tariq Ali was among those quick off the
mark with the next stage in the process: Bush-bin Laden equivalences. Ali swiftly published *The Clash of Fundamentalisms*, the
cover of which showed Bush's face superimposed onto that of
Osama bin Laden. Throughout his book, which suppurated
with that unique mixture of pathological self-regard and passé
Marxism, Ali attempted to demonstrate why the United States,
indeed any western government, is not morally eligible to act
against any other country. After all, Ali would repeat in broad-
casts, books, and articles, "the US had created Osama bin Laden
and his gang during the first Afghan War."[14] Case closed: you
created him, therefore you must eventually allow him to kill
you. This line became so popular that the man whose career
was built on such notions, Noam Chomsky, enjoyed a come-

back tour, even going to London and preaching his gospel of equivalence from the steps of the altar of St. Paul's Cathedral.

After 9/11, Chomsky's sole career line—"America once did this and therefore has no right to do that"—rose to levels of fantasy unmatched even in his own earlier career. As early as September 15, he was comparing the attacks of four days previously to President Clinton's 1998 rocketing of the Al-Shifa chemical plant in Khartoum, and then with the allied bombings in the Kosovo war.[15] Chomsky was also one of the first to claim that the attacks of 9/11 were the result of "grievances" suffered by the people of the Middle East, in particular over the situation of the displaced peoples of Palestine (a concern on which Chomsky and Co. pre-empted bin Laden, who had never shown any particular concern for the sufferings of the Palestinian peoples). But if such analysis was unhelpful for understanding the threat outside, it was exceedingly helpful for understanding the threat within. Over the following years, many people were going to follow down the logic-paths of planet-Chomsky. One of the places they would arrive was at the suspicious place identified by Christopher Hitchens when he wrote that "Chomsky's already train-wrecked syllogisms seem to entail the weird and sinister assumption that bin Laden is a ventriloquist for thwarted voices of international justice."[16]

Eleven days into the American forces' action in Afghanistan, on October 18, 2001, Chomsky excelled even himself in a broadcast speech: "The New War Against Terror." In it he spoke of what American forces were doing in Afghanistan, declaring "Looks like what's happening is some sort of silent genocide." He alleged that there was a concerted American attempt to starve and kill between three and four million Afghan people.[17] Chomsky's lunatic claim that the United States was deliberately committing an act of genocide was no slip, however: as David Horowitz and Ronald Radosh pointed out, Chomsky's intention with this startling remark was to say, "We are moral monsters; we are coolly planning the murder of not merely thousands of innocents like the desperate crew who brought down the World Trade Center—and whom we are about to punish—but *millions*."[18] Of course the "silent genocide" was so "silent' because it didn't happen. But Noam Chomsky is not a statesman, and his admirers cannot, and do not, hold him to account even for libelling an entire race with glib and false charges of genocide.

Two years later, when Chomsky was asked where his "silent genocide" had got to, he replied:

> That is an interesting fabrication, which gives a good deal of insight into the prevailing moral and intellectual culture. First, the facts: I predicted nothing. . . . All of this is precisely accurate and entirely appropriate. The warnings remain accurate as well, a truism that should be unnecessary to explain. Unfortunately, it is apparently necessary to add a moral truism: actions are evaluated in terms of the range of anticipated consequences.[19]

Of course, Chomsky's language can be opaque when it suits him, just as it can be memorably plain when certain other points are being made. Mark Steyn had a good go at trying to explain Chomsky's manner of weaseling out of the genocide accusation: "In Noam's rabbit hole, the buck never stops with him. . . . He doesn't deny that he used the words . . . he simply denies that the words mean what they appear to mean to anyone whose first language is non-university English."[20]

The reason this matters is that the habits of Chomsky were picked up more and more widely after 9/11. His increasingly lazy books (latterly consisting of leaden interviews) sold and gave a vaguely intellectual flavor to dissent in the war on terror. But West-haters and self-haters weren't reading him to pick up on knowledge of American iniquity; they were reading him in the hope of American iniquity—because they wanted there to be American iniquities. And they went along with the imagined genocides because they wanted there to be genocides, silent and otherwise, committed by America. Because if Chomsky was right, then America would not have the right to act, and if America did not have the right to act, then war would not be possible under any circumstances, and Chomsky readers would feel they'd done their bit in stopping it.

Except that a war had to be fought—a war with more than one battle. And it was a war that had to be won, not just because three thousand people had been reduced to human ash in New York and Washington, but because millions of people across the globe were living in countries which approved such an act, and would go on suffering under dictatorships that encouraged such slaughter both in other countries and in their own. It had to be fought because the Bush administration and its allies in London and elsewhere understood that a new threat existed. The likelihood of great stand-offs between nuclear superpowers had receded, and the populations of the world were safer as a result. But the likelihood of small terror cells colluding with tyrannical and isolated regimes, and achieving a one-off nuclear attack, or dirty strike, was proportionally higher than it had ever been. Unstable states were the means by which the US and her allies could continue to be hit. Al-Qaeda affiliates could not thrive in democratic states which opposed them and their nihilistic creed. But as the dust and debris from the Twin Towers settled and was swept away, people in America became more and more sanguine and cocky about the threat. The threat was there, however, and, in this new situation, a peace brought about by universal guilt was not going to save the life of anybody. As Hitchens wrote in disgust at Chomsky's unhinged frippery, "these opinions are a recipe for nothingness."[21] But they were more than that. They were a recipe for forgetfulness—forgetfulness of the horror of that morning, and also, in other hands, a recipe not for inaction, but for action against the West.

Yet they remain opinions that have a particular appeal to large numbers of people who pride themselves on being at the forefront of cultural thought. In her printed advice to the people of the United States, the novelist Arundhati Roy included the simple commandment: "Read Chomsky."[22] The shrill Roy has taken her own advice, for in a succession of almost child-like rants against American power since 9/11 she has demonstrated that she has picked up both Michael Moore's political simplicity ("The US government's recent military interventions in the Balkans and Central Asia have to do with oil"[23]) and Chomsky's habits, minus the intellectual casuistry.

Though no one could say Roy's thoughts were necessarily influential, they certainly expressed what a lot of people were thinking. A year after 9/11, as attention was turning to Iraq, she wrote:

Relativism and the Iraq War

What if Iraq does have a nuclear weapon, does that justify a preemptive US strike? The United States has the
largest arsenal of nuclear weapons in the world. It's the
only country in the world to have actually used them on
civilian populations. If the United States is justified in
launching a preemptive attack on Iraq, why then any
nuclear power is justified in carrying out a preemptive
attack on any other.[24]

Hiroshima and Nagasaki may have been nearly sixty years in
the past, but by this formula the US had no right to disarm Saddam Hussein (even—note—if he had a nuclear bomb) because
of the inherited guilt of Hiroshima and Nagasaki. So the
descendants of the Americans of the Second World War had
no right to prevent a potential nuclear strike on them because
of the actions of their forefathers? Like Chomsky, Roy does not
inflict this racist judgment on her own or any other particular
race, but America is fair game, and much the most dangerous
beast in town. "The whole world," Roy raved in the 2002 piece,
"would be better off without a certain Mr Bush. In fact, he is far
more dangerous than Saddam Hussein."[25] Though they paid
occasional lip-service to the notion of Hussein's nastiness,
Roy, Chomsky, and every other two-bit peacenik-poseur never
presented a solution for getting rid of the Iraqi menace. If
your business is equivalence, then you don't have to; you just
dig around in your nurtured repertoire of western crimes, and
assume that the people of Afghanistan and Iraq would—if
they could—be sitting back in their chairs reading your liber-
ated thoughts and thanking you for your bravery.

The ultimate expression of futile equivalence is yet to come,

Neoconservatism

but the route by which it finds its way is Israel. Western hostility to Israel since its birth, and particularly over the last thirty years, is a cause for concern, not just because of the attitude itself, but because of the means by which it has become implanted. That route found its origin and end-point in suicide-bombing.

It is hard to determine exactly how the sentimentalization of Palestinian suicide-bombing began, but the guilty party—whoever it was—created a precedent that now haunts the West in Iraq and on our own streets. For in the case of Israel, equivalence found itself mixed with a good dose of contemporary pseudo-compassion to produce the first modern point at which terror became acceptable.

As was pointed out in Chapter 2, neoconservatives are committed to supporting Israel. And this support has strengthened since 9/11 for one very clear reason: the events of 2001 confirmed what many neocons had held all along—that in the mine of twenty-first century terror, Israel had long been the canary. The warnings that what had happened to Israel would happen to the West went unheeded. The warning that Islamic terror was aimed at the West and would strike there if, or when, it could also went unheeded. In 1995 Benjamin Netanyahu had written:

> It is impossible to understand just how inimical—and how deadly—to the United States and to Europe this rising tide of militant Islam is without taking a look at the roots of Arab-Islamic hatred of the West. Because of the Western media's fascination with Israel, many today are under the impression that the intense hostil-

ity prevalent in the Arab and Islamic world toward the
United States is a contemporary phenomenon, the result
of Western support for the Jewish state, and that such
hostility would end if an Arab-Israeli peace was eventually reached. But nothing could be more removed from
the truth. The enmity toward the West goes back many
centuries, remaining to this day a driving force at the
core of militant Arab-Islamic political culture. And this
would be the case even if Israel had never been born.[26]

Yet for those in America and the West who picked up on the
"Israeli-Palestinian peace is the issue" line after 9/11, nothing
would throw them off that scent. Like the CIA-al-Qaeda connection, the Israeli-Palestinian question could be dropped into
any argument to show both "compassion" and "understanding" of the issues. Unfortunately, as a result, many amid the
western populations simply fell on the wrong side of the fence.
When figures like the British Prime Minister's wife, Cherie
Blair, professed sympathy for the young men and women who
boarded buses and blew up Jews, they not only committed a
moral inversion, confusing victim and aggressor, guilty and
innocent, they also stripped the Palestinian people of the dignity of free will. The Palestinians became, and remained, the
pawns of the professedly "liberals" in the West, as much as they
had always been the pawns of the Islamic peoples. Arundhati
Roy made a characteristic attempt to describe the situation: in
her version, Palestinians "never know when their homes will
be demolished, when their children will be shot." And in the
face of this unrestrained and insatiable Jewish thirst for killing
children, "Young Palestinians who cannot contain their anger

Neoconservatism

turn themselves into bombs ... suicide bombing is an act of individual despair."[27] The sentimentalization of suicide bombing as an act of "despair" fails so comprehensively to fit the political reality that it could only be employed as a result of ignorance, or as a piece of propaganda in an attempt to influence some other outcome.

And so it was no surprise when the ignorant sentimentalization of the Palestinian cause conflated with equivalencing over the slaughter of Jews and accelerated within months of 9/11 into the open acclaim of Jihad and the "intifada" on western streets. For neocons, Netanyahu's warnings had proved accurate. "The democracies have wasted much time in addressing the question of resurgent Islamic terror," Netanyahu had warned in 1995. "They are approaching the twelfth hour. They can wait no longer."[28] Yet wait they did, and the twelfth hour arrived in the skies of New York, Washington, and Pennsylvania. For the opposition, those acts of terror were not an extension of the hatred being inflicted on the Israeli people, but a reaction to Israel's self-defense. Neocons knew that the events were linked in a different way. The attacks on Jews in Israel had long been permissible in the West because the attacks were meant to be on the state, not on its people. This ongoing piece of casuistry is seen as a clear lie by neocons, who know the attacks for what they are: attacks on the Jews because they are Jews, attacks on the free West because it is the free West, and attacks on democracies because the perpetrators hate democracy. The inability of western governments to call Islamic terror by its name and root it out as the absolute enemy of the free West cost thousands of lives on 9/11. Political correctness, moral equivocation, and the notion that Israel's experience of terror might be unique to Israel all assisted on the path to inaction and unpreparedness. But neocons learned from Israel's lessons, knowing that Israel was our ally, not our enemy. First Israel, then America, and next Europe were under attack from the same enemy. The enemies and guilty parties were those who were perpetrating the attacks, and no amount of equivalencing could change that.

If this line was simplistic, neoconservatism's opponents were perfectly happy to repeat an even more simplistic mantra: "Peace in Israel/Palestine is the key." Neoconservatives always knew that this line was not only simplistic, but that it was— and remains—disingenuous. The ignorant do not mean what they say: they merely repeat a slogan. But those who are acquainted with the situation know something else, which is that, if peace does come to Israel/Palestine, it is not coming any time soon. They know that calling for a resolution to the Israeli–Palestinian conflict before waging another war is like calling for postponement until the seas run dry. One must then ask why they are stalling like this; why they are opposed to the West acting.

Plainly it is a tactic to prevent action by America, Britain, and their allies, an attempt to neuter us into inaction. But when some of the perpetrators saw this tactic was not working, they became more fevered, more desperate, and many of those involved in the stalling game came out into the open. Even before the start of the Afghan war it became clear that many of those who, we thought, were equivalencers were no such thing. It was not that they were interested in peace, or com-

mitted to justice, or any other such slogan. These were distrac-
tions and alibis. The fact was that they were dedicated to
defending the causes and actions of Islamic terrorism.

The New Counterculture

Since 2003 many of those opposed to the conflict in Iraq
have pretended that it was only that conflict to which they
objected, that they are pragmatists, not anti-Western idealists.
Since there have been so many attempts to rewrite recent
events, it is well to recall the anti-war movement's position
before 2003. For it was not only Iraq that caused rifts: the
rifts that were widened by the Iraq conflict were opened from
the moment the Twin Towers were attacked.

The perennial objectors to America's right to self-assertion
were active within days of 9/11, organizing—by their own
estimation—247 "anti-war" demonstrations in the US alone
between September 11 and the end of that month. College
campuses, spurred by the radical professors lucratively tenured
there, saw around 150 "peace vigils" and "teach-in" protests
in the same period.[29] The public were meant to see such reactionary protests in a benevolent light, but if they did they were
fooled. Professor Eric Foner from Columbia University took
the opportunity to voice his views within days of the attacks
by saying, "I'm not sure which is more frightening: the horror
that engulfed New York City or the apocalyptic rhetoric
emanating daily from the White House."[30] In reality no such
uncertainty existed in the minds of the anti-war leaders. Their
movement had shamelessly organized from the very moment
America was hit, not just in order to blame America first and
prevent America from acting, but to claim that America has no

right to act even if it wanted to. This problem might have had its origins in the Western self-absorption which Bloom identified, but it ended in support for barbarous tyrannies abroad and in superciliousness towards those seeking security at home. It also found an early and easy alliance with terrorism.

The anti-war movement was not demoralized by its failure to prevent the liberation of Afghanistan, but, on the contrary, maneuvered itself immediately to gain wider support and a wider say in opposing the then upcoming liberation of Iraq. The first major coordinated demonstrations against such a war were held across Europe and America in September 2002. This was not an accident, for by now socialists had joined forces with a movement with which they now had much in common—the forces of reactionary Islam. Movements like the Hamas-championers of the American Muslim Council (AMC) and the Council on American-Islamic Relations (CAIR) —an offshoot of the Hamas-created Islamic Association for Palestine—leapt into action.

September 2002 was chosen as the date to march for one particular reason: it marked the second anniversary of the terrorist "intifada" in the Holy Land. Some socialist organizations subsequently claimed not to know the significance of this date when they originally linked up to organize and march with Muslim organizations. Muslim organizations across the West by no means kept the significance of their marches a secret, and when they were told the facts, none of the socialist organizations which claimed ignorance were bothered enough to consider breaking what had become an incredibly useful alliance. The demonstrations organized in the US by ANSWER (Act Now to Stop War and End Racism) made plain that the

September demonstrations comprised an expression of "soli-darity" with the Palestinian terrorist cause. By the end of October, the "anti-war" yet pro-Palestinian terrorist demon-strations in America alone had attendances of hundreds of thousands. The figures were significant for many reasons, but not least because (as David Horowitz pointed out in his book on the subject, *Unholy Alliance*) "these numbers were larger than those that had been achieved in the first six years of protest against the Vietnam War."[31] A new counterculture was on the move.

The marches organized by this socialist-Islamist pairing amply reflected the view of those involved, and did so across the Western world. In September 2002 in Europe, young Muslims paraded dressed as suicide bombers; anti-Israeli plac-ards abounded, as did open anti-Semitic attacks. Swastikas and Stars of David were superimposed onto one another to accom-pany chants and slurs against the Jewish people. A number of Jews on marches, who had been protesting against the possi-bility of war in Iraq, left horrified at the "hate-filled chanting and images in which anti-Israel and anti-Jewish imagery were blurred [leaving] us feeling deeply alienated."[32] What they learned, and what many others would subsequently learn, was that the prime target of the anti-war movement worldwide was not Saddam Hussein (indeed it remained entirely silent on him). Its first target was not even George Bush or Tony Blair. Its first target was the Jewish state, and its right to exist. Its secondary targets were Britain and America.

In America and across Europe, the banners handed out by Muslim associations carried an anti-Iraq war slogan on one side and "Freedom for Palestine" slogans on the other. From the very beginning, the anti-war movement was characterized by overtly anti-Israeli propaganda. Muslim associations were delighted and emboldened by the success of their campaign. In a lengthy and furious denunciation of a newspaper piece which had dared to criticize it, the most prominent British Muslim association (the Muslim Association of Britain) wrote: "Zionism is a movement which was until recently condemned by the International Community and the United Nations as a racist ideology."[33] Even a quarter of a century after his notorious UN resolution, Idi Amin was still giving them hope.

The anti-war coalitions across the West went on to gain the support of extremist racists and white supremacists who agreed with Muslim and far left organizations that world policy was being dictated by Jews, and they also gained the support of such luminaries as Colonel Gadaffi. They also earned the thanks of Saddam Hussein himself, who declared the support of the anti-war demonstrations a victory for the Iraqi people.

There is no doubt that the period leading up to war in Iraq included much of the most divisive debate in the West for a generation. The fact that for most people living here there would be little immediate physical impact on their lives, whether or not their troops fought, seemed if anything to heighten emotions. The problem with this was not just that much of the protesting was cheap—but that it came free. With conscription a thing of the past, and the prospect of multiple suicide bombings still seeming only a possibility, there often seemed—physically—nothing much to play for. Yet many went along with the antagonists, and were swept up in the chants of the anti-war movement not from convictions that could withstand any form of test, but from a form of moral laziness. It is worrying when swathes of people are hostile to their government, but it is more worrying still when ordinary citizens can become hostile to their country as their default mode. When the first or second instinct of a citizen is to lambaste his own, then we know that there is a wider rot that has set in, albeit a rot that can be mended.

There was no more conspicuous "bravery" in opposing the conflict than there was in supporting it. The matter was simply one of morality and philosophy. By February 2003, when millions of protestors marched in cities across the West, it was clear that there were many who felt angry about the prospect of war, but who were neither socialists nor Islamists. Some objected to war in general. Others had specific reasons for objecting to this war in particular. Yet hundreds of millions of people did not march, many taking the view that, on matters of intelligence, national security, and statecraft, their governments knew better than they did. Of course the frivolity, self-absorption, and comprehensive lack of constructive opposition offered by the anti-war movement was most reminiscent of another movement that had left its mark on American culture. The legacy of the Sixties, and specifically the legacy of the Vietnam anti-war protests, persuaded the remnants of a nostalgic generation, as well as a generation eager for its own great cause, to have a go at being anti-warriors. Once again, this was not a debate about war abroad, but a debate founded in a war at home—a culture war impelled by those antagonistic to Western society and those pursuing a nostalgic search for meaning in an age even more morally confused than that of the Sixties. The legacy of Vietnam was a legacy of division and misrepresentation, a legacy that a new anti-war conglomeration now picked up and took to its own illogical conclusions.

During the 2002–2003 demonstrations, American and European streets were turned not just into a theater of anti-Semitism and its pretty indistinguishable twin anti-Zionism. They were also turned into the clearest demonstration yet of the feeling of contempt and antipathy held by many socialists and Muslims in Western societies towards Western governments and Western society. When young Muslim children chanted hate-slogans on the streets and an imam could call on the National Mall for "revolution time," crying, "We have to get rid of greedy murderers and imperialists like George Bush in the White House,"[34] then some people realized that these were more than demonstrations of hatred for the wars in Iraq or Afghanistan. When pro-Palestinian terror activists scorned the reasons for war in Iraq or Afghanistan, some people realized that they were opposed not only to these specific wars, but also to the actions and defense of both the Jewish state and the states of the West—the very states that harbored them.

Since the events of 2001, America has seen many mass mobilizations of people on the streets of its cities. It has, like its allies, learnt of specific cases of treachery among its citizens who have left to fight allied forces overseas and plotted acts of terror at home. It has read of the encouragement in this by imams in Western cities and organizations based on their shores. We have also seen, in the pages of national publications and on university campuses, the encouragement of a movement not merely critical of our interests, but specifically opposed to those interests. This movement arose and became prominent thanks to the attacks of 9/11, but it represents forces that have

Neoconservatism

existed for many years. The important point about what has happened since 2001 is that foreign ideologies and other ideologies that cannot be assimilated have found common cause with socialists who were left cause-less by the disintegration of their communist idol. And both have found a sympathetic ear among the mainstream because, by 2001, too many Western peoples and their intellectual and political leaders proved incapable of speaking or thinking plainly in defense of their own society. With their learned presumption that "liberalism" was the right, as well as the nice, position to adopt, publications and politicians proved all but incapable of facing down their enemies.

What America and Europe have seen over these years has been the emergence of a new counterculture. Like the first counterculture, this movement is not merely an alternative culture, or a culture that is critical of our culture, but an assemblage of people specifically and consistently opposed to this culture. They are opposed to Western interests, and bitterly sarcastic about the notion that any such thing exists. Its immoral members openly celebrate violent attacks on western society; its more moral members are simply incapable of coming up with any but the most hollow reasons for why such attacks are wrong. The bad among them desire caliphates or socialist dystopias, while the better talk of newly invented international courts and supranational institutions. In other words, all of them dream and plan the end of America's right to behave as a sovereign nation. None have come up with any serious propositions for toppling tyrants. All expend their considerable venom on the elected leaders of Britain, America, and their allies so that they have none left to express even formulaic distaste for dictators. Their employment of relativism has sapped their one historical allusion, the Holocaust, of its moral impact, and they are now dulled to the possibility that any difference exists between absolute evil and British and US policy.

None considers defense of the West and its way of life to be a serious priority. They regard the appalling and pressing problems of our time as some kind of smokescreen constructed by George Bush and Tony Blair—a grotesquely flippant charge which also happens to absolve them of any serious consideration of the issues. The movement combines antipathy towards Western society with—at best—apathy towards terrorism and terrorism's supporting tyrannies. Since so-called "liberals" have once again crumpled before this counterculture (when they haven't joined it), the task of defending our culture against this creeping nihilism falls to conservatives, and it is they who must, once again, be strident in defense of what they know to be right and good.

The Iraq War

It is possible that the war in Iraq will be the last major intervention of its kind for some years. There is little stomach for any further such intervention (for instance, in Iran or Syria). For this reason, among others, it is still possible that many people will persist in regarding our objective in Iraq as having failed. It is therefore worth explaining frankly why the war was necessary and why it remains right.

It is a fact of life that in politics there is a difference between what one would like to do and what one can do. In an ideal society, the government is restrained but not shackled, and there is a relationship of trust between the people and government that permits the government, on occasion, to take decisions that may be unpopular and occasionally inexplicable to the public. The Iraq conflict was just such a conflict. But, as Kristol and Kagan discuss in their contribution to *Present Dangers*, it was spurred by reasons either too numerous or too opaque for large proportions of the population to go along with.

What occurred over Iraq—and in particular over the issue of WMD—was certainly not, as the neocon-bashers have tried to label it, a "noble lie." This accusation has, for some time, been the calumny of choice for discerning critics. Yet the accusation is ignorant. The notion of the "noble lie" certainly arises in Plato, and it is true that Strauss and many neoconservatives admire Plato. But what Plato described (in his *Republic*) was that, on occasion, leaders have to conceal truths from the masses in order to lead them most wisely. He certainly did not (as one commentator put it with wild hyperbole) claim that "it is practically a duty to lie to the masses."[35] Still less did Strauss, or his most direct pupils, believe any such thing. Plato described how in matters of grave importance, occasions arise in which a leader will know best, and in which the less well-informed masses, if given the opportunity to decide on a specific matter, might decide wrongly. There are very few who would disagree with this, and the profession of outrage at the very notion of the "noble lie" is, to put it kindly, an example of faked outrage.

But the allegation that neocons, or anyone else in either the UK or US administrations, told a "noble lie" over Iraq to achieve their goals is not merely "stretching it"[36]: it is glib and offensive nonsense. And it is nonsense not merely because those who have peddled the line (such as Geoffrey Wheatcroft in the *Guardian*[37]) have misrepresented their Plato and not read their Strauss. It is not even nonsense simply because the accusation is a further blithe attempt by members of the press to claim that prominent politicians are liars. No, it is wrong because, far from concealing anything from their people, the governments of the US and the UK told their people everything they knew. If they did make a mistake, it was that they provided the people with every complicated and messy truth that they possessed at the time. And in telling everything they knew at the time (including publishing single-source intelligence which should never have been disseminated), they discussed and made available intelligence that was incorrect, information that was unclear, and a certain amount of raw intelligence that may turn out to have been comprehensively mistaken.

The fault of the US and UK governments was not in "lying" to the people, but in telling the people too much, revealing information that no previous government would have revealed, and, through this process, seriously compromising and embarrassing their security services. In their thorough investigation into the British matter, Anthony Glees and Philip Davies quoted the observation of Daphne Park (a former senior controller at the security service M16) that the government's fundamental error was its wish to share intelligence with the public—a public "who were increasingly anxious about government 'spin' and 'sleaze.'" The mistake therefore was not a desire to lie or dissemble, but to be "too ready to pander to public opinion."[138] Had the public not been deluged with a vast quantity of information, plus numerous additional reports into the matter, then the accusations and counter-accusations would have been proportionately fewer, less confused, and less bitter. Government openness, both in providing informa-

Neoconservatism

tion and in providing opinion before the Iraq war, was more comprehensive than at any other time in British or American political history. Talk of lies, cover-ups, and neocon-led conspiracies is a diversion—a diversion created by the sinister and agenda-laden, and carried on by the confused. The facts about why the war in Iraq took place are really far clearer than any conspiracy theorists or Strauss-fingerers would have us believe, and neocons have laid them out perfectly openly, time and time again, in print, in public speeches and through an unashamedly consistent public record.

The truth—which, as Paul Wolfowitz noted, so many people are unwilling to acknowledge—is that 9/11 changed things. It may not have changed the nature of America, but it changed its dynamic. When administration figures who had never been neoconservative seemed to come over all neocon, it was because neoconservatism represented, on one level, a form of exuberant Republicanism that many on Capitol Hill had either forgotten or were new to. But the Iraq war was not led by neocons—not even by the highest-ranking neocon, Paul Wolfowitz. Deputy defense secretaries do not create US foreign policy. Neocons had already provided much of the background, the explanations for the moral imperative of action, and much-needed clarity throughout a situation mired in unworkable status quos. But the conflict was decided on, and led by, non-neocon Republicans who had come to realize, as the neocons had realized years before, that the old way of doing things had failed them. To the extent that they became opponents of a status quo that was damaging America, Iraq, and the Middle East, the highest members of government became foreign policy neoconservatives.

Relativism and the Iraq War

An opportunity arose in the wake of 9/11—an opportunity for change. All the neoconservative complaints during the previous decades over the preservation of a status quo that was hostile to American interests were starkly highlighted that day. Countries that were meant to be America's allies turned out to have had a hand in events; countries that were allegedly "contained" were harboring supporters of those who committed the atrocity and others who aimed to carry out similar atrocities. This status quo was being sustained at a colossal cost not only in dollars and global respect, but now also in American lives. This status quo had been called "realism," but as Muravchik had said years before, "Just what is realistic about it?"[39]

The outrages of 9/11 demonstrated the need for a shake-up in the world, and specifically a shake-up of the role in the world of America and her powerful allies. The impetus provided by the atrocity made it possible to confront a number of the lingering global nightmares to which the weary post-Cold War world had turned a blind eye. What this impetus allowed were confrontations with regimes that needed to be confronted, but which, under the status quo, had not only gone unconfronted but (for America and the UN) often humiliatingly so. The new opportunity was amply summed up by Tony Blair in a conversation in Downing Street a few days before the Iraq war began. It is an ideal neoconservative expression—a perfect blend of humanitarianism, national interest, and hyper-realism:

> What amazes me is how many people are happy for Saddam to stay. They ask why we don't get rid of Mugabe, why not the Burmese lot. Yes, let's get rid of them all. I don't because I can't, but when you can, you should.[40]

Neoconservatism

After 9/11 the "can" was there; the "should" was clear in Washington and London; and if the status quo was ever to be broken for the better, now was the time.

The war to topple the Taliban and dismantle al-Qaeda's Afghan infrastructure was by no means as unopposed at the time as many now pretend, but a majority of the American people understood that America at least had the right to return fire on those who had attacked its cities. But when the opportunity to overthrow another threatening tyranny arose, was carried through, and succeeded—this time in Iraq—confusion grew. It is worth explaining frankly, then, the first truth of the Iraq war, which is that it was—and though the phrase is callous, it cannot be avoided—a "free war." That is, after 9/11 and after Afghanistan, there was still the momentum, within government and much of American society, for one further act against those who represented a world in which such atrocities could be carried out.

With the Taliban out of the way, there was no government left in the world that openly harbored so many participating al-Qaeda operatives. But one government did remain that had openly celebrated the acts of 2001 and that had long been a magnet in the region and the world for anti-western aggression and anti-western defiance. Particularly since, by turning his defeat in the first Gulf War into an opportunistic imitation of "holy war," Saddam Hussein had encouraged and given assistance to anti-western Islamic terrorists of all shades.

One of the examples Paul Wolfowitz often quotes is the case of Abdul Rahman Yassin, one of those indicted for the 1993 bombing of the World Trade Center, which killed six people and injured around one thousand others. Yassin was the only one of the 1993 WTC perpetrators at large. After escaping US jurisdiction he headed straight for Baghdad, where he was given sanctuary for the next ten years.[41] The case of Yassin is not exceptional; it is representative. Abu Abbas, the Palestinian terrorist who had led the hijacking of the *Achille Lauro* in 1985, received sanctuary in Iraq; the terrorist organization he headed, the Palestine Liberation Front, moved its headquarters with Abbas from Tunisia to Baghdad after their murderous hijacking of the Italian ship. There are many similar examples, such as Abu Nidal, of a community of committed terrorists being welcomed and encouraged by the Ba'athist regime. This, combined with the Hussein regime's financial rewarding of Palestinian suicide terrorism (a reward provocatively upped by Hussein, in March 2002, to $25,000 for the family of each man or woman who went out to kill Israelis), served to ensure that, with or without card-carrying al-Qaeda members, after the fall of the Taliban, Iraq became the most prominent haven for Islamic terrorists. That is also why Abu Musab al-Zarqawi and his "al-Qaeda in Iraq" group moved to Iraq. After fighting in, and fleeing from, Afghanistan, al-Zarqawi and his terrorist group sought sanctuary in Iraq— not after, but *before* the war in Iraq began. By 2002 it was the only country in the world to assure them a warm and supportive welcome. This is a world away from the peaceniks' ill-informed and repetitive cry that Islamic militants and Saddam Hussein somehow "didn't get on." In the years after the invasion of Kuwait, Hussein had made every effort—and with considerable success—to appear as the religious and military leader of the anti-western jihad. He had become the terrorists' magnet, and their patron.

Neoconservatism

Hussein's heroic image in certain parts of the Muslim world was, of course, grotesquely far removed from reality. No dictator in modern times has slaughtered more Muslims, both in genocides perpetrated in his own country, and in wars against his neighbors. America and her allies knew that Iraq had weapons of mass destruction because (uniquely among modern tyrants) Hussein had used them in attacks—like that on Halabja—of which the whole world knew. Yet he retained a degree of, if not popularity, then respect among the "brother" Arabs and Muslims of those he had slaughtered. His country may have been cowed by his regime of torture, mass execution, and fear, but what respect and admiration he was held in throughout the region—despite his genocidal habits—was entirely due to his defiance and resistance to the West. This was his salient position (in a period in which his personal power should have been diminishing): he was the totem of anti-western hatred, and the meeting-point for anti-western forces. Under any circumstances this should have been unacceptable to Britain, America, and the West. Yet the situation was allowed to continue, and for more than a decade after his forcible and humiliating expulsion from Kuwait, the West played a largely soft-power game with Iraq. Sanctions imposed by the West were manipulated by Hussein to terrorize "his" people, keep his family and favorites in luxury, and—as we now know—buy and bribe those politicians and others in the West and elsewhere who were willing to be bought.

Even before 9/11, this situation was unappealing to all parties. Sanctions were crumbling; since 1997, France, China, and Russia on the UN Security Council had been pressing for a relaxation and eventual lifting of sanctions.[42] In each case the attraction was not just that each country would be able to benefit from the increased oil trade, but also that they would be able to recommence the arms trade with Iraq. Saddam Hussein himself knew which way the wind was blowing, declaring in 2000, "We have said with certainty that the embargo will not be lifted by a Security Council resolution, but will corrode by itself."[43] Neoconservatives and realists of all shades knew that when sanctions ended the world would see—and this could be foreseen with absolute certainty—the re-arming of the Iraqi dictator by regimes that wished to benefit financially.

France, with its President Jacques Chirac, enjoyed a particularly close relationship with the Hussein regime and its arms interests, and was among the nations most eager to see a lifting of sanctions. France's pose as a peacenik in the run-up to war was not only an act of retrogressive opportunism, but a continuation of its role as an ally of Iraq. France's supporters among the street protestors enjoyed making jokes about American and British arms sales to Iraq during the Iran-Iraq war (when both had rightly regarded Iranian dominance in the region as the principal threat), yet it is no thanks to Jacques Chirac that America, Britain, and their allies had not met a nuclear Iraq in 1991, never mind 2003.

It was after a triumphant visit to Paris in 1975 to see President Giscard d'Estaing and Prime Minister Chirac that Saddam Hussein was offered a French nuclear reactor for $300 million. Though this was twice the "list" price, the deal was accepted and the French reactor paid for. "We were happy to pay," recalled one of the Iraqi nuclear team, adding, "After all, who

else was going to sell us a nuclear reactor?"[44] The French-sup-
plied nuclear reactor at Osirak had money poured into it by
Hussein in his desperate bid to become the holder of the first
"Arab bomb," and thus the pre-eminent Arab leader. But the
effects of such a destabilization in the region's politics, even in
those days before Hussein had become an explicit threat to
the wider world, was recognized by Israel. Before the reactor
went "hot," the Israeli government ordered its destruction.
The raid (on 7 June 1 9 8 1) was mounted in the crucial period
before the reactor was able to create the materials which—if
they leaked out—could destroy the surrounding area after a
hit. This model pre-emptive attack was highly controversial.
Every single one of Israel's friends and allies condemned the
attack. Yet time proved how right the Israelis had been. Had
they waited until the reactor could supply bomb-making mate-
rial, the destruction of the facility would have had disastrous
consequences in the region. Had they waited until the bomb
had actually been made, an attack would have been unfeasible,
and would have led to nuclear conflict. By attacking in this
window of opportunity, they forestalled a nightmare possibility ten years on—something America was to recognize when
Dick Cheney (then Secretary of Defense) acknowledged, with
great understatement, "You made our job easier in Desert
Storm."[45] Not so much "easier" as "possible." Had Hussein
been armed with a nuclear bomb in 1 9 9 1, there is little doubt
that he would have been able to keep Kuwait, and anything
else he liked.

The prospect of a resurgent nuclear Hussein was not one
that the United States was willing to contemplate, and after
9/1 1 it was a prospect that it knew it had to act on. Reports

Relativism and the Iraq War

from British intelligence (reiterated in President Bush's January 2003 State of the Union address) of Iraqi officials shopping for uranium in Niger were widely dismissed after the invasion, but found by a detailed Inquiry in 2004 to have been "well founded."[46] Other intelligence pointed to diverse renewed efforts by Hussein, though many of the details were not to emerge until after the invasion. But if British and American intelligence were concerned about a resurgent Saddam Hussein seeking and acquiring weapons of mass destruction, certain other western governments hardly seemed bothered.

Within months of 9/11, German intelligence informed Gerhard Schröder that they believed Saddam Hussein's quest for nuclear power had restarted. The chief of the BND (the German intelligence agency), August Hanning, stated plainly, "It is our estimate that Iraq will have an atomic bomb in three years."[47] It would be untrue to say that the German government under-reacted to this information—it didn't react at all. Even informed that Iraq was within reach of having the bomb, Gerhard Schröder continued to oppose regime change in Iraq.

Then, in the summer of 2002, while UN inspectors were still in Iraq, German officials received new information indicating that Iraq possessed previously unknown stockpiles of the smallpox virus. Instead of taking any action, or passing the information on, the German government kept silent on the matter—indeed covered it up completely. Gerhard Schröder had run his re-election campaign (in a very marginal race) on a populist platform, during which, as William Shawcross wrote, "the German Chancellor deliberately created an atmosphere of anti-Americanism."[48] In an atmosphere where the German government was scrabbling for every vote to stay in office, it

Neoconservatism

was unsurprising that Schröder's Justice Minister, Herta Däubler-Gmelin, should have taken a public opportunity a few days before voters went to the polls in September 2002 to compare President Bush to her country's very own Adolf Hitler. In this situation, the German government decided it was best not to throw away the anti-American course of their election by revealing evidence of Iraqi WMD, which could only bolster the case for war, and so the details of the smallpox discovery were kept quiet, both from the country and from the UN.

When the story finally broke in February 2003, the German press was awash with reports of how, if targeted, twenty-five million Germans could be killed by the smallpox virus.[49] German papers began debating how and when Islamic terrorists might try to wreak this terror on the German people. In an attempt to quell the public fear, two government ministers claimed that there was little likelihood of "American-hating" terrorists attacking Germany with the smallpox virus: Germany was, after all, against any war.[50] A further underlying motive of France and Germany in opposing the war became clear: appease the threat, and let America and Britain take whatever came. As Andrew Sullivan wrote, "by taking the anti-American line, they risk nothing. They know the U.S. will deal with the threat; but by appeasing the Islamo-fascists, the Franco-German axis hopes to avoid any blowback."[51] If Germany kept its head down, it would avoid the kind of provocation that might lead to an attack: after all, if America was going to be targeted anyway, why get in the way?

This "let them take care of it, while we keep our hands clean" attitude permeated the thinking of certain countries that had once been US/UK allies. It could also be heard throughout the streets of Europe and America, where civilians, who had no answer to the threat of Saddam Hussein, nor any sensible notion of how to deal with him, loudly demonstrated to keep their consciences "clean," even if this meant allowing Hussein to keep W M D (which they generally believed he held, even if they now ridicule governments for having believed likewise). Just as the equivalencing that had spread throughout the continent reached its zenith in the echelons of the German cabinet, so renunciation of personal and global responsibility stretched from the streets of America to the cabinet rooms of Europe. In Europe especially, a popular determination to confront a present and growing threat was, at best, lacking. This moral and political failing was partly the result of Europe's peculiar post-war belief that, because it was bad, war should be avoided at all costs. But it was also the result of immediate strategic convenience. In 2 0 0 3 William Kristol and Lawrence Kaplan criticized those European allies of America who "spend on social programs and allow the United States to guarantee their security, and then condemn their American cousin for being too aggressive." [52] Not only were countries like Germany unwilling to act, they were also largely incapable of acting. In that situation, inaction was strategically, financially, and "morally" advantageous. The UN had proved incapable, unwilling, and (necessarily considering its constituencies) antagonistic towards the idea of removing this enduring threat. But someone had to stop the re-emergent menace of Saddam Hussein, and in 2 0 0 3 America and Britain led the way.

Because of the failure to locate the stockpiles of W M D, which every intelligence agency in the world believed Iraq to possess, many American civilians now think they were fed a not-so-noble lie by their government. They were not. Many people, however, press the claim that the government lied became a matter not of copy, but of pride. A stand-off was initiated by portions of the media. In these circumstances they skewed, misread, and wilfully failed to report aspects of the story that did not accord with their argument. This situation led to the unhealthy situation of a rapacious Western media setting out to be hostile opponents of their governments. Thus the press increasingly gave itself over to moral arbitration rather than to gathering facts. So Britain's *Mirror* ran (before the start of the conflict) a front-page photo of Tony Blair with red hands and the caption "blood on his hands." Inside was the full, demented "story" from that Australian arbiter of morality, John Pilger. In the article (described by the editors as "his most damning verdict on Tony Blair") the not noticeably butch Pilger attacked Tony Blair as "effete," compared him and George Bush with Adolf Hitler and those tried at Nuremberg, and then described the American administration as "the Third Reich of our times."[53] This was the level at which much of the media across the West began to conduct its coverage.

Pride, self-absorption, and political wrong-headedness became not just widespread, but endemic in certain papers before and after the war in Iraq. Before the invasion, many media reactions to events on the ground in Iraq were misinformed and unrepresentative, but by the end of the conflict the most gaping biases had emerged. Partly due to the security situation, most of the press remained within the walls of the Al-Hamra and Palestine hotels. As one of the most admirable reporters confessed, "The dirty little secret is that the endless 'stand-ups' you see on your screens are based on no reporting at all."[54] What was incredible about this, though, was not that the reporting from many journalists abandoned any pretence at reportage, pitching straight for positions as the next crusading Pilger-figure, but rather that such a large proportion of the free press became open in its desire for American and British interests to fail. Some declared these wishes only in private, hoping for more casualties, so that George Bush's re-election could be derailed.[55] Others openly declared themselves for the other side.

"It is to be hoped," wrote Tariq Ali, "that the invaders of Iraq will eventually be harried out of the country by a growing national reaction to the occupation regime they install, and that their collaborators may meet the fate of Nuri Said before them."[56] Ali was not alone in hoping for the execution of those Iraqis who "collaborated" with American and British forces, and the "occupation" equivalence became useful for those opposed to British and American interests. On the BBC's *Newsnight*, British MP George Galloway, friend of the Iraqi thug Tariq Aziz and the late terrorist Yasser Arafat, was asked whether there was any difference between Nazi occupation of France and the Allied occupation of Iraq: "no difference at all," he replied. Galloway was speaking not only as an enemy of American and British troops, but also as an apologist for the terrorists. Curiously ignoring the murderers who were targeting men, women, and children across the country, Galloway lied: "Actually, the Iraqi Resistance does not target its own civilians." He went on to pretend that the "resistance" was only attacking "people who are working for the occupation."[57]

To those who hated the liberation of Iraq more than they

Neoconservatism

hated the Hussein tyranny, Galloway and his ilk became "out-spoken" heroes.

And the genuinely ignoble lie became commonplace there-on throughout the anti-war movement. Some of it was caused by self-hatred; some of it was simply open proselytizing for terror. In September 2004, Naomi Klein reacted to the "up-rising" against American forces in Najaf by using the pages of the New York *Nation* magazine to declare, "It's time to bring Najaf to New York."[58] Three years was all it had taken for New York to turn from a city shocked by terrorist outrages to a city in which journalists like Klein could frivolously call for more jihad. Professor Ward Churchill of the University of Colorado, meanwhile, had attacked (and continued to attack) from another angle, impugning the innocence of those who had died on 9/11. To him and those who thought like him, the victims of 9/11 weren't human beings with even the rights of any other innocent civilian killed in conflict. To that college professor the victims of 9/11 had become guilty parties—"little Eichmanns" who were, in his foul description, "civilians of a sort. But innocent? Gimme a break."[59]

Creeping equivalence was leading to its natural end points. What this represented was not merely fallout from a contro-versial conflict, but the counterculture generation expressing, with spite and racism, their hatred of Western society, and their desire for the troops and civilians of those societies to be taught a brutal lesson.

But in Washington, the knowledge that the right thing was being done did not change. Donald Rumsfeld wrote of a meeting before the Iraq war with a South Korean journalist, who had asked him: "Why should Koreans send their young people halfway around the globe to be killed or wounded in Iraq?" "It's a fair question," Rumsfeld replied. "And it would have been fair for an American to ask, fifty years ago, 'Why should young Americans go halfway around the world to be killed or wounded in Korea?'" Rumsfeld, who had lost friends in the Korean war, continued:

> Korean freedom was won at a terrible cost—tens of thousands of lives, including more than 33,000 American killed in action. Was it worth it? You bet. Just as it was worth it in Germany and France and Italy and in the Pacific in World War II. And just as it is worth it in Afghanistan and Iraq today.... Today, as we think about the tens of thousands of United States soldiers in Iraq —and in Afghanistan and elsewhere around the world fighting the global war on terrorism—we should say to all of them: "You join a long line of generations of Americans who have fought freedom's fight. Thank you."[60]

The press, however, and much of the public for whom it was the sole source of information were not only unwilling to feel gratitude to the US and UK soldiers dying in the cause of Iraqi freedom; they were actually willing more of them to die. And they were more than willing to scoff and ignore the sacrifice taking place—which is why, when the Abu Ghraib scandal erupted in April/May 2003, the press not only covered it, but relished and savored it.

The events in Abu Ghraib received the coverage they did because they fitted into a portion of the press's ideas and agenda. Terrible though the events were, the glee with which they were picked up on displayed once again the press's desire to see the Allied efforts in Iraq fail. Once again, the combination of equivalence and grand displays of outrage and "compassion" ruled the day, with the *New York Times* running the Abu Ghraib scandal on its front page thirty-two days in a row —longer than any balanced reader could have wanted. The 'investigative reporter' Robert Fisk (famous for having been beaten up in Afghanistan and for declaring that—as a Westerner—he had deserved it) led the UK *Independent*'s front page with a pornographic display of pseudo-moral self-flagellation. "Take a close look at the leather strap, the pain on the prisoner's face," Fisk enticed his readers, in an article intriguingly entitled "An illegal and immoral war, betrayed by images that reveal our racism." "No sadistic movie could outdo the damage of this image," he went on. "In September 2001, the planes smashed in to the buildings; today, Lynndie smashes to pieces our entire morality with just one tug on the leash," he wrote of one picture.[61] It is a sign of just how degraded and barely defended public morality had become that a national newspaper could blithely make such an untrue claim.

In the *Nation* magazine, Katha Pollitt declared that "the United States has just lost its last remaining rationale for the misbegotten invasion of Iraq." "The big winners," she went on, "are Islamists and al-Qaeda. To their ideological bag of tricks, already bulging with religion, nationalism, misogyny, ethnic pride and antimodernism, they can now add the defense of civil liberties, human rights and the Geneva Conventions."[62] In a *New York Times* piece (coincidentally entitled "Shocking and Awful"), the op-ed columnist Maureen Dowd went straight

Relativism and the Iraq War

for the critical point on the Abu Ghraib scandal by complaining that Paul Wolfowitz and Donald Rumsfeld should not have attended a White House Correspondents dinner which Ms. Dowd was at after the Abu Ghraib scandal. "When a beaming Wolfowitz stopped at my table to greet an admiring Republican, I wanted to snap, 'Get back to your desk, Mr. Myopia from Utopia!'"[63] Not all comment on the scandal was so mature.

Mary Ann Sieghart wrote in *The Times* of London: "That's it! I've had enough. I'm fed up with justifying the war in Iraq to skeptical friends, family and acquaintances."[64] As Mark Steyn responded, "The standard rap against us armchair warriors is that we can't stand the heat of real war, but poor Mary Ann can't stand the heat of real armchairs."[65] Abu Ghraib provided some of those who had never understood the urgent and compelling necessities for going into Iraq with an excuse to jump off this smallest of bandwagons. But those who had been opposed to the war from the outset were just given another opportunity to show their true colors.

What the Abu Ghraib scandal, and all the other great and small setbacks in Iraq, displayed was a retrospective version of the gleeful quagmire and "gates of hell" predictions before the war. The hopeful pre-war talk of massive British and American casualties was off key because the propagandists of the theories wanted them to be true. So it was with Abu Ghraib. And so it was when, in October 2004, gleeful anti-war types seized on a dodgy *Lancet* survey which declared that 100,000 Iraqis had been killed by the conflict. They seized on this—the highest figure provided—because they *wanted* 100,000 Iraqis to have been killed. Because, if 100,000 Iraqis had been killed, then they could pretend that they had been right all along. Again, modern rage and self-absorption—the desire to be proved right triumphing over the desire for 9 0 ,0 0 0 more people not to be dead—plunges not so much into "activism" or "compassion" as into out-and-out nihilism.

Which is why, when George Bush declared that he had sent American troops into Iraq "to make its people free, not to make them American,"[66] these same people either ignored what he said or were overcome with sarcasm and irony. But by the time the war was over and the choice for the Iraqi people was between democracy and terror, it was also a little late for sarcasm, and a little late for irony. And when Bush spoke of the way in which a democratic Iraq would "serve as a dramatic and inspiring example of freedom for other nations in the region," much of the media saw not an opportunity to report or support the democratic sacrifices taking place in Iraq, but just another amusing opportunity to hit Bush. When Bush continued that "it is presumptuous and insulting to suggest that a whole region of the world or the one-fifth of humanity that is Muslim is somehow untouched by the most basic aspirations of life,"[67] they avoided taking on the question, felt some outrage at their own insults being used against them, and continued to pretend this was a personality-led P R battle. When, in early 2 0 0 5 , even die-hard opponents of the American government's policy began to concede that democracy spread appeared to be happening in the Middle East, many Democrats and counter-government journalists soldiered on, like Japanese troops sticking in the jungle long after 1 9 4 5 , waging their own particular brand of sardonic warfare on the aspirations not only of the US and UK governments, but by that time—and unforgivably—on the Iraqi people themselves.

Relativism and the Iraq War

A brutally serious and seismic moment in a people's history was treated with unimaginably sustained vanity, levity, and small-mindedness by those not so much expected, as employed, to know better.

The press, and therefore much of the public to which it was preaching, believed what it wanted to believe. And what it wanted to believe was the "liberal" consensus opinion—that the war in Iraq had been something to do with oil and abusing Iraqis. They wanted British and American troops to die, and they wanted them to have killed 100,000 Iraqis because that would prove them right in their perverse beliefs about British and American society. What they showed was their nihilistic hatred of the society in which they were fortunate enough to live.

Naturally, there are elements of bias in all journalism. But what was significant about this bias was that it was bias against our side—against the allies and allied troops. The press was trapped in a self-absorbed world of dossiers, Washington insider intrigues like the Plame case, and faked pity for sources chewed up, spat out, and then passed onto someone else. Yet the media continued to miss the big stories. They almost entirely missed, even after the referendum and two elections in January 2005, the story of Iraq's brave movement towards democracy—indeed it was a movement towards which the *New York Times* and other papers seemed not only skeptical, but almost hostile. If Iraq turned out to be a success, then they would have to concede that George Bush and the neoconservatives had got the war right, and that the people of the Middle East were indeed ready for democracy. In its desperation to prove the neoconservatives wrong, many observers simply missed out any story that might appear to back up the case for war. The discovery of mass graves in Iraq was given scant attention compared with front page after front page on dossiers, memos, and Abu Ghraib. And of the almost entirely unreported stories, two startling examples remain. Because they didn't fit into the "Iraq had no W M D" argument, they went briefly reported where they were reported at all.

The first is the story of Mahdi Obeidi, who came forward shortly after Allied troops arrived in Baghdad. Obeidi had been high up in Saddam Hussein's military-industrial projects, and one of those who had been repeatedly questioned by UN teams investigating Iraq's W M D capabilities. He had never revealed a thing. Under a regime of fear, and with his family held hostage by the tyrant, Mahdi Obeidi never would have said anything. But once the liberation of Iraq was complete, Obeidi came forward, led American officials to the garden of his own house, and pointed them in the direction of a rose bush. Hidden for twelve years under that rose bush were the components of a nuclear centrifuge for enriching uranium—the very piece of equipment that is central to making a nuclear bomb. Buried with the components were the blueprints and instructions for assembling the materials to create the bomb. The "bomb in his garden" was buried by Mahdi Obeidi under the direct orders of Saddam's son, Qusay Hussein, and, throughout a decade of sanctions and inspections, the secret had been kept by a scientist terrorized by the regime into silence and cooperation.[68] And of course it wasn't only Obeidi who had worked on the Iraq bomb. As he wrote in 2004, "Hundreds of my former staff members and fellow scientists possess knowledge that could be useful to a rogue nation eager for a covert nuclear weapons program."[69]

As former weapons inspector David Kay told CNN of the Obeidi discovery, "There's no way that that would have been discovered by normal international inspections. I couldn't have done it. My successors couldn't have done it."[70] Though Obeidi's revelation did not mean Iraq had a nuclear capability by 2003, it certainly demonstrated something that both the British and American governments were unaware of, and that inspections would not have found even if they had continued for another decade. The Hussein regime had successfully, and silently, retained the capability to assemble a nuclear bomb. With sanctions slipping, and the impetus for continued isolation of Iraq eroding, there is no doubt that, in the very near future, facilities like those in Mr. Obeidi's garden would have been dug up and put to use.

Just one other example of a Hussein-threat story ignored by the British press was the discovery—thanks to post-war investigations—of the trading links between members of the much-derided "axis of evil." In the colossal Duelfer report it was revealed that, as late as 2003, Saddam Hussein was in the process of buying long-range missiles direct—"off the shelf" —from North Korea. He was also negotiating for further military technologies that were banned under sanctions but purchasable from fellow isolated axis-member North Korea. By 2001 Iraq had made downpayments of $10 million to North Korea, signed contracts, and arranged meetings with suppliers from the country. In addition to meetings in Damascus, North Korean firms visited Iraq in 2001.[71] Clearly, even if the unanimously unsatisfactory sanctions had remained in place, the Ba'athists in Baghdad would still have explored every avenue until they achieved the capabilities they dreamed of.

Ignoring stories that do not fit in with the pre-agreed narrative is a problem for the press that should be addressed; a problem that only a fundamental wake-up call can reverse. A culture exists in which reporters are not merely content with being reporters, but wish also to be commentators on the story. But there is an orthodoxy as to what is legitimate "comment." All too often, being a commentator means approaching each story from the same angle—hostile and cynical of government's intentions, in favor of the rights of the Palestinian peoples over those of the Israelis, anti-war and so on. In other words, "establishment" commentators possess every routine trope of foreign and domestic radicals. It is in every way a lazy culture —where flippant and unjustifiable accusations can be thrown around at will. It is a culture in which cartoonists across the broadsheet papers casually, ignorantly, and without censure, portray the elected leaders of Britain and America as war criminals. It is a culture in which the person who makes the most extreme and untrue claim—far from being shunned—is the one who becomes famous, and whose career advances.[72] A media which is meant to inform has repositioned itself as a moral arbiter. Yet it does not have the foundations, knowledge, or accountability to perform such a task. Its behavior during the Iraq war shows not only that its credo is the propagation and promotion of the self, and that its only final measure is its own ego, but also that its morality is the morality of nothingness. This is a status quo that is emblematic and needs to be removed.

Relativism and the Iraq War

The force and entrenched nature of this status quo is rooted in the countercultural ethos. This is a modern problem, which has grown up because those who absorbed the counterculture did not. An anti-conservative status quo is in power in the media and swathes of political governance. It revels in a mode of consensus which behaves as though it is brave and outspoken, but is truly not just powerful, but all-pervasive. Privileged insiders behave as though they are fascinating and dangerous outsiders. This is a status quo that is lazy and immoral, for it is a status quo that permits people to think they are brave for walking down an American street with hundreds of thousands of other people, or dissident because they attack the President of the United States. It is a status quo rife, from the top down, with what Oriana Fallaci rightly terms "phony revolutionaries"[73]—the sort of people who seriously believe that they are outside the establishment (and pathetically try to demonstrate as much) even when they are presidential candidates, tenured university professors, or heads of multi-million dollar foundations.

These are deep and complex social problems that need addressing. But what is neither deep nor complex, and can be addressed easily, are those people who have surfaced, thanks to the Iraq war, not as critics, but as opponents of western society. These people are people whom we should now discount. All societies have their enemies, but the pervasive methods of political correctness, equivalence, and relativism have allowed these opponents of our society to become absorbed into the status quo and cosseted within our midst. Whether it is in the House of Representatives, the networks, the press, or in society at large, neoconservatives should lead the way in pointing the finger and isolating those who have, for too long, been allowed to get away with being traitors and opponents of the very country which gives them sanctuary.

Writing about an anti-British critique by an especially unpleasant Scots socialist, Roger Scruton once noted that the deliberate faults and excessive bitterness in the man's work brought home a clear if uncomfortable fact—that the writer in question was "writing as an enemy."[74] Moral and practical problems emerge from this, but Scruton has hit on the only possible explanation and way of dealing with the extremes of violent hatred now routinely expressed in Western newspapers, on our televisions, and on our streets against the West itself.

Many of the people who espouse moral equivalence and who rage against Britain and America do so out of an attempt at moral—or at least moralistic— seriousness. But many others simply hate our society. They are haters for one of two reasons. Firstly, there are those who attack the Western way of life, and who desire the death and destruction of our people. Secondly, there are those who attack us because they feel no loyalty to the country in which they have settled: they are not a part of it, and do not truly desire to be so.

Extreme examples of such hatred appear in the mainstream (though left-leaning) UK newspaper *The Guardian*, which publishes pieces that spiral ever lower into the moral cesspit. Its pages host writers like the socialist Terry Eagleton, who (in an article entitled "A Different Way of Death") has tried to absolve Palestinian suicide bombers of moral culpability for their murders by equating the manner of their deaths with that of the victims who leapt from the World Trade Center on 9/11, claiming that both killed themselves only because they have no other

option.[75] Eagleton is only a socialist, but fellow *Guardian* con-
tributors have plainer loyalties to justify their equivalences.
Richard Gott was brought in by the *Guardian* on the eve of the
2005 British general election to proclaim Tony Blair a "war
criminal" and denounce the United States as a country "that
presents a global threat similar to Germany in the 1930s."[76]
What *The Guardian* did not, and would not, reveal, is that Gott
is not simply a fellow-traveling socialist and Stalinist. Gott was
outed a decade ago by Oleg Gordievsky as a Soviet agent in the
pay of the KGB. The *Guardian* did not, and would not, reveal
such information when it published his anti-Bush and Blair
piece. But it is worth reflecting that a major British newspaper
has covered for a KGB spy, allowing him to accuse Britain and
America of being an "evil empire," even while being aware
that the writer had spent his life extolling the virtues of his pay-
master, the real "evil empire." This is significant, for it allows
us to reflect that this is not a paper that engages in legitimate
criticism, but rather one bent on propaganda, and on the dis-
semination of attacks against the Western allies.

Among others smoked out by their rage over the Iraq war
are those whose criticisms are not only ideological, but racial.
When Arundhati Roy criticizes America and Britain, we should
note her descriptions of what these countries have done to
"us natives."[77] She is showing us that she is an opponent of us,
because we are people she regards as colonialists and different
to her. Likewise the British-based columnist Yasmin Alibhai-
Brown. When the handover of Iraqi sovereignty took place in
June 2004, Alibhai-Brown confessed in London's *Evening
Standard* that "there have been times when I wanted more chaos,
more shocks, more disorder to teach our side a lesson. On

Neoconservatism

Monday I found myself again hoping that this handover proves a failure because it has been orchestrated by the Americans."[78]

Alibhai-Brown is at least being honest in admitting that she wants more British and American troops and Iraqi civilians to die, and that the vindication of her own opinion is of more importance to her than the lives of these people. But her dishonesty in the passage comes in referring to "our" side. It is clear from this passage, and many others by people like her throughout their careers, that such people dislike the West and are antagonistic towards the West. They believe that the West is made up of racists and xenophobes, and remain discontent with their adopted nations when they are not going in the awful direction in which they wish them to go. This attitude can be adopted from without or from within. It is equally destructive and inexcusable in both cases.

In April 2004, the filmmaker Michael Moore took relativism to its endpoints when writing of the Iraqi "insurgency." Moore described contractors working in Iraq (who have, in a number of cases, been abducted and murdered in Iraq) as "not contractors," but MERCENARIES" [*sic*]. Moore's equivalence doesn't end there, however. Though he claims to see blood on the hand of civilian contractors, he sees none on the hands of the terrorists and gangsters who have brought such bloody misery to Iraq. On the contrary: "The Iraqis who have risen up against the occupation are not 'insurgents' or 'terrorists' or 'The Enemy.' They are the REVOLUTION [*sic*], the Minutemen."[79] It requires a distinctive pathology to condemn the innocent and absolve the guilty, but in comparing the cold-blooded murders of the Iraqi people with "Minutemen," Michael Moore puts himself on the other side, joining a long

line of people who live in the West, but yet despise the West and
—not content with despising it—have become opponents of it.

This monumental modern confusion of morality, pseudery,
and lies helps neither our own societies nor Iraq to get onto
the right track. I said at the beginning of this chapter that the
problem—the very starting point for this confusion—lies in
the "tyranny of relativism." This tyranny, which mocks those
who speak in absolutes, has demonstrated through the period
of the years since 9/11 that relativism is not simply a game to
sound clever, as some would have it, but the road to nihilism.
It is the road along which the confused, the lost, and the wicked
have traveled for a generation. And it is a road that today has
led many people to absolute hatred of the West, inversion of
morality, and comprehensive nihilism.

The Australian writer John Pilger was asked, in February
2004, which side those who opposed the war should be on,
now that the Iraqi regime had been defeated. As someone who
had built his career on moral judgments consisting of equivalences against the West, Pilger was faced with a simple choice
—the armed forces of Britain, America, and his own country,
or the so-called "insurgents," a collection of gangs of remnant
Ba'athist thugs, al-Qaeda terrorists, bandits, head-hackers,
assassins of men, women, and children. His answer could not
have been clearer. "Do you think the anti-war movement should
be supporting Iraq's anti-occupation resistance?" he was asked.
"Yes, I do," Pilger answered. "We cannot afford to be choosy."[80]

In May 2005, Amnesty International, an organization that
has morphed since its founding from a human rights organization into a politically slanted campaigning group, described
Guantanamo Bay as "the gulag of our times."[81] Nothing could

be done to persuade the organization that equating Guantanamo, where nobody had been killed, with the Soviet gulag, in which fifteen to thirty million people were killed, was wrong or offensive. They did not mind that the claim was offensive to the families of the millions of innocent Russians murdered, and they certainly did not mind that they were telling a flagrant lie about America.

And in December 2005, the Chairman of the Democratic Party, a man who had for a time the previous year been the Democrats' frontrunner in the race for the presidential nomination, summed up what all these fraudulent and warped claims meant to him. Howard Dean seized the opportunity just days before Iraqis once again went to the polls in record numbers to declare his verdict on the Iraq war. "The idea that we are going to win the war in Iraq is an idea which is just plain wrong."[82]

This is where relativism has led. It starts by encouraging the perception that America and her allies have no moral authority over terrorists, tyrants, and genocidal dictatorships. It continues by excusing, then supporting, the terrorists and tyrants. It finishes by saying why the terrorists and tyrants have the right to win over us, trying to persuade us that they will win over us because the West does not have the right to conquer or destroy evil. Relativism culminates by helping terrorists to win and evil to triumph.

FOUR

NEOCONSERVATISM
FOR AMERICA

I N T H E United States it was by no means inevitable that neoconservatism would find its home within the Republican party. In neoconservatism's formative years, the Democrats also provided a good and solid home for some neoconservative thinking.

Yet today, neoconservatism's natural home is in the Republican party. This is perhaps most obvious on issues of foreign policy. But Republicans have also embraced (even if intermittently) neoconservative principles on domestic policy (lower taxes, for example, or issues of social justice) as well. One should be under no illusion here, though. There is no point in pretending that the neoconservative measures that the Bush administration has adopted are due to any especially widespread appetite within the Republican party for a forceful realist-humanitarian foreign policy. Far from it. Much of the current consensus relies simply on post-9/11 doggedness and a hope that the situation in Iraq continues to improve. As a party, the

Neoconservatism

Republicans are still as commonly suspicious of neoconservative foreign policy ideas as are many members of the Democratic party, albeit for different reasons. Many instinctive conservatives remain suspicious of a neocon foreign policy whose humanitarian impetus they think will make the American armed forces little more than the armed wing of the Red Cross. This suspicion remains at least as prevalent in the Republican party as fear of militaristic expressions of self-interest (in which only "convenient" humanitarian catastrophes are addressed) is among the party's opponents.

In any case, it is useless to pretend that any neoconservative foreign policy would have found its way into the Republican's orbit had it not been for the personal conviction and advocacy of President Bush who in 2001 rebelled against his own earlier foreign policy stands and embraced the neoconservative vision. This was not an inevitable stance for him to take, especially as his own instincts during the Nineties had often been to keep America out of troubles such as those in the Balkans. And there were after all other options open to President Bush after 9/11. He might for instance have followed his predecessor's tactic of kicking the ball down the field. He could have saved members of his administration countless personal attacks, and sustained his own high approval ratings for a time by arresting a couple of suspects, talking tough, and perhaps launching some cruise missiles against a few targets. Many people from all sides now wish that perhaps he had done just that, allowing America to stand back from the world, and not have—as it currently does—an almost uniquely high stake in the wellbeing of at least two foreign countries. But Bush did take a leap, and America took it with him, electing him to a second term even as the situation in Iraq looked as bad as it ever had.

What Bush has led his country to is—neoconservatives believe—a return to policies of which America should be proud, the instinctive policies of America and America's founders. President Bush has reminded people that America's concerns are the world's concerns, and the world's concerns are the natural concerns of America. He has led the way in showing that America's interests are best served not by selfish isolationism or abnegation of responsibility, but by being a world leader with a humanitarian urge.

But this forceful humanitarianism will not necessarily outlive Bush's premiership. Many possible successors, including many from Bush's own party, lack the stomach for forceful interventionism. The difference between many of those who perpetually call for action in failed states and neoconservatives who call for action in failed states is that neoconservatives actually want troops deployed and are prepared to see through the conflicts that will arise. This lack of stomach affects humanitarians as much as it does realists. The most verbal humanitarianism often loses its stomach the moment conflict is involved, and sometimes a long time before. Without the enforcing knowledge that self-interest is at stake, the desire to cut and run always arises, the humanitarian instinct softening amid moral confusion and war's fallout. Neoconservative policy is now assaulted from all sides. The effects of this are more than administrational—they are deadly for the wellbeing of America and the world. Telling outbursts from Democrats and Republicans, both before and after the second Iraq war, make it clear not only that many are unlikely to agree to such a conflict in the near future, but—more damagingly—that they may not be led into one either.

Though many Republican Senators remain hostile to the precepts of interventionism, for the time being theirs is nevertheless the party which provides the safest home to neoconservatism. To begin with, national self-interest remains a deep-seated Republican instinct. With time and argument, there is no reason why more Republicans might not come round to the idea that the welfare and security of fellow democracies always has been and always will be directly in the interests of America. If that argument can be more comprehensively enshrined, then most of the impetus for neoconservative action is already there. From the party's support during the Bush-led interventions of 2001–2003, it is clear that, with the appropriate explanation and justification, Republicans are at least amenable to arguments from humanitarian angles and more amenable than their Democratic colleagues to arguments from national self-interest.

But there is another reason why the Republican party will inevitably provide the better home for neocons, and that is its willingness to adopt the harsher policies of domestic neoconservatism. Certain of those policies will be new to a current generation of Republican representatives, but none will be as indigestible to them as they would be to many Democratic members. For many Republicans, neocon attitudes may be adopted with a sense of homecoming. Many Republicans have, for nearly a decade, too often shied away from certain conservative issues—issues which neoconservatism refuses to sidestep. Neoconservatism argues for, and provides intellectual justification for, a raft of policies which many conservatives have of late often been too fearful to utter. But it is also a form of conservatism that has made its peace with much of the modern world, including the welfare state, accepts the existence of the welfare state, and criticizes it as a friend bent on helping.

But we should begin with the why. Why must America, irrespective of the party of governance, develop, and extend its neoconservative moment?

Why?

It has been clear since his neoconservative epiphany in 2001 that George W. Bush is among those who firmly believe in the principle of the "End of History." He spoke in his speech at West Point (cited in Chapter 2) of the fact that at the end of the twentieth century there was "a single surviving model of human progress," a model which involved freedom, justice, and tolerance. As his colleague Tony Blair said in his famous 1999 Chicago speech, the familiar battles between left and right are over, with liberal democracy having emerged triumphant.[1] Though this is the case, it is still vital that America knows where it is in such a world, so that it can sustain its place in it.

America of course remains the pre-eminent world power, a position it has earned and deserves. It remains the largest and most powerful economy in the world. Its armed forces are rarely equalled in skill, and never superseded in technological capability. Its record of assistance to its allies leads those with open minds to know that America can be trusted as an ally because it has responded to the call of its allies in the past. Why, then, do so many people within America persist in considering America to be plummeting towards the bad?

Neoconservatism

The last decade has seen a number of powerful arguments put forward to the effect that America itself is lost, that what was good has been destroyed. These tracts have ranged from the forceful and declamatory works of the Buchananite right to the civil-liberties laments of the "liberal"-left. Almost all have assumed that what has been lost cannot be regained. This is not the case, and I would argue that even much of the premise is wrong. America should be glad to see much of the social and economic injustice of the past firmly left in the past. Much that was often concomitant with that past should go unmissed. The barriers that held people back—whether due to race, class, or wealth—are hardly desirable things, or reasons for nostalgia. But what people often lament are specifics that have been lost along the way. That is, they are lamenting things that have been cast aside too lightly. But most are things that can be regained. Neoconservatism does not want to return to the past; it simply wants to pick up those things that were wilfully and unjustly discarded, and take us to a better and more hopeful future.

There is justification for concern. That is—there is a justification, and an attitude. Conservatives of all stripes should be particularly wary of the latter, which is easier to identify, though not necessarily any less intractable. Some people appear to like just a little too much the idea of a glorious past from which we are slipping. Claiming that the country is going to the dogs or to hell in a handcart has often become a means of absolving oneself from involvement in the tough action required to prevent unwise changes. Just as the counterculture spawned the unsavory sight of nihilism adopted as an attitude among the "radicals" and the socialists, so, one should ask, has not the myth of decline become a free acquisition of conservatism? Has "Owl of Minerva-ism"—the heady idea that we are living in the fading light—become the conservative nihilism? More than one generation of conservatives has been born and come to maturity since perhaps the highest moment of civilizational pride after the Second World War, yet conservatives continue to be born who, from their earliest days, spout the mantras of collapse and decay. Neoconservatism should argue that it is the duty of any conservatives indulging in such an attitude to wake from this nostalgic reverie and start fighting for what they see is right and good.

What is required is not the sort of conservatism which revels in archaism, and anachronism. Conservatism cannot afford to adopt such attitudes, which, while sometimes gratifying to indulge, are damaging to the causes of conservatism and the cause of America.

Which brings us to the fact that underlies the "it's all downhill" attitude. This is something that can understandably be held up as justification for the view of decline—the unarguable fact that portions of American life are gross and affect the life of the nation to its detriment: a yobbish culture, high crime rates, excessive levels of illegal immigration. All are examples that declinists might cite to justify their stance.

But the examples would be wrong. Conservatism's job is to preserve that which is good in the nation, as well as to fight to get rid of that which is bad. The preserving is still periodically done, but the offensive position needs to be assumed more often. The war against the culture is constant enough to require continual refutation. The success of that anti-culture war is due in part to the fact that socialists have preached their gospel of

Neoconservatism

irrevocability to the people: the pretense that immigration must necessarily continue rising, that yob culture and soaring crime rates cannot be prevented because they have something to do with liberality or are the unsavory but inevitable sideshows of greater "freedom" and less "oppression." Conservatism must not just expose these myths—it must shatter them. The offensive position must be resumed, and if socialists say that these methods are methods of the past or unsavory methods of the present, we must not give them their pyrrhic P R victories, but must press ahead, because we know that what we believe is not only for the good, but the right thing to do.

Changing the status quo

The rest of this chapter sets out some of the neoconservative-based attitudes which should be adopted at home and abroad if America is to retain and enhance its position as a strong and powerful voice for freedom, liberty, and justice across the globe. Some of these suggestions may seem to some readers to be impractical, impossible, or unimaginable: they are not. In any case, the assumption that great and sweeping change cannot occur is the single aspect of politics that most disenfranchizes voters. Where there is a problem, that problem must be addressed. The electorate know this, and their political representatives must reflect the fact. Americans should address their concerns by doing whatever is necessary to solve them, not by considering whether they have the right tools, or by trying to find a way to pretend that the problem is not a problem. America should decide what it wants, and then work out how to achieve it.

When officials insinuate that taxes must rise, the American people are entitled to ask "Why?" When politicians and policy pundits tell people that immigration cannot be halted, the American people have a right to demand "Why?" And if, in answer, they are told that this or that has already been decided upon and nothing can be done, then the American people should boot that politician or government out of office.

Many people seem to think that we live in an age in which nothing is sacred. That is not true—the twenty-first century has an especially lengthy list of things deemed beyond criticism. It is time that such newly invented taboos were eradicated.

The myth of decline is a self-fulfilling prophecy. A new conservatism will help eradicate the myth and improve the reality. This is not about halting progress: it is about recognizing that the "progress" we have often been force-fed is a fallacy. Neoconservatism is about turning the tide away from the corrosive "progress" of socialism. It is about giving hope and ambition to the conservative cause, and recognizing that, in the drive to make people's lives better, government must never say that something cannot be done. Neoconservatism can provide the impetus to begin this process, and, like all good things, neoconservatism starts in the home.

Tax

People are made most easily free by being allowed to save or spend as much of the money they earn as possible. One of the advantages that America for the time being enjoys over its European cousins is that American governments tend to understand this fact. But it should always be one of the first principles of any conservative-minded government not just to reduce, but to cut taxes dramatically. One of the corollaries of this is that public services must also be reduced.

Neoconservatism

As Irwin Stelzer has said, neoconservatives long ago "broke with traditional conservatives in the domestic-policy arena by making their peace with the welfare state, on which conservatives had waged war for decades."[2] Neoconservatives understand that welfare should provide basic support to those who have fallen to the bottom of society, and provide a safety-net for them. But they also understand the threat of, and should lead the assault upon, "welfarism"—the appalling notion that anyone is continuously "owed" a living by society. Such an idea (and that is all it has to be to create a problem) inculcates all kinds of mental, emotional, and physical laziness. It can never be in anyone's interests to believe that a life lived at the expense of the state is a good thing. Such an idea only arises when there is provision to create such an impression.

But welfare is not the only thing that should be cut. Government should also take a check on its ever-increasing payroll, and especially the grotesque swallowing-up of money without noticeable results. When it transpired in 2005 that the CIA was receiving an annual budget of $44 billion, many people considered that money well spent. But they epitomize the unwise spending of sclerotic government agencies. The CIA's inability to train or employ sufficient Arabic translators as well as its claim that it needs another decade to have good sources within al-Qaeda are the results on a grand scale of what we see so often on a personal level—the result when somebody assumes government money will simply continue rolling in.[3] The government must scrutinize all its agencies. None work so well that cuts cannot be made. The public sector needs to be more careful by far with its treatment of public money: it is not money which the population simply donates to them, but money which they must earn, and become far more cautious about wasting.

In the end, no one will be anything but richer from the government's constraining its vast payroll. Government must never spend money and enlarge its non-vital payroll through habit, simply permitting the ballooning of posts which are, by their nature, self-justifying. In addition, expansion of the state's payroll does too much damage in diminishing the independence and reach of the private sector. Meddlesome expansionism ossifies government and non-government services. But there is one outreach of government that needs especial derision and that is the current administration's adoption of faith, equality, and all manner of other social-policy advisers. Such positions speak all too loudly of an administration pasting over gaps in its thought with other people's money.

Government should always minimize its spending on public relations advisers. Such figures are, among stiff competition, the most vapid waste of money. Government is not a brand, and government's job is not to win PR battles. Government's job is to govern. If the people do not agree with a policy, and if after the government has tried through debate to persuade them of the policy's merits the public remains unconvinced, then the government should either give up an unpopular measure, or forge ahead and risk losing power for its principles. It is not government's job to use taxpayers' money to tell taxpayers what they should think. Conservatives of all stripes must regain the initiative. To begin with, we must abandon as demeaning, and ultimately self-destructive, the political PR obsession.

Conservatives must continually take a lesson from—and remain as far away as possible from—the European social-democrat philosophy, by which, in return for providing the citizen with a good life, the state presumes to have the right to all of a citizen's money, generously allowing him to retain a portion. This social-democrat dream is in fact a nightmare, and a nightmare whose end can never be reached. Government alone cannot make people happy. It should protect its citizens, and sustain a limited number of other duties, but otherwise its motto should be "Less is more." It should try to hold people back from degradation, while at the same time realizing that it can never do this comprehensively. Government can only act palpably through limited and clear social structures, within a financial environment that permits people to be free to fulfil their highest potential. The opposite (and still prevalent) idea in Europe—that the state knows better than both the people and the markets—is a dangerous nonsense that finds its endpoint in communism. As a fundamental, collectivism has been utterly shown up, appropriately described by Robert Skidelsky as "the most egregious error of the twentieth century."[4] It is arrogant and extraordinary that any government today should believe it can manage people's earnings any better than its predecessors did.

Avoiding collectivism, the US government must constantly favor supply-side economics. That is, it should not provide a benefits-rich society, in which the priority is keeping inflation low, but rather a benefits-poor society, in which full employment, individual liberty, and self-advancement are the aims. The situation of those out of work in America is currently alleviated —as though there were no other option—through benefits. Huge bureaucratic and financial investment sustains what is, in some areas, an entire underclass of people (often more than one generation of the same family) permanently out of work. We must make a priority once again of returning all people to any work by any possible means.

The essential element in impelling people back into work is constantly to reject the fallacy that a high-taxing state can deal on its own with unemployment. The only solution for unemployment is employment: no mid-way alternative exists. Any conservative government should make the encouragement of proper investment in the jobs market and the creation of businesses that provide jobs as a priority. Tax cuts help do this. Conservatives know that when people have more money in their pockets they are freer to exercise their choices and ambitions. They are also freer to invest in their own society, and to use their earnings in the way they believe will best increase their earnings. Better prospects for employers lead to more opportunities for employees. Government should be ever restricted, while the jobs market is ever freed.

Benefit payments of all kinds must be recognized as a sop —a comprehensively wrong approach. People must be encouraged to recognize the difference between government giving something to the people and government handing back a tiny portion of the money it has taken from the people.

Conservatives must restate and reclaim their ground on taxation. Their ground starts with a public acceptance of the fact that politicians do not know best how to spend other people's money—indeed, evidence suggests that they are always more than usually bad at it. Taxation should cover the cost of a limited government, sturdy defense, and very limited public services. Few other aspects of government expenditure should be safe from the neoconservative scalpel. After all, what do people palpably get from vastly increased state expenditure?

Neoconservative economic policies have already found their way into economic policy in countries other than the US (notably Australia[5]) and Americans should be proud of the good this has done. But they should also be wary of those whose desire is to undermine American economic success. For instance, at present, much economic talk in America centers on the budget-deficit which the Bush administration has run up. This is regarded by many as a demonstration of fiscal irresponsibility, especially when considered alongside the Bush administration's limited keenness for tax-cutting. But the budget deficit has been run up because it has been used to pay for what is needed. Some of that money might have been used better, and lessons will have to be learnt. But what the administration has done is to decide what needs to be done and then to do it. Despite what some old-guard conservatives think, balancing the books in government is simply not enough. Government —especially since 2001—has special duties to its people and duties to the world. The current budget deficit will be paid off, but in the meantime the American people should be proud that they have had a government that has put principles before book-balancing in a time where fiscal prudence in certain areas would be irresponsible in more than a financial sense. America and its conservatives must always first try to agree on what they need, and then spend accordingly.

Education

In education, conservatives must argue for two primary policies: the first relating to universities, the second to schools. Firstly, we abolish any quotas for university attendance or the make-up of universities. The universities should provide the country with an intellectual elite, one that feels sufficiently privileged to appreciate its duty to repay the investment society has made in it. The brightest pupils, whatever their background, whatever their race or ethnicity, should enter the finest universities. The expansion of the university system, where pointless courses are taught on second-rate campuses, is a disaster. This development has devalued university degrees and duped students into incurring massive debts rather than going straight to work and becoming productive members of society.

But the particular position of the universities should be directly relevant only to the small percentage of the population who go to them. What is of direct consequence to everyone is the standard of schooling and general education in the country. In this, as in everything else, conservatives must stand up for what they believe in again, ignoring the flak they will receive from implementing controversial policies and saying things that often seem as if they cannot currently be said.

There is no doubt that the disastrous effects of the counterculture are felt most acutely among the young—a generation brought up in an environment which so denies the notion of natural right or cultural difference that many people are incapable of distinguishing good from bad. The perfect example of this lies in so-called "black culture" (which is not only not culture, but a gross dishonor to culture that is "black"). The effects of "black culture" currently run rampant. Celebrated by television, lauded in the national press, and pandered to by those in authority, no one dares stop it, or speak out against it, because to do so would be "elitist" or "prejudiced." Black culture, as it is currently presented, is a cesspit of degradation, violence, and nihilism. Tolerance of it demonstrates relativism's awful appeal to the populace. As Fukuyama writes, "Relativism ... does not lead to the liberation of the great or strong, but of the mediocre, who were told they had nothing of which to be ashamed."[6]

But "black culture" is far worse than mediocre. It is the epitome of the low and the destructive. Young people exposed to it without being aware of its idiocies and pitfalls enter a world in which women are debased, casual and cowardly violence is glorified, and absurd machismo goes not only unchallenged, but unsatirized. Populist comedians and media figures, who pretend to be brave by satirizing those who defend or do not threaten our culture, dare not even attempt to challenge this destructive movement. This nihilistic societal tendency is allowed to spread precisely because it goes unchallenged. America and Western culture can overcome such movements only by being clear from the outset that they are unappetizing, unworthy, and beneath us—not because they are alien, but because they are unfulfilling and nihilistic. As Irving Kristol wrote in another context, "Different gardeners will have different ideas, of course, but there will be a limit to this variety. The idea of a garden does not, for instance, include an expanse of weeds or of poison ivy."[7] Until a stand is made against a culture that glorifies and encourages rape, murder, gun crime, hate crimes, and grotesquely unchecked materialism, that culture will continue to cause palpable and visible damage to American society.

Since many of the problems in our society arise from the outset directly because of a lack of ethics, or because of nihilistic ethics, conservatives of all persuasions must argue for and implement a vast increase, rather than a decline, in faith-based schools. Such schools invariably produce better educated pupils, and consistently turn out better behaved pupils. Society owes a great debt to these schools, to their teachers and staff, and it is time we started acknowledging that debt and repeating our successes. Certainly, we should not avoid repeating our successes simply for fear of upsetting our failures. Such a pandering to the lowest denominator is a recipe for national degradation, and a vanity for which future generations should not forgive us.

And we should be clear what we mean by faith-based schools. It does not mean a marketplace of faiths, or the institutionalization of the idea that any faith will do. Government-funded state schools should, with the exception of a small number of Jewish schools, be Christian. This should be the case not only because it is the right thing to do, and the best way of securing the finest possible education for America's young, but because America should continue and further the inherited faith of the country. Both believing and non-believing neoconservatives agree that Judeo-Christian values should pervade our actions. As Richard John Neuhaus put it, "politics is chiefly a function of culture, at the heart of culture is morality, and at the heart of morality is religion."[8]

Increasing every year the number of children able to benefit from a traditional-values education will allow a new generation to reconnect with the nation's cultural and spiritual heritage. It will allow them to grow within a moral and religious framework, and set them up in the best possible way for their lives as free and responsible citizens. There are many benefits from education within the Judeo-Christian tradition: not only are children allowed to start off from the right moral place, but they are also provided with the earliest—and for many of them, the only—opportunity to understand the basis of western art, history, and philosophy. Children ignorant of their nation's faith are most likely to feel alienated from the country they live in, precisely because, from the earliest age, they have been denied an opportunity to feel part of it. Their civilization's literature becomes opaque, and walking around a great art gallery is all but meaningless.

None of what has been said means enforcing religious observance on adults, or any other such thing. It should be recognized that while adults are free to make their own decisions, children should not be treated in the same way. The best way to bring up children in America is to bring them up in the tradition of Judeo-Christian ethics and morals, with the benefits of the great books this entails. The effects of taking these morals away can be seen every day on America's streets. We should recall T. S. Eliot's warning from 1934:

> Do you need to be told that even such modest attainments
> As you can boast in the way of polite society
> Will hardly survive the Faith to which they owe their significance?[9]

It is time that grown-ups owned up to their most fundamental duty to the young, and once again gave them the best possible start in life.

The attitude towards Muslim educational institutions should be to consider them exceptions. Islamic extremism is today the most explicit enemy of our society. It is the declared intention of Islamic extremists to undermine the traditions of America and replace them with subservience to the *dar el-Islam*. Though the number of people intent on violent jihad against the country may possibly be small, we must also take into account those intent on jihad by other means. Islam is a proselytizing faith, and one that is incompatible with Western history, law, and society.[10] With the number of unknown millions of Muslims currently living within America's borders, no risk whatsoever should be taken. Exclusively Muslim madrasah-like schools and colleges are breeding grounds for segregation and anti-western hate, and even some within the Muslim community acknowledge this. If any Muslim academies are allowed to exist, they should be funded entirely privately, with no taxpayer assistance, and should be subject to uniquely strict regulation and inspection. If such conditions are considered unbearable, then Muslims will have to try their luck in other countries. America has no obligation to entertain peoples opposed to or antagonistic towards its way of life. The hatred expressed not only towards the American government, but also towards American society by Muslims since the war on terror began is ample evidence that the Muslim community is innately hostile and opposed to any integration within American society. America must start implementing its response.

For we have allowed the Straussian-nightmare endpoint of relativism to arrive, in which intolerance towards our society is treated as a value "equal in dignity" to tolerance.[11] Our only possible reaction to this situation is not to allow our tolerance to destroy us—we must not allow tolerance to prove the Achilles heel of freedom. To defend our tolerance we must be intolerant to those who are opposed to us. Some people will claim this is racism, but it is not—it is not about race, but about ideology, and about America protecting her own.

Recent years have shown that the threat of Islam is real. Throughout Western cities, Muslims have been allowed to preach a variant gospel of hatred towards Western society. And we have funded them: we have supported their mosques; we have paid welfare to their people. Yet even after the first attacks on the American homeland, the American government's reaction has lacked direction. In the wake of the 2001 attacks, violence against Islam, and not the violence of Islam, was portrayed as the pressing problem. The White House and all government departments remain intent on demonstrating how pro-Muslim they can be, celebrating Muslim religious festivals and arranging constant photo-opportunities with Muslim "leaders." These are the early signs of societal suicide. Welfare-reliant imams have been allowed to stay in the States, and their murderous disciples have, with savagery and cowardice, attacked the States. In the face of this the government has been unwilling—because scared—to recognize that its immigration and multiculturalism policies have to an extent allowed this threat within American society. The moves to counter it must be harsh, and mosques and centers that have been preaching hatred must be closed down entirely. Treating the Islamist threat seriously means being wary of allowing the Trojan horse into our midst. At the very least it means ensuring that the Trojan horse is not built from our own materials of tolerance and fairness.

Our Western failure to defend ourselves at home and stand up to our enemies at home is founded in our relativism. American schools and universities should begin the fight back against relativism and the other forces hostile to our society by rooting themselves in the nation's faith. But they should also be rooted in a proper understanding of the nation's past. The teaching of history in schools in particular must be radically altered, not only in order to teach American children what it is that makes them American, and why they should be proud of their identity, but also in order to strengthen their ability to stand against the forces of relativism and Islamism. But in the West today, the intelligentsia have a pathological aversion to celebrating their own culture. This is the area in which culture wars are of most value.

A young British journalist writing in 2003 single-handedly demonstrated the problem: the ignorance of a generation in the West that has too often been brought up on narcissism and nothingness. Confessing that he and his fellow university-educated friends had no idea who had won the battle of Waterloo, he rightly used the opportunity to criticize the teaching of history in British schools. But he went on to say that, though he was entirely ignorant of British history before the Second World War, and critical of the education system for letting him down, nonetheless he was "not one of those people who think we should go back to teaching 'our proud island history' and all that propaganda."[12] This is a perfect representation of the effect of an abysmal historical and moral education. The young may be so ignorant of their country's history that they do not know whether they won or lost major battles in their country's history, but they still have an opinion about what they are ignorant of. They may not know anything about the past, but they don't like what they don't know.

Neoconservatism

The presumption in the West that even adequately teaching one's own country's history constitutes "propaganda" is an ingrained attitude of a poorly educated generation. They may know very little about their country, but they know that to appear clever or sympathetic they should be cynical, critical, and hostile to the past they don't know. As in the case of Allan Bloom's pupils in Chapter 1, this is an attitude assumed for free. Throughout the West today, criticism of one's own and one's culture's past has become a short-cut to giving off an appearance of learning and moral seriousness: it assumes the rest is all known. Cultural relativism and an unwillingness to celebrate one's own culture have spurred this modish form of vanity, most especially on American university campuses. The result is something which is not just a vanity of outlook, but a vanity of moral and intellectual presumption.

Of course, this classic campus attitude is not a serious attitude; it is a false and frivolous set of opinions, cheaply assumed to be a demonstration of sophistication, but truly a veneer covering acres of ignorance and self-doubt. People have jumped to this endpoint without either the vital labor or the absorption of knowledge that true learning entails. Pupils and students in this situation are not merely likely to grow into bad citizens. Because they have left themselves open to it, they are more likely to be converted to all sorts of violent and vile creeds—political, spiritual, and feral—that cannot be absorbed.

They have arrived in an end-place of sorts, but because they have not themselves done the intellectual journeying, they have neither sympathy nor understanding. What they have instead is an increased sense of rage and indignation. Young people who demonstrate against wars with countries they cannot find on a map are useless citizens, all emoting and no understanding. They are what their society needs least.

They are the pupils of the countercultural generation that now dominates America's educational institutions, giving their own peculiar spin on world affairs to a generation of children now worse educated in the basics of their own country's history and culture than any previous school-educated generation. When a strong dose of historical "guilt" is added to a class of students who know nothing of the basics of history, of course the result is a morally skewed product. Teach a generation of children to "feel" the burden of slavery without teaching them the origins of the trade or ever even suggesting that pupils might feel concomitant cultural pride in its abolition, and it's no wonder you get a generation whose persistent reflex reaction as a society is to self-absorbedly ask, "What did we do wrong?"

This lack of knowledge is yielding morally, as well as intellectually, impoverished results, for there is a meeting-point here of ignorance, nihilism, and the cult of "self-esteem." The educational system in America has, for more than a generation, cultivated the nurturing of esteem over the nurturing of knowledge and expertise.[13] Concern that some pupils may feel loss of esteem if they are tested on facts has meant that much of the school curriculum (notably in history and literature) has become little more than an empathy test. To begin to overcome this, we should start caring less about how people feel, and instead judge students on what they know. The nurturing of self-esteem is clearly a problem, not the solution, when that self-esteem smothers the teaching of productive competitiveness and excellence. As Irving Kristol wrote thirty years ago,

Neoconservatism

"The only authentic criterion for judging any economic or political system, or any set of social institutions, is this: what kind of people emerge from them?"[14] As anyone walking through a city center today can testify, a large proportion of the people the educational systems are producing are not very nice. This is not something that is inevitable, and nor is it the result of a freakish nationwide coincidence. It is the direct result of cultural relativism, society's modish unwillingness to defend the supremacy of its values, and an unwillingness, from the top down, to resist lesser and expressly obnoxious creeds.

In his portrait of his friend Allan Bloom, Saul Bellow described how:

> He didn't ask, "Where will you spend eternity?" as religious the-end-is-near picketers did, but rather, "With what, in this modern democracy, will you meet the demands of your soul?"[15]

This, at least, is the question we must be asking of—and answering with—the young. Nearly forty years ago Leo Strauss wrote: "Liberal education reminds those members of a mass democracy who have ears to hear, of human greatness."[16] That greatness is what the young must once again be encouraged to aim for and extol. To do the opposite—to elevate the pedestrian and encourage the base—is not just to do a disservice to a generation: it is to abandon them, from the beginning of their lives, to thwarted existences of bafflement, ignorance, and rage. With no light to climb to, they will not simply remain in the cave—they will see no reason why they should wish to leave it.

* * *

Social policy

Neoconservatism holds that people are most able to achieve their potential when they are free and able to be heard within a genuinely democratic society. While they do not believe that it is society's business to inject itself into people's lives as a matter of course, as socialists do, neither do they believe, as some traditional conservatives do, that society should be minimalist in taking responsibility for the well-being of individuals. To this extent, neoconservatives are the only conservatives who formally recognize that there are limits to what can be achieved without the state.

Alone among contemporary political philosophies, neoconservatism is properly liberal on issues of personal freedom, without allowing personal freedom to trespass on society's well-being. The problem with contemporary liberalism is that it can find no rational reason for preventing the extremes to which unchecked "liberalism" has taken people. So, though neoconservatives are among those who believe innately in racial equality, they certainly do not believe that racial equality is best served, for instance, by introducing all-black schools (as do some among the "equality" lobby) or indeed by giving any special treatment because of skin color. The negative policy of "positive discrimination" is—and always has been—absolute anathema to neoconservatism. Likewise, while neoconservatives obviously believe absolutely in sexual equality, they believe that women find neither equality nor freedom by being freed to ape the lowliest male thugs in their behavior. And neoconservatives' attitude to homosexuals may be said to be along the same lines. Neoconservatives have absolutely no issue with gay rights. But they would say that gay rights do not include, and do not stretch to, rights that heterosexuals do not possess, or practices that would be criticized in heterosexuals. In other words, neoconservatives believe, on all such issues, that the wars of rights have been won, but that the war to keep "rights" within the acceptable limits of civilized society remains very much alive. Without any restraints on liberalism, the culture itself, as one neocon has put it, begins to "unravel." [17] "For those who see in modernity admirable principles but also worrisome tendencies," writes Adam Wolfson, "their persuasion will be neoconservatism." [18]

Like all conservatives, neocons recognize the individual as uniquely valuable—the test of political order, not a mere cog in its machinery. For this reason, individuals must be free—not free to do absolutely anything they wish (the endpoint of "liberalism" [19])—but safely free so as to avoid anarchy or tyranny. To achieve this, the institutions that safeguard and protect us must be strong. All conservatives would agree on that. But neoconservatives recognize that institutions can only safeguarded by emphasizing individual responsibility. People should be held as directly responsible for their misdemeanors as for their achievements. In recent years, figures from all political sides have too often talked the socialist language of opting out and spreading the blame. Since neoconservatives hold individual liberty sacred for its ability to free people, so too they believe that, if individuals are to be treated with respect, they must be held responsible for all of their behaviour. So neoconservatives must, for instance, lead a radical overhaul of the welfare benefits system. One example may suffice.

Teenage pregnancy rates in America today remain trou-
blingly high. We should conclude not simply that the system
for combating teenage pregnancy is not working, but also that
there is something actively wrong with it. Neoconservatives
might be said to believe that people should never be penalized
or praised for things over which they have no control. So, for
instance, people should not be singled out for either negative
or favorable discrimination because of the color of their skin.
Likewise, people should be given the same opportunities for
educational advancement, and not be penalized if they are
bright and come from a low rather than an average-income
family. But if people are rightly not to be held responsible or
judged on what they cannot affect, it is only right that they be
held responsible for those things that definitely do result from
their own decisions and actions. Today the difference between
the two is blurred, and often oddly inverted.

Within the welfare system, neoconservatives suggest that,
while society should not "punish" single mothers who have
babies early, neither does society owe them special support.
There is still a perception that a life of ease begins once the
welfare life has been embarked upon. The only way to change
the situation is to take away that perception. Whether the
young girls involved intend to become welfare mothers or not,
it cannot be denied that the consequences of their actions are
insufficiently dissuasive. This should change. As Irving Kristol
has suggested, "These girls should be made to look upon welfare not as an opportunity, but as a frightening possibility."[20] It
is, as Gertrude Himmelfarb noted of the Victorians, more
important to do good to others than to feel good oneself. For

all its faults, Victorian society was at least aware that people sometimes needed to "restrain their benevolent impulses in the best interests of those they were trying to serve."[21]

While society should always provide welfare support for children to ensure that they have the best opportunity to escape from the unfortunate environment into which their mothers have borne them, the mothers themselves should be compelled to live with partners, parents, or other relatives. In other words, the prospect of life-long support and accommodation should be withdrawn. People who enter such a life must be made aware that they do so of their own free will, and that they, and not the state, are ultimately responsible for their future. Certainly there will always be shrieks of protest at such a policy, but the effects of the removal of the welfare incentive will have palpable effects on teenage pregnancy rates, and society as a whole will benefit.

This is just one application of the neoconservative philosophy that rights cannot exist without responsibilities. The present generation has done nothing to earn the rights it believes it possesses, and furthermore it remains ignorant of the origins of those rights. Like Locke and Hobbes, neoconservatives believe that the fundamental right is the individual's right to life. Other rights can and should be argued for, but the rights boom over the last generation has produced a raft of laws that are, as Fukuyama put it, both "ambiguous in their social content and mutually contradictory."[22] There is no innate right to a flat, free flow of free money, or never-ending welfare. Society needs, from the top down, to re-evaluate its priorities. At the moment it is selling itself wrongly: as an endlessly beneficent cash-machine rather than as an occasionally charitable donor.

Those reliant on welfarism are a drain on the country for more reasons than their mere lack of productivity, for this underclass is responsible for numerous societal defects.[23] One such associated problem is crime, a matter that is rightly one of the greatest concerns of voters. Crime is the place where the effects of the counterculture and other societal misjudgments are directly felt by the public. Neoconservatives know that the private use of drugs is not simply a matter of private arrangements between consenting adults. They know that the drug problem, and the post-Sixties acceptance of it, is a scourge that directly affects public experience, for it lies at the root of a majority of burglaries, muggings, and other crimes. A user's habit is a problem for society, not just for the user, because society pays, through colossal increases in crime, for what is often misguidedly presented as an issue of individual "liberty" or "liberalism."

The method of dealing with the drug problem comes under the neoconservative policy on crime and policing, as expressed by James Q. Wilson and George L. Kelling in the "broken windows" approach. It was this approach that was famously— and successfully—adopted in New York by Mayor Giuliani. The "broken windows" policy argues that when a window is broken and goes unmended, other unsavory aspects of society have the opportunity to encroach. People take less care of their environment because their efforts hardly seem worth it. Soon no one does anything good because a gargantuan effort would be needed to effect an overhaul. Areas become crime-ridden and unsafe for the free citizen because untended aspects of a neighborhood spread. Property is abandoned and left derelict as people move out.

Neoconservatism

Many areas in America—inner cities and outskirts—experience the reality of this theory. The neighborhood declines and, as it looks more and more shabby, good families and good people do not want to live there—but drug dealers, gangs, and other criminals do. People who are not rich enough to move out of the area have no option but to remain, and in order to remain they must keep clear of areas of their neighborhood, and avoid intervening if there is any trouble. In other words, to remain safe the good people are forced into the position of having to do nothing.[24] This is a microcosm of societal breakdown, where the criminal dictate to the decent how the decent must live. Government in America has put up with this situation for too long.

The first thing needed to combat this situation is a strong police force, freed from restraints and governmental undermining, and able to use any force it deems appropriate to deal with the situation. Only the police fully know what is required on the streets, and the authorities must trust the police again. The police force's job is simply to find a way to police successfully. It has not gone unnoticed that this is not happening in some areas.

It is time a dose of realism was reintroduced in the matter of law-enforcement. By having to tiptoe around the issue of race and bend over backwards so as not to offend, the police in America are having their job made not just harder, but very often impossible. For as long as a disproportionate amount of crime is committed by young black males, young black males should be disproportionately targeted by police. For as long as Muslims, largely of Arab stock, commit terrorist acts within western society, the law enforcement agencies should disproportionately target young Middle Eastern-looking men for stop-and-search. This is not racist—it is responsible policing, and the least that is required to make American citizens safe. As soon as middle-aged Chinese women start committing a disproportionate quantity of crimes, then they should be disproportionately targeted by police. As soon as blond Swedish men get into the habit of plotting and committing acts of terrorism against western society, then blond Swedish men should be repeatedly stopped and searched.

All this should be perfectly obvious to the US government, but apparently it is not. The specific refusal to use ethnic profiling at airports is an appalling end-point of this law-enforcement failure. According to the Transportation Secretary Norman Mineta, there are no circumstances in which ethnic profiling should be employed. In a CBS interview with Steve Kroft, Mineta was asked, "If you saw three young Arab men sitting, kneeling, praying, before they boarded a flight, getting on, talking to each other in Arabic, getting on the plane, [would there be] no reason to stop and ask them any questions?," Mineta replied, "No reason."[25] This is not political correctness, and it is not even suicide: it is government deciding that the lives of American citizens are of less concern than the feelings of ethnic minorities.

The restraining of the police and security services through the tyranny of "racism" accusations puts the public at considerable risk. The police must target those who have committed, or are likely to commit, crimes. The criminals brought to trial or apprehended should not be "representative" of any class: they must simply be the people—of whatever creed, class or color—who are committing crimes. The police should not be "sensitive to ethnic concerns," but should simply do whatever they have to in order to prevent crime. Any ethnic or religious group likely to be turned against the state because they have been, for instance, stopped and searched, is a group whose loyalty to the country is clearly not even skin deep.

The fact that a swathe of law-makers and opinion-formers in America are willing to risk the lives and property of millions of their countrymen for the sake of peoples' feelings demonstrates how little the countercultural forces actually care for their society. To care more for an ideal than for a population is strangely reminiscent of a political creed that had been presumed dead.

Immigration and National Identity

In all domestic decisions, neoconservatism offers a refreshing clarity. This does not mean that all decisions or all issues become easy, but what neoconservatism offers (and what mainstream conservatism often dares not) is clarity on where we are coming from, as well as where we should be going. The debate over immigration is a good example of what happens when that clarity is missing.

Immigration rightly preoccupies many Americans, yet successive Democratic and Republican administrations have been unable to deal with it because the natural argument has become unacceptable to them. As Bloom and Fukuyama highlighted, the western elites cannot find a "logical" reason why they should not let anyone and everyone into their countries. Though it has bypassed the attention of the political class, it has not bypassed the notice of the public that the "morality" of immigration "works in only one direction." (As Peter Brimelow pointed out in *Alien Nation*, the multiculturalism enthusiasts still seem strangely unwilling to "diversify" Saudi Arabia or Yemen.)[26] As Samuel Huntington said of the influx of illegal immigrants from Mexico, "The economic and political forces generating this threat are immense and unrelenting. Nothing comparable has occurred previously in the American experience."[27] On this matter it is no wonder that the views of the Colorado Congressman Tom Tancredo are now being listened to, protective fencing round America's border and all.

Neoconservatives understand that the reason we have for closing the immigration floodgates is eminently rational—a reason that the public knows and the politicians try to hush up. It is simple: America does not want unstoppable immigration across its borders because it wants to remain America, to remain identifiably American, and to remain so in perpetuity.

Only those who dislike American culture or feel envy or malice towards it wish the submergence of the culture. But even now it is not they who have the upper hand. Those behind the willing submergence of American culture are often those who simply feel ambivalent about an identifiably Western or American culture. They are not sure if they can express pride in it and are unwilling to declare "for" this particular side. This is vain foolishness, and a foolishness that neoconservatism must cut through.

A nation that dares not mention matters of race and culture is a nation that lacks the confidence needed to survive, let alone be a global leader. And it is a country that leaves itself open not only to the strongest, but also to the weakest of alien creeds. The prevalence of the vacuous and indefensible creed of multiculturalism is a manifestation of this. Multiculturalism has become such a rampaging force that it can end careers and force the populace as a whole to live under a petty tyranny of political correctness.

America has a particular identity, which would have been very different had America been settled by different people. Multiculturalism, however, is very often maliciously motivated, corrosive, and disastrous for America's way of life. As Huntington has put it, "Multiculturalism is in its essence anti-European civilization ... an anti-Western ideology."[30] Irving Kristol absolutely agrees, adding that multiculturalism is "as much a 'war against the West' as Nazism and Stalinism ever were."[31] To avert multiculturalism's triumph, we must become absolutist again—for our own good.

American society is right to welcome and encourage the benefits that limited immigration has brought, but that does not mean immigration should be perpetual, or limitless. The director of the Pew Hispanic Center estimated a few years back that 35 to 45 percent of all Hispanic immigrants currently in the US are in the country illegally.[28] This is a scandalous figure, and one which government should have to act upon. But it seems that they cannot. Samuel Huntington put forward a striking analogy:

> If each year a million Mexican soldiers attempted to invade the United States and more than 150,000 of them succeeded, established themselves on American territory, and the Mexican government then demanded that the United States recognize the legality of this invasion, Americans would be outraged and would mobilize whatever resources were necessary to expel the invaders

and to establish the integrity of their borders. Yet an illegal demographic invasion of comparable dimensions occurs each year.[29]

Once a people are secure in the knowledge of who they are, and unashamed to declare that what they are is a good thing, it will be possible to begin a sensible debate about asylum and immigration. But only when the populace knows that their government will never allow their country to be turned into a caliphate or ghetto will the concept of immigration as a whole stop being threatening. There are many ways in which government can contain immigration, and every way in which it can halt it. Any government that says otherwise is simply repeating banal and weak-willed lies. They are also storing up problems.

The campaign against this prevailing trend is vital to the American sense of national identity and a crucial element in America's continuance as the influential power with global responsibilities. America's job is to lead the world. But to do this, it must be confident in who it is. America must face down her enemies by declaring for herself. We must not allow those who dislike the US to make the country a test case for a fantasy society, in which all opinions—even nihilistic ones—are equal and all faiths and beliefs equally valid. Nor should the presumption that America's population must inevitably keep growing be allowed to persist.[32] We need to open out this debate more honestly if we are going to sort out this issue. Above all, Americans need to say again: "This is America, this is what we stand for, and beyond this line we will not budge."

* * *

Neoconservatism

Europe

It is no secret that the European Union presents problems for all types of conservatives. Though they may feel far away from it at times, Americans should take a deep and involved interest in Europe and Europe's well-being. They should mind because on the continent of America's first-cousins a generation is in power—or coming to power—that is busily steamrolling ahead with the creation of an entirely new society, a society that is hostile to Europe's—and America's—past, and capriciously inventive with its future.

The society that professional EU politicians are creating is woefully ill-conceived, a utopia based on school-boyish and long-disproved presumptions about human nature and the course of our future. They are perpetuating the most danger-ous of contemporary myths—a myth many of them inherited from their days as fellow-travelers of communist ideologies. Reformed or closet socialists may not talk today of socialism, Marxism or communism, but instead of the more pleasant-sounding "integration," "unity," and "perpetual peace." But they are, nevertheless, spreading the most socialist trope of all—the myth of human perfectibility, a myth that not only led to the twentieth century's camps and gulags, but that has always led such ways. In persistently seizing on simplified notions of collective guilt for the Nazi horror, they are in danger of entirely overlooking the root causes of the other evil ideology.

The notion of human and societal perfectibility exists as a substitute for faith in humankind, not as an expression of it. At its root lie an idea and a myth that are, as Irving Kristol would have it, "woefully blind to human and political reality."

Even as they scoff at the simple neoconservative idea that freedom and democracy are things that could belong to all people, the socialists of Europe drag their people towards a far more impractical "post-historical" state entirely of their own imagination.

They do not ask why if their vision of a peaceful, harmonious, state-free, multicultural future is inevitable, then why it is so? Or who made it inevitable? They do not ask the question because these individuals are themselves both the inventors and propellers of this "inevitability"? This is not a "progressive" or inevitable course of human history, but a means of inflicting alien ideology on the people of Europe. Conservatives must expose this and explain how and why an ideology that is spurred on by personal nihilism and relativism must never be permitted to set up a new order. Foundationless "progressive" politics is vacuity in search of meaning. The itinerary of this socialist agenda must be stopped at the same time as its lack of philosophy is exposed.

An undoubted effect of the Second World War was that a wide distrust and outright suspicion of nationhood arose in Europe. "Nationalism" was identified as the problem, and as the "nation" was responsible for nationalism, it was obviously the cause of the problem. At the time of the sixtieth anniversary of VE Day, this argument was baldly stated by the EU Commissioner Margot Wallström, who claimed that the war had been caused simply by "nationalistic pride and greed, and ... international rivalry for wealth and power." Ms. Wallström was joined by her fellow Commissioners in restating the modern EU's basic presumption: that the way to avoid an otherwise inevitable second holocaust is ratification of the draft constitution of the European state and the abolition of the nation state.[33] Before Holland's 2005 vote on the EU constitution, the Dutch government bombarded the people with television "Yes" adverts filled with footage of Nazi concentration camps. "If you say 'No' to the European project, this is what you will go back to," they implied, apparently with so little faith in the people of Europe that they are convinced they will engage in genocide, given the slightest opportunity.

The lesson went that, since nation states had gone to war, war could not happen if you got rid of nation states, or created really big nation states.[34] This is the ideological twin of the presumption voiced by proselytizing atheism that "bad things have been done in the name of all faiths, therefore all faith is bad." These instances of *reductio ad absurdum* are entirely based in relativism. Besides, without relativism, perpetrators could not have assumed the role of victim, and from there, leadership. This is demeaning for a continent which others (not least in America[35]) have revered for what was learned there, and what Europe's past offers.

Roger Scruton recently noted that "those who believe that the division of Europe into nations has been the primary cause of European wars should remember the devastating wars of religion that national loyalties finally brought to an end."[36] But to remember such wars, of course, one would first have to know of them, and for too many Europeans historical reference begins and ends with the Nazis.

Under such circumstances, no wonder someone might consider the state to be the problem. Sixty years after the war, German public figures are persistent in their attempts to explain why Germany is once again uniquely wise, and its vision of the future superior. The German ambassador to London has complained that Germans are misunderstood and that the British are "obsessed" with the Nazi period.[37] His brother (Matthias Matussek of the German magazine *Der Spiegel*) has taken the argument a step further, claiming, "We have learnt the meaning of mourning and have a determination never to allow another genocide. In contrast, our British neighbors have not learnt much more than the triumphalist trumpeting of the victor."[38] Never mind, for the moment, that this claim is both a lie and a fantastical moral inversion, that enables Germans to portray themselves not merely as victims, but as uniquely wise. The assumption of personal guilt under these circumstances becomes not merely simple, but beneficial. So it is no coincidence that Germans are prominent among those pushing for a super-state. For understandable reasons, the best of them have no faith in their own country's ability to remain within its own borders. But that is no reason to impel a loss of faith in the state across the board. To read the German experience as a lesson to be taught to other European states—let alone those who put an end to German aggression—is to indulge not in victor's, but loser's justice. As Leo Strauss observed in a related context, "It would not be the first time that a nation, defeated on the battlefield and, as it were, annihilated as a political being, has deprived its conquerors of the most sublime fruit of victory by imposing on them the yoke of its own thought."[39]

Neoconservatives should be particularly opposed to Europe because it resembles a prototype of anti-democracy. Britain had one referendum on the Common Market, and from that it has been strong-armed into (and has been too weak-willed to resist) a raft of legislation, which today has a practical impact on the life of every Briton. The aim of the EU now in passing laws is, as George F. Will has observed, "to put as many matters as possible beyond debate. Beyond the reach of majorities. Beyond democracy."[40] The elite is not only not keen to seek the opinion of the people, it is actively finding ways in which it can avoid hearing the opinions of the people.

If the governments of France and the Netherlands had decided, like many of their European colleagues, not to give their electorates the chance to say "*Non*" or "*Nee*," the progress towards super-statism may have proceeded unchecked. But Brussels now works on the presumption that electorates are holding back "progress." These are the foundations of tyranny. Of course, Europe is not going to have another holocaust like the last one. If anyone starts dressing troops in stormtrooper outfits and herding Jews onto trains, Europeans would not permit it any more than would Americans. But totalitarianism mutates, changes, and adapts: evil never returns in the same guise. In obsessing over the fire last time, Europe has taken its eye off the next storm.

It is in keeping its eye on the next story that Europe must comprehensively reject all attempts by Turkey to join the European Union. America should support its European allies in this act of rejection, but sadly it is not doing so. Even some of the brightest American neocons argue for Turkish entry. They argue that Turkey could act as a "bridge" between the Middle East and Europe, a meeting point of cultures. If Turkey joins, it will be no such thing. Turkey will provide not a bridge but a tunnel, through which, under open borders, anyone, including terrorists, would be able to enter the EU by crossing from Iraq or Syria into Turkey. Rejecting Turkey might mean giving offense, but offense is necessary. Even a common-trading Europe must be a Christian club, a meeting place of Christian-based states with a common cultural interest. The Turks should be courted and afforded courtesy as friends and allies, but their entry into Europe in the twenty-first century is no more desirable today than it was three hundred years ago.

The UN

In the run-up to the Iraq war, one overwhelming presumption prevailed in the West among those who opposed the war—and even among some who were in favor. This presumption was that the UN had at least some authority to say whether the war was justified or not, and—even more strangely—whether it was "just" or not. This last fallacy took in a good many who should have known better. A prominent Bishop in England stated that "there was never enough international consensus" for the Iraq war, and Anglican bishops seriously debated the international legal conditions necessary for a war to be "just."[41] This is not, perhaps, what Thomas Aquinas had in mind. As they are among the few people able to pronounce doctrinally on just war, it is greatly disappointing to see bishops talking of UN mandates. The UN has no spiritual authority, no legal authority, and not even any very impressive track record in getting such things right. In truth, what has happened in recent years (as David Frum and Richard Perle have observed) is that the UN has become "exactly what it pretends to be: the parliament of the world."[42] But the UN is not the parliament of the world. And it is certainly not an organization that can deliver a balanced—let alone a truthful—opinion to America and her allies.

Neoconservatism

In 2003, on the eve of the liberation of Iraq, the UN was displaying qualities that would have been familiar to Jeane Kirkpatrick and Daniel Patrick Moynihan. For instance, the rogue state Libya was elected at this time to chair the UN Commission on Human Rights. Libya may be temporarily back in the fold, but Americans should not be quick to forget Libya's years, under its current ruler, of terroristic antagonism towards their country. We should not forget the Pan Am terrorist attack over Lockerbie or the numerous other acts of Libyan-sponsored terror. Libya holding any position, let alone that of chair, on a commission on human rights is an idiocy only possible at the UN.

In another UN coup, May 2003 was meant to see Saddam Hussein's Iraq (the only regime in existence to have used weapons of mass destruction) assume the presidency of the UN Conference on Disarmament. The fact that Saddam Hussein did not assume this position was only thanks to the removal of his regime by force in an action of which the UN (as with the Kosovo conflict) did not approve. Meanwhile Syria continues to sit on the Security Council, despite its rightful designation as a linchpin member of the axis of evil. This is a country which until recently occupied one of its neighbors, is led by an inherited dictatorship, and currently provides a training ground for terrorists preparing to cross the border into Iraq.

The UN's inability to recognize right and wrong, or to discern any moral distinction between the two, is not its only failing. Its failings are practical as well as moral. Too often it resembles the League of Nations, an organization that led Niebuhr to write "the prestige of the international community is not great enough . . . to achieve a communal spirit sufficiently unified, to discipline recalcitrant nations."[43] And no wonder that prestige is still lacking when the UN fails as signally as it did in Bosnia, in Rwanda, and in the Congo. All speak of an institution which, even if it means well, is hopelessly inept in acting on such good intentions as it has.

In 1995, inaction in the Balkans led a number of neocons to sign a broad coalition statement declaring that refusal to use force "has relegated the U.N. to irrelevancy at best and complicity at worst."[44] Examples of its ineptitude abound, even when non-military aid is called for. The UN response to the Asian tsunami in 2004 was woefully slow and weighed down by procedure. Comparisons with the swift humanitarian responses of, for instance, the American and Australian armed forces, are not merely unflattering—they are shaming. For the UN to act more effectively, it will demand more power, more backing, and more money. None of these could possibly be given to the UN in its current state.

Conservatives of all creeds must explain why the UN is a false construct and not what it pretends to be. The UN is a nice idea: it is an organization founded on hopefulness and good intent. But the League of Nations was built on the same principles. Things do not become true because they are well-meaning, or become right because they seem nice. The UN does provide a useful focal point for some global discussion. It does provide a physical symbol of international striving. But as the diplomat Robert Cooper has observed, the UN was founded in order "to defend the status quo and not to create a new order."[45] It is neither democratic, nor representative of our interests. Resolutions passed by the UN are significant, but must not dictate to us when they are wrong and influenced

Neoconservatism

by tyrannies. To be dictated to by UN resolutions is to accept that we have offered up some of our sovereignty, or that our sovereign status has changed on the say-so of people who are unelected by, and unanswerable to, the people of the West, and many of whom represent governments that are neither free nor democratic.

As a country, America must realize that the UN in its current form will never represent the interests of America or her allies. The organization is weighted against us. The interests of the community of nations are not always America's interests, any more than are the interests of the international courts. But America's interests and the interests of the UN will often coincide, and hopefully coincide more often than they diverge. It should be a source of interest and satisfaction to us when we are in agreement with the UN, but we in the West should not consider ourselves ruled by the reactions of the body, nor seek its praise. We should not assume that our compatibility with it will grow, any more than we should assume that it will significantly decline.

America should certainly not withdraw from the UN, as some have argued.[46] We should make the argument—and make others see—that the UN is a dream, not a reality. It should gain no more power than it has, because it is unelected, undemocratic, and as such uniquely prone to misguidedness and tyranny. And it should receive no more financial assistance than it does: money paid to the UN is money siphoned off to causes that would better benefit from direct assistance. Most importantly, it must be shown that neither our national interests, nor the interests of the world as a whole, are best served by an organization whose record has consistently been one of sinking to the lowest moral denominator on the grandest of scales. The UN cannot define "just war," and it certainly cannot define, or pretend that it especially cares for, America's specific national interest. An organization that presumes to represent the interests of hostile dictatorships can never represent the interests of great democracies. A generation disposed to view the UN's verdict as binding is a generation disposed to global relativism. It reveals itself to be attracted by merely a more pleasant-looking form of unrepresentative tyranny.

The war on terror

America's allies in Europe still bask in their post-World War II peace dividend, and try their hardest to prolong it. The desperate final phase of this flight from reality is now epitomized by the European Union, an assault on national identity always intended to persuade the populace of Europe that—as Roger Scruton has put it—"lay[ing] down one's life for a collection of strangers begins to border on the absurd."[47] The experiment was planned to make war illogical, indefensible, and impossible. This is a tremendous mistake on the part of the European project. The EU has relied on the possibility that the peace divided can be eternal at the very moment that it has run out. Since 9/11, the gulf between America and Europe has been between a people who still largely recognize that a threat to our civilization exists, and a people whose majority lives in the fond hope that it does not. For some people, none of the wake-up calls from the jihadists has had any effect—neither the foiled atrocities, nor those that have succeeded. This should be of grave interest to Americans and all people who value freedom.

Neoconservatism

In Holland, two prominent figures—the politician Pim Fortuyn and the film director Theo van Gogh—who addressed the problem of Islamic terrorists in Europe were assassinated in broad daylight on Dutch streets. In both the Netherlands and Belgium, politicians like the brave Hirsi Ali, Mimount Bousakla, and Geert Wilders who have spoken out against the jihadists, are now forced to live on army bases and require round-the-clock police protection. As with the assassinations, responses to such intimidation across the European press range from the silent to the celebratory (with the British-based *Index on Censorship* shaming itself utterly by lauding this particular form of censorship on van Gogh[48]). The "liberal" press and the "liberal" establishment have been silent—not relatively silent, but utterly silent. American "liberal" reaction has been little better. It has all been too reminiscent of that earlier collapse of "liberalism" in the face of black violence on the campuses during 1968–1969. Just as then (as Muravchik observed), "Liberals just collapsed.... I didn't understand it then, I don't understand it now."[49]

Van Gogh was not a conservative, but it was only conservatives that spoke out against his murder. The "liberals," the mouthy celebrities and politicians in America and Europe who had spent the previous years shouting and demonstrating against the use of force in liberating Afghanistan and Iraq, had between them not one word to say when the jihad arrived on Europe's streets. In a number of cases, they had worse than nothing to say. Many papers implied that van Gogh had brought his killing on himself, and should not have been so "provocative" against Islam. In Rotterdam, a local artist who painted a mural of a dove and the legend "Thou shalt not kill" as a protest against the killing of van Gogh was ordered by the local police to remove his work—they had received complaints that the message was an incitement and racist. Meanwhile, Hamas supporters were allowed to gather on the streets cheering the bloodletting. Cowed by political correctness, Dutch reporters stated not that the groups were Islamists, but that they were "Moroccans" as if their nationality and not their religion was the nub of the matter. Though there have been moments of tough-talking, the general reaction of the Netherlands authorities has been that of a child who believes that, if it closes its eyes hard enough, the bogey-man will go away.

A similar but even worse phenomenon occurred in Spain after March 2004, when Islamic militant immigrants (paying their way in Spain as drug dealers) killed two hundred people and injured many more when they bombed the morning commuter trains of Madrid. This was strategically planned to affect the outcome of the election later that week, and the Spanish electorate duly responded by voting out their government and electing the opposition socialists, who had promised (and were true to their word) that if elected they would order a Spanish retreat from Iraq. Despite this appeasement of the terrorists, more bombs (fortunately discovered and defused) were planted later. Yet, not content with its servile attitude to terror, the new socialist government in Spain has spent the time since its surprise election waging war on the Roman Catholic Church in Spain, slashing funding of the Church, and simultaneously funding massive increases in the state teaching of Islam. Even though terrorists have attempted to bomb Spain again since his election, the socialist Mr. Zapatero remains convinced that the problem is with his people, not the terrorists, and that the Spanish terrorist swamps must be placated rather than drained.

We have seen how Germany tried to respond to Islamic fundamentalist attack by diverting attention towards America. A similar trick was performed by France. Having done everything they could not to engage in the war in Iraq, the French nonetheless found that it was an oil tanker of theirs that was attacked off the coast of Yemen in October 2002. Europe still does not get it. Trying desperately to pretend that there is no jihad and no problem of millions of dissident, angry Islamists inside its borders, Europe is still asking: "What did we do?" and "Was it something we said?" The terrorist war against the West may only be in its earliest stages, but Europe's first reactions are unpromising. Its governments are choosing to opt out when it ought to be clear that opting out from terrorist attack is not an option. In the ultimate gesture of ultra-appeasement, some Europhiles, like the serially wrong Timothy Garton-Ash, even believe that the terrorist attacks demonstrate a need to let more Muslims into Europe, as a gesture of goodwill or, amazingly, penance.[50]

And whither Britain? The question for America's closest ally is now whether it should keep itself allied with America, go the way of Europe, or try to do a freestyle approach somewhere in the middle. The answer is obvious, and Americans should understand how important it is that Britain make the right choice. They must persuade their ally that the only possible choice is to maintain distance from the disastrous politics and military of Europe, and re-arm for a new and strategically challenging conflict.[51] In 2002, and many times since, Condoleezza Rice has "exhort[ed] our freedom-loving allies, such as those in Europe, to increase their military capabilities."[52] Britain's European allies are not taking these warnings seriously, seeming to believe that some elaborate and expensive game of bluff is being played by Washington. But just as, in their early days, it was the neocons that were most aware of the communist threat, so now they are more in tune with the seriousness of the current situation.

British re-armament, including the development of increasingly high-tech missile technology, is vital if Britain is going to continue to be able to assist America in the targeted warfare of the new century. We are entering a time when regimes could be deposed by the use of a single missile, and widespread "collateral damage" could become a thing of the past. To meet such needs, we should, as Richard Perle and David Frum have suggested, form a new coalition, in which a closed circle of allies forms a mutually beneficial defense-procurement market. Perle and Frum suggest that Britain, America, Canada, and Australia could form such a club—each benefiting from the advances made by the others.[53] To this list we should add Israel, which is as much at the front line of the war on terror now as it has always been. This would not merely enhance the development of advanced weaponry on our side, but would solidify an axis, and highlight to our erstwhile allies the immediate consequences of appeasement, buck-passing, and attempts at opting out.

The wars of the new century will necessarily be pre-emptive, be localized, and require shifting coalitions. There is nothing new in any of this. As Michael Gove has argued persuasively, this allegedly "illegal" policy of pre-emption is historically a solid British policy, having, on a number of occasions, saved

Neoconservatism

a world "where international law could still be practiced."[54] In an age of WMD proliferation, where western cities can be targeted by rogue regimes or stateless terrorist groups, pre-emption is the only possible policy. Even Mutually Assured Destruction (MAD) is no deterrent to the enemies we now face, and so there is no room for benefit of the doubt.

It is in such a situation that the Western allies must keep a close eye on Iran's nuclear project. Iran looks likely to provoke the Osirak moment of this decade. Neoconservatives and others should be clear: Iran must not be allowed to develop a nuclear device. This is not just because the nuclear spread is already too wide; that Iran is, with North Korea, the foreign regime most hostile to the West; or that Iran has extensive links with every Islamic terrorist network in the Middle East. It must be prevented from developing a bomb because, uniquely, Iran has expressed (not least in the words of Mssrs. Rafsanjani and Ahmadinejad[55]) the desire to use it. Iran's intention to strike Israel and wipe it off the map has emboldened Iranians to believe they would only need one bomb. And they may be right. No such attack on a democratic ally by a regime like Iran can be contemplated. Israel, America, Great Britain, and other powers must use whatever force is necessary to dissuade or physically prevent Tehran from developing nuclear weaponry. Tehran is no ally. A pre-emptive strike on its nuclear facilities must be planned and welcomed, unless Iran can prove beyond any doubt that it is not developing nuclear energy for a missile. Due to the speed at which Tehran is subverting the diplomatic process, a strike before the end of 2006 looks essential.[56] Anyone who thinks such a strike immoral or hawkish must simply state why they would be content and secure in a world living with the threat of a Tehran bomb.

Each and every country has a choice: to work at prosecuting the war against the terrorists and tyrannies, or sit it out with those intent on policies of inaction. Europe's display (with noble exceptions, such as Italy under Berlusconi) of "kicking the ball down the field" shows little determination to deal with the root problem or its effects. Too many Europeans believe that history has stopped for them. A 2003 poll revealed that fewer than half of all Europeans believe that *any war at all* can be just.[57] They are dreaming of a peace that they are no longer willing to protect. With European countries' combined military spending less than half that of the US, it is again no wonder that inaction seems financially attractive to the governments of Europe, as it did to the German government when it kept quiet on WMD before the Iraq war. If European countries do not vastly increase the percentage of their budgets spent on defense, their armies will not only remain dwarfed; they will lag behind technologically and become all but inconsequential on the battlefields of the twenty-first century.

If many European governments were truly honest, they would have to admit that the reason they do not support the war on terror fully is not just because they cannot afford it, or know that they can leave America to deal with it. Their inaction is largely due to the fact that they are scared of it—and rightly so, because the war is not on their horizon, or on their borders, but in their towns and streets. The inaction of Europe is caused not just by a laziness or stupor, but by the numbed realization that it might be too late to take any but the most drastic measures to clear its countries of hostile terrorist cells and populations. The stomach for these drastic measures is only slowly emerging in the populace, and principally in the country most demographically threatened—the Netherlands. The Netherlands will have Muslim-majority cities within this generation, and the Dutch people are beginning to wake up to the fact that they never asked for this and do not want it. This may not be where multiculturalism was meant to lead, but it is certainly where it has led. It has led to host countries being unable to stop Hamas, Hezbollah, and al-Qaeda demonstrations and supporters, because they have given such people rights that cannot be breached. This problem has arisen and will—if not checked—grow in the United States as well. The degradation of one Western state can easily show the way in which the degradation of the others will be achieved.

In all our countries of the West, multiculturalism and the rule of "rights" are now used as weapons to beat us, and have become demonstrations of our weakness, not our sophistication. An al-Qaeda training manual found in 2003 had as its Rule 18 that their terrorists, if captured, "must insist on proving that torture was inflicted on them" and "complain to the court of mistreatment while in prison."[58] Such has been their tactic—they have used it in Guantanamo and everywhere else they have been incarcerated. Meanwhile, Muslim representatives have repeatedly condemned and expressed concern over the arrest of any Muslims at all in the West.[59] We are allowing the advances that our society has fought for to be used against us, and used to drag us into darkness.

America cannot afford to let this threat continue, on its own shores or within the shores of its closet allies. Britain's jihadists were already at work there before the first bombing of London. In writing (in 2003) that London is "the real bridgehead of terrorism in Europe," Bernard-Henri Lévy was only giving voice to a well-known fact in the intelligence and policing communities of Europe.[60] Lévy was writing in his book on the killing of the Jewish *Wall Street Journal* reporter Daniel Pearl, beheaded in Pakistan in 2002 by a graduate of the London School of Economics, Omar Sheikh. By the time Sheikh murdered Daniel Pearl, the London college had supplied Osama bin Laden's service with three of its graduates[61]— that's three that we know of. Richard Reid, the "shoe bomber" who tried to blow up and murder the passengers on a flight from Paris to Miami in December 2001, went to school in London. Asif Mohammed Hanif and Omar Khan Sharif were granted every luxury of the British welfare state before they flew to Israel in April 2003 to murder Jews outside a Tel Aviv bar. And there are numberless others who have flown to join the jihads in Iraq, Afghanistan, and elsewhere.

And of course on July 7, 2005 the plotters finally succeeded in launching a wave of suicide bombings against the people of London. Before those attacks, many people in Britain had become sanguine about the terror threat, preached to by Michael Moore, the BBC's *The Power of Nightmares*, and other lies that there was no threat—that it had all been made up by neocons. But this line was as unsustainable after July 7 as it had always been. For too long certain Britons had decided they did not need to worry about the jihad, and ignored Britain's use as a base from which terrorists worked, and as a breeding ground from which terrorists were sent out to murder people abroad. For four years, dozens of Islamist terror attacks on Britain were foiled by the police and security services, and the glad fools of the anti-war-on-terror lobby contin-

ued attacking the security services, interpreting news of security successes as government propaganda and evidence that
there was no terrorist threat.[62] And as long as British Muslims
only killed Jews in Israel, or British servicemen in Iraq, their
crimes were forgiven, excused, and equivalenced around by
the British Muslim "community" and their voluntary apolo-
gists on the "left." After the London bombings all the old
faces like Tariq Ali and new faces like the *Guardian*'s very own
openly Islamo-fascist intern explained that Britain (the country which hosts them) deserved these attacks.[63] When they and
others of their ilk equivalenced an attack on London with the
attack on the terrorist stronghold of Falluja, not merely did
they betray where their sympathies lay, they also performed
the final prostration before the jihadists by claiming that terror
is caused by reacting to terror—by prosecuting and punishing
terror.

Not everyone, mercifully, is under the impression that the
response to terror should be to cower and ensure that in
future we do not even offend the terrorists. Some people still
have enough self-respect not to live their lives at the behest of
the new fascists and their creed. But surrender is not the only
wrong path: to be only on the defensive in this situation is also
to commit suicide. The only response to terror is attack, and
the only viable plan of attack is the neoconservative one. By
this formula, Iraq as much as Afghanistan was a test of our
seriousness; a test (as Frum and Perle have put it) of "whether
we truly intended to wage war against our enemies—or whether
we would revert to the pin-prick tactics of the past."[64] The
9/11 atrocity was a wake-up call to the West that we could no
longer tolerate the terrorists breeding in our midst or massing

under hostile foreign dictatorships. And, just as 9/11 woke us up, the overthrow of Saddam Hussein was, as Niall Ferguson put it, "the mother of all wake-up calls" to the enemy[65]—proof that the war would be dictated on our terms, not on theirs.

As Spain has proven, the terrorists cannot be appeased, and their cause cannot be negotiated with. When Osama bin Laden rails of "the tragedy of Andalusia" he is talking of a deed carried out in 1492, some time before even Jacques Chirac came into politics. When the former Hezbollah leader Hussein Massawi tells us, "We are not fighting so that you offer us something. We are fighting to eliminate you," there are still people, even now, who think perhaps he's bluffing, or that he'll come around if we give him a few more centuries to get over Cordova. This is madness, self-delusion, and an invitation to destruction. No accommodation can be made with these people. They are not after a political settlement, but after an absolute military and religious conquest.

The fact that portions of the West cannot muster the energy even to fight a verbal war with the jihadists is an appalling fact we currently face. This is not a war in which every family is giving up its sons. Contrary to Norman Podhoretz's claims, it does not deserve to be called a "World War," because it is a war currently waged by a professional army only.[66] The enemy is clear. Yet, even though the enemy presently in Iraq are the sub-bandit thugs of Zarqawi and Co., the West is still replete with public and private figures who silently or openly desire the victory of what they call the "insurgents"—terrorists. When the choice is clear—victory for the Iraqi people, the US army and their allies, or for the terrorists—it takes an elaborately wicked enemy of western society to wish victory for the terrorists, people who daily target women, children, and the elderly in Iraq. It takes a wicked relativist to condone terrorism, but in this so far largely armchair conflict, the number of armchair terrorists across government, public life, and media—especially in Europe—bodes exceedingly ill for the future. In this respect, America must take the degradation of its erstwhile allies in Europe especially seriously. If it has not already become so, this conflict may yet descend into a full-scale clash of civilizations. In that situation, as Tony Blankley has argued in *The West's Last Chance*, "a defense of the West without the birthplace of the West—Europe—is almost unthinkable. If Europe becomes Eurabia, it would mean the loss of our cultural and historic first cousins, our closest economic and military allies, and the source of our own civilization." [67] In other words it would result in the isolation of America.

So what should we do?

The terrorists must be attacked wherever they are. Government should ignore how minority communities "feel" about the war, and prosecute the war as best it can. This is war, not PR, and the prosecution of this war contains two strands. The first is at home, where those who are against our societies must no longer be tolerated within our societies. Detention and imprisonment are our strongest weapons, but we have other tactics that we fail to use, such as deportation of culprits and suspects to their countries of origin, or to countries where they will face charges. Deportation of suspects—even between allies— takes far longer than it should and is often made impossible. This is the result of impractical international agreements. That is why those like the notorious cleric Abu Hamza, have been

allowed to continue preaching jihad against the West and indoctrinating young men even while the US requests their extradition to America. Under Article 2 of the ridiculous and newly
invented European Convention on Human Rights, European
countries are "forbidden" from deporting or rendering culprits if their lives may then be in danger. Not surprisingly,
then, lawyers argue that their clients' lives are in danger wherever they are requested. It took until December 2005 for
Britain to deport to France one of the chief suspects in the
1995 Paris metro bombings: that's ten years to cover about as
many miles of water. There is a mistaking of priorities here.
To win this war the lives of terrorists and inciters to terrorism
should be considered as pitilessly on our streets and within our
society as they are on foreign battlefields. The "human rights"
amnesty must end. It is a symptomatic and sickening indictment
of the present system that under current procedure, the extra-
diting of terrorists even between Britain and the United States
is made near-impossible by "human rights" objections.

It is time for America and her allies to withdraw from all
conventions and treaties which restrict our ability to deport suspects between allied countries. We can no longer satisfactorily
prosecute a war in which there is so much international interference in our laws and multiple obstacles put in the way of
justice and victory. America is still a sovereign country, and if
it cannot do what it needs to protect itself, including demand-
ing the right to try suspects living in sympathetic countries,
then it needs to find out who is stopping it and act accordingly.
The rights of the West's people override those of the Islamists
in their midst. And extradition should also include sending suspects away from our shores. If those within America who incite

others to murder Western people and culture—were made aware that the choice is between America and Yemen or Saudi, they might be less abusive of current hospitality. But if that abuse continues, we should not extend the rights we cherish to those who neither earned nor believe in them, yet daily abuse them. The peoples of the West have fought for, and earned, many rights, but these are rights that must be refused to terrorists and terrorist-sympathisers.

Clerics and "community leaders" who claim (as the leaders of nearly all Muslim organizations in America still do) that suicide bombings targeted at Jews are legitimate, even if those targeted at Americans are not, must be exposed to the contempt and trial they deserve. Subsidiaries of Hamas and Hezbollah must be pursued with as much fervor and conviction as al-Qaeda. Yet it is not enough only for the terrorists to be removed from our society—the preachers must be removed too. For this to happen we must extradite, render, and imprison. But we must also be unsparing in our criticism of those who have put American lives at risk in their quest to fulfil an unsupportable and naïve belief in extreme multiculturalism. In other words, time must be called on the period in which America became a guinea-pig for an experiment with no justification or support, but every conceivable risk.

America's duties to freedom, security, and democracy exist at home and abroad. The spread of democratic liberal states is our best hope for a world genuinely free from tyranny and from the threats to our security that hateful, unstable and hostile regimes pose.

The comprehensive success of this mission is still far off,

and there are many both within and without our society who wish that mission to fail. They have consistently crowed over the slow progress in Iraq and scorned the neoconservative belief that democracy, once encouraged in Iraq, would spread in the region. "The promised democratic domino effect ... shows no sign of materializing," claimed Stefan Halper and Jonathan Clarke in 2004.[68] Yet if they had held publication for a year they might have seen the beginnings of that very effect.

In an extraordinary set of events after the Iraqi election in January 2005, Paul Wolfowitz's Iraqi vision began to be vindicated. As he wrote in 2003, "Terrorists recognize that Iraq is on a course towards self-government that is irreversible and, once achieved, will be an example to all in the Muslim world who desire freedom."[68] Syrian troops were peacefully forced out of their occupation of the Lebanon, and elections were then held. And Condoleezza Rice's tough style of diplomacy in her new role as Secretary of State has led to the promise of greater democracy in elections in Egypt, Saudi Arabia and other countries of the region. The Lebanese Druze Muslim leader Walid Jumblatt, no crony of the West, put it plainly in February 2005:

> It's strange for me to say it, but this process of change has started because of the American invasion of Iraq. I was cynical about Iraq. But when I saw the Iraqi people voting three weeks ago, 8 million of them, it was the start of a new Arab world. The Syrian people, the Egyptian people, all say that something is changing. The Berlin Wall has fallen. We can see it.[70]

Neoconservatism

It is a Berlin Wall that has fallen despite, not thanks to, the hordes of free people in the West who turned out to be all noise, and who possess not a quarter of the courage of those who took their chance to vote in 2 0 0 5 in Iraq.

Those who deny that change is happening are now looking more and more desperate, and are ever more openly eager for the terrorists to defeat the free people of Iraq. That misguided and appalling hope flows from a simple, perverted desire to prove George Bush and the neocons wrong.

Therefore our fight should be prosecuted not only by the army and police forces, but by the general public, intellectuals, politicians, and anyone with a sense of civic responsibility. For most of us, this is mercifully a conflict without continuous civilian death tolls. This war is, for most people, still a war in the world of ideas and abstractions. But this matters. For, as Irving Kristol has said, "What rules the world is ideas, because ideas define the way reality is perceived; and, in the absence of religion, it is out of culture—pictures, poems, songs, philosophy —that these ideas are born."[71] It is as a direct result of our rotten thought-culture, our relativism, and our inability to defend the good, that the war against western civilization and freedom has won so many associates, converts, and sympathisers.

Our enemies at home and abroad have repeatedly shown that they understand us in the West better than some within our societies know themselves. Cultures which have forgotten about war, or believe it is a thing of the past, can neither imagine, nor imagine the need for, conflict. Portions of America are as attracted to such dreams as their European cousins. Their societies are rich in accountants and bankers, but "lacking in princes and demagogues."[72] Though they cannot imagine the apocalypse, only a generation brought up on self-esteem would draw from that the conclusion that the apocalypse cannot therefore happen.

We all understand that other prosperous societies do not want to lose the privileges they possess any more than we do. We understand each other in this. But, though this pacific stand-off is all very well between democracies, the same reciprocal understanding cannot exist with our enemies. Our present enemy cannot be negotiated with; our success in defeating that enemy will only be assured by the force with which we unite against it and the fire with which we fight it. If we forget that, or ignore it, then our peace and the future of liberal democracy will be in real danger.

Many in the West believe there is no danger: they have been told as much by munificent propagandists and agenda-filled media outlets. Others support the danger threatening us. Yet others fulfil Fukuyama's "Last Man" thesis, where people become enraged *because* they have nothing against which to struggle, and so struggle "*against* the just cause" and "struggle for the sake of struggle." In this scenario, "if the greater part of the world in which they live is characterized by peaceful and prosperous liberal democracy, then they will struggle against that peace and prosperity, and against democracy."[73] You do not have to watch the ugly hordes protesting against meetings of the world's democratic leaders to see that this movement is now growing unchecked. And you do not have to single out the July 2005 London bombings—during the G8 meeting in Gleneagles—to notice how useful a diversion, as well as moral support, the anti-globalization lobby has become to the terrorists.

Some talk, and always will talk, of ulterior motives in the

new world conflicts. They will talk of profits and undeclared agendas. They will talk of oil pipelines, even when such pipelines do not exist. And, of course, they will talk of Semitic conspiracies in the new century, as surely as they did in the old. They will say that we invaded Iraq, or toppled the Taliban, as part of a Jewish conspiracy, just as some of them claimed the war against Nazism was a Jewish-led war, and just as others saw the world war before that one as organized by and for Jews. The accusation is perennial, and as wrong now as it was then. Jews have always provided a scapegoat for those intent on attacking freedom and democracy by other means. It is not surprising that this age-old defect continues, but it is saddening and surprising to hear it taken up again in its latest guise with such vigor and bile by a generation brought up on racial equality— by people who turn out to believe in the concept completely, with the acceptable exception of one race.

All these ways of criticizing our society are caused by the paucity of public and educational morality, the denial of natural right, and lack of awareness of the weaknesses within a culture we have taken for granted for so long that we are now unable to defend it. But the choice is clear: it is, as President Bush has it, "us or them." We will certainly go on arguing about tactics and approaches, but to deny that there is a conflict, or to claim that that conflict is other than it is, is to be either ignorant and lazy or wilfully mendacious.

This conflict's destructiveness, its amazing possibility to harm us, is caused not by the strength of our opponents' arguments or their strength of arms, but by the weakness within our own society. Many people have rightly stated that militant Islamism cannot possibly provide the coherent ideological threat that, for instance, communism did.[74] Though there is truth in this, it is mistaken on two levels. Firstly, you can never predict (as I hope was shown in Chapter 3) what depths of shocking contrariness socialists are capable of: they will always surprise even the most profound pessimist. And, though the current alliance between the forces of jihad and the forces of anti-globalization and socialist reaction has been neither inevitable nor entirely comfortable, the experience of observing it over recent years confirms that it is the product of two groups playing good old realpolitik in a combined attempt to attack our culture.[75] They and their colleagues cannot win unless we allow them to. We are allowing them to by not adopting a rigorous enough stance in defense of ourselves and against them.

In his second inaugural address, in 2005, President Bush spelt out the neocon dream:

> We are led, by events and common sense, to one conclusion: The survival of liberty in our land increasingly depends on the success of liberty in other lands. The best hope for peace in our world is the expansion of freedom in all the world.
>
> America's vital interests and our deepest beliefs are now one. From the day of our Founding, we have proclaimed that every man and woman on this earth has rights, and dignity, and matchless value, because they bear the image of the Maker of Heaven and earth. Across the generations we have proclaimed the imperative of self-government, because no one is fit to be a master, and no one deserves to be a slave. Advancing these ideals is the mission that created our Nation. It is

the honorable achievement of our fathers. Now it is the urgent requirement of our nation's security, and the calling of our time.[76]

That calling is one in which Britain, Australia, and many other nations have nobly joined, and one in which we should all persist. As the free West it is the sum of our inheritance, our faith, and our responsibility.

Flush with success from Kosovo, in 1999 Tony Blair set out five precepts for humanitarian intervention: sureness of case, exhaustion of diplomatic options, practical plausibility, willingness to endure in the long term, and national interest.[77] It was and is a perfect neoconservative list. Intervention and, where necessary, pre-emption must become the certainties of all Western foreign policy whatever the governments of the day. As the strong, we have a duty to defend the weak—but we can only do that if we remain strong. We must be forceful in our own authority and in the resulting assertions that human rights are something for which we are willing to fight, and that any tyranny is a regime we should aim to topple. This is not some new imperialism; it is rather, as Tony Blair put it, an expression of "the universal values of the human spirit ... freedom, not tyranny; democracy, not dictatorship; the rule of law, not the rule of the secret police."[78]

Nor is it a new doctrine—it is the expression of forces of right and justice, which have always been the aim of Western society and Western law. For most of us, our responsibility is not on the battlefield; it is in taking part, whatever we do, in a society with everything to offer. But if we fail to defend it—if we even become lax, or petty or absent-minded about our society—we sow the seeds of its loss. It does not seem, when set alongside what previous generations have done, to be such a challenging calling. But, as Pericles had it, though the threat may be less, that is not any reason to meet it any less vigorously.

Neoconservatism—whether or not it is called such—is the route back to the right path; the path by which true liberalism returns, strengthened and defended for the good of all. Through it conservatism regains its optimism, sense of purpose and mission—encouraging the good in the modern world and identifying, rejecting, and fighting the bad. Through it we will show that the forces of the counterculture, which have so blighted our society, are not here to stay and are no more inevitable than Western decline or societal breakdown. Critics and even one-time advocates of neoconservatism have claimed that neoconservatism's time is up, or at least "appears to have passed."[79] But we have been here before. The neoconservative moment—the conservative revolution—is not over. In America the forces that make it possible are awake and will not go back to sleep. With confidence in its power, knowledge of a just cause, and the myth of inevitable decline banished, the American people can reaffirm their instinctive ambition and hope, and the conservative revolution can truly begin.

ENDNOTES

―――――

INTRODUCTION

1 Francis Fukuyama, "After Neoconservatism," *New York Times*, 19 February 2006.

2 Giuseppe di Lampedusa, *The Leopard*, trans. Archibald Colquhoun (London: Collins and Harvill Press, 1960), p. 31.

3 David Brooks, "The Neocon Cabal and Other Fantasies," *International Herald Tribune*, 7 January 2004, repr. Irwin Stelzer (ed.), *Neoconservatism* (London: Atlantic Books, 2004), p. 42.

4 Leo Strauss, "Relativism" in *The Rebirth of Classical Political Rationalism* (Chicago: University of Chicago Press, 1989), p. 13.

5 Andrew Kenny, "The End of Left and Right," *Spectator* (UK), 5 February 2005.

6 T.S. Eliot, Choruses from "The Rock," VI.

CHAPTER ONE

1 Joshua Muravchik, "The Neoconservative Cabal" in Irwin Stelzer (ed.), *Neoconservatism* (London: Atlantic Books, 2004), p. 245.

2 Lyndon LaRouche, "Insanity as geometry" in *Children of Satan*, 26 March 2003.

3 Jeffrey Steinberg, "The Ignoble Liars Behind Bush's Deadly Iraq War" in *Children of Satan*.

4 Robert Bartley, "Joining LaRouche In the Fever Swamps," *Wall Street Journal*, 9 June 2003.

5 Jim Lobe, "The Strong Must Rule the Weak: A Philosopher for an Empire," *Foreign Policy in Focus*, 12 May 2003.

6 See—or rather don't see—Tim Robbins' "Embedded" and its inane caricatures of Strauss's thought.

7 Mary Wakefield, "I don't lie. Whoops, there I go again," *Daily Telegraph*, 9 January 2004.

8 Will Hutton, *The World We're In* (London: Little, Brown, 2002), p. 96.

9 Will Hutton, "Time to stop being America's lap-dog," *Observer*, 17 February 2002.

Endnotes

10   Will Hutton, "A dark week for democracy," *Observer*, 10 November 2002.

11   Hutton, *Observer*, 17 February 2002.

12   Kenneth R. Weinstein, "Philosophic Roots, the Role of Leo Strauss, and the War in Iraq" in Stelzer (ed.), *Neoconservatism*, p. 204.

13   Jeet Heer, "The Philosopher," *Boston Globe*, 11 May 2003.

14   Willian Pfaff, "The Long Reach of Leo Strauss," *International Herald Tribune*, 15 May 2003.

15   Muravchik, "The neoconservative cabal," p. 247.

16   Shadia Drury, "Saving America: Leo Strauss and the neoconservatives," Evatt Foundation, online, 11 September 2004.

17   Robert Locke, "Leo Strauss, Conservative Mastermind," *Frontpage Magazine*, 31 May 2002.

18   Weinstein, "Philosophic roots," p. 204.

19   "Interview with Sam Tanenhaus," *Vanity Fair*, 15 May 2003. Complete transcript available from United States Department of Defense, 9 May 2003.

20   Max Boot, "Myths about Neoconservatism" in Stelzer (ed.), *Neoconservatism*, p. 51.

21   Werner J. Dannhauser, "Strauss and the Social Scientist," *Public Interest*, Spring 2003.

22   Werner J. Dannhauser, "Allan Bloom: A Reminiscence" in Michael Palmer and Thomas L. Pangle, (eds), *Political Philosophy and the Human Soul: Essays in Memory of Allan Bloom* (Lanham, Md. : Rowman & Littlefield, 1995), p. 5.

23   Ibid. p. 4.

24   Irving Kristol, *Neoconservatism: The Autobiography of an Idea* (Chicago: Elephant Paperbacks, 1999 edition), p. 7.

25   Anne Norton, *Leo Strauss and the Politics of American Empire* (New Haven and London: Yale University Press, 2004), p. 109.

26   Letter from Werner J. Dannhauser to the Editors, *New York Review of Books*, 24 October 1985.

27   Thomas L. Pangle, Introduction to *The Rebirth of Classical Political Rationalism, Essays and Lectures by Leo Strauss*, 1989, p. viii.

28   Leo Strauss, *On Tyranny* (Chicago: University of Chicago Press, 2000), p. 23.

29   Kristol, *Neoconservatism*, pp. 7–8.

30   Danny Postel, "Noble Lies and Perpetual War: Leo Strauss, the Neocons, and Iraq," an interview with Shadia Drury, *Open Democracy*, 16 October 2003.

Endnotes

31   Pangle, Introduction to *The Rebirth of Classical Political Rationalism*, p. viii.

32   Dannhauser, "Strauss and the Social Scientist."

33   Leo Strauss, *Natural Right and History* (Chicago: University of Chicago Press, 1999), p. 93.

34   Christopher Hitchens, "Bloom's way," *The Nation*, 15 May 2000, repr. in Hitchens, *Unacknowledged Legislation* (London: Verso, 2000), p. 227.

35   Strauss, *Natural Right*, p. 5.

36   Nasser Behnegar, "The Liberal Politics of Leo Strauss" in Palmer and Pangle (eds), *Political Philosophy and the Human Soul*, p. 255.

37   Strauss, *Natural Right*, pp. 2–3.

38   Ibid. p. 5.

39   Leo Strauss, *Liberalism: Ancient and Modern* (New York: Basic Books, 1968), p. 5.

40   Ibid. p. 5.

41   Ibid. p. 24.

42   Pangle, Introduction to *The Rebirth of Classical Political Rationalism*, p. xiii.

43   Strauss, *Natural Right*, p. 34.

44   Cited by Peter Berkowitz, "What hath Strauss wrought?" *The Weekly Standard*, 2 June 2003.

45   Published with *On Tyranny*, 2000.

46   Allan Bloom, *Giants and Dwarfs: Essays 1960–1990* (New York: Simon and Schuster, 1990), p. 11.

47   Saul Bellow, *Ravelstein* (London: Viking, 2000).

48   D. T. Max, "With friends like Saul Bellow," *New York Times Magazine*, 16 April 2000.

49   Martin Amis, *Experience* (New York: Talk Miramax Books, 2000), p. 225.

50   Allan Bloom, *The Closing of the American Mind* (New York: Simon and Schuster, 1987), p. 17.

51   Ibid. p. 19.

52   Ibid. p. 25.

53   Ibid. p. 25.

54   Ibid. p. 26.

55   Ibid. p. 27.

56   Ibid. p. 38.

57   Ibid. p. 40.

58   Ibid. p. 40.

59   Ibid. p. 60.

60   Plato, *The Republic*, Book VII.

61   Bloom, *The Closing of the American Mind*, p. 67.

62   Ibid. p. 67.

Endnotes

63 Ibid. p. 85.

64 Ibid. p. 192.

65 Ibid. p. 80.

66 Christopher Hitchens, "The egg-head's egger-on," *London Review of Books*, 27 April 2000, repr. in Hitchens, *Unacknowledged Legislation*, p. 221.

67 Bloom, *The Closing of the American Mind*, p. 74.

68 Ibid. p. 266.

69 Ibid. p. 147.

70 Hitchens, "The egg-head's egger-on," p. 221.

71 Bloom, *The Closing of the American Mind*, p. 312.

72 Ibid. p. 27.

73 Ibid. p. 329.

74 Ibid. p. 121.

75 Ibid. p. 382.

76 Ibid. p. 204.

77 Palmer and Pangle (eds.), *Political Philosophy and the Human Soul*, p. 5.

78 Irving Kristol, *Reflections of a Neoconservative: Looking Back, Looking Ahead* (New York: Basic Books, 1983), pp. xiv–xv.

79 Mark Gerson, *The Essential Neoconservative Reader* (Reading, Ma: Addison-Wesley, 1996), p. xiii.

80 Kristol, *Neoconservatism*, p. 6.

81 See "Memoirs of a 'Cold Warrior'" in Kristol, *Neoconservatism*, p. 457.

82 Irving Kristol, "'Civil Liberties,' 1952—A Study in Confusion," *Commentary*, March 1952.

83 Irving Kristol, "On 'Negative Liberalism,'" *Encounter*, January 1954.

84 Irving Kristol, "My Cold War," *The National Interest*, Spring 1993, republished in Kristol, *Neoconservatism*, p. 485.

85 Kristol, *Neoconservatism*, p. x.

86 Irving Kristol, "Confessions of a True, Self-confessed—Perhaps the Only—'Neoconservative,'" *Public Opinion*, October /November, 1979, p. 50.

87 Quoted in Michael S. Joyce, "The Common Man's Uncommon Intellectual" in Christopher DeMuth and William Kristol (eds), *The Neoconservative Imagination: Essays in Honor of Irving Kristol* (Washington: The AEI Press, 1995), p. 66.

88 Kristol, "My Cold War," p. 486.

89 Interview with Mark Gerson, quoted in Gerson, *The Neoconservative Vision* (Lanham, Md: Madison Books, 1997), p. 7.

90 Kristol, "My Cold War," p. 486.

91 Ibid. p. 486.

Endnotes

92 Philip Selznick, "Irving Kristol's Moral Realism" in DeMuth and Kristol (eds), *The Neoconservative Imagination*, p. 19 ff.

93 Kristol, "My Cold War," p. 484.

94 Cited in Gerson, The Neoconservative Vision, p. 17. Niebuhr quote, in *The Children of Light and the Children of Darkness* (New York: Scribner's, 1944), p. xi.

95 See Leon R. Kass, "The Need for Piety and Law: A Kristol-Clear Case" in DeMuth and Kristol, *The Neoconservative Imagination*, p. 112.

96 Robert Glasgow, "An interview with Irving Kristol," *Psychology Today*, February 1974.

97 Irving Kristol, "Spiritual Roots of Capitalism and Socialism" in Michael Novak (ed.), *Capitalism and Socialism: A Theological Inquiry* (Washington: AEI, 1991).

98 Interviewed on *The Power of Nightmares*, aired on BBC2, 27 October 2004.

99 Kristol, *Neoconservatism*, p. 34.

100 Michael Novak, "Review of 'Two Cheers for Capitalism,'" *Commentary*, July 1978.

101 Irving Kristol, *Two Cheers for Capitalism* (New York: Basic Books, 1978), p. 90.

102 Ibid. p. 91.

103 Irwin Stelzer, "A Third Cheer for Capitalism" in DeMuth and Kristol (eds), *The Neoconservative Imagination*, p. 105 ff.

104 Kristol, *Two Cheers for Capitalism*, p. 57.

105 Gerson, *The Neoconservative Vision*, p. 352.

106 Irving Kristol, "Congressional Right has it wrong," *Wall Street Journal*, 18 November 1985.

107 Irving Kristol, "From the Land of the Free to the Big PX," *New York Times Magazine*, 20 December 1964.

CHAPTER TWO

1 Kenneth Weinstein, "Philosophic Roots, the Role of Leo Strauss, and the War in Iraq" in Irwin Stelzer (ed.), *Neoconservatism* (London: Atlantic Books, 2004), p. 208.

2 Irving Kristol, *Neoconservatism: The Autobiography of an Idea* (Chicago: Elephant Paperbacks, 1999), p. 7.

3 David Brooks, "Lonely campus voices," *New York Times*, 27 September 2003.

4 Max Boot, "Myths About Neoconservatism," *Foreign Policy*, January/February 2004, repr. Stelzer (ed.), *Neoconservatism*, p. 47.

5 Stelzer, *Neoconservatism*, p. 4.

Endnotes

6   Norman Podhoretz, "Neoconservatism: A Eulogy," *Commentary*, March 1996.

7   Irving Kristol, "The Neoconservative Persuasion," *Weekly Standard*, 25 August 2003, repr. Stelzer (ed.), *Neoconservatism*, p. 33.

8   James Q. Wilson, "Neoconservatism: Pro and Con," *Partisan Review*, Vol. 4, 1980, p. 509.

9   Kristol, "The Neoconservative Persuasion," p. 36.

10 Daniel Moynihan and Nathan Glazer, *Beyond the Melting Pot* (Massachusetts: Massachusetts Institute of Technology, 1965), p. v.

11 Mark Gerson, *The Neoconservative Vision* (Lanham, MD: Madison Books, 1997), pp. 98–101.

12 March 1975.

13 Daniel Moynihan, *A Dangerous Place* (Boston: Little, Brown, 1978), p. 158: on Waldheim, see Simon Wiesenthal, *Justice not Vengeance* (London: Weidenfeld & Nicolson, 1989), pp. 310–22.

14 James Q. Wilson, "Gentleman, Politician, Scholar," *Public Interest*, Summer 2003.

15 For the complete text of Moynihan's speech, see Mark Gerson (ed.), *The Essential Neoconservative Reader* (Reading, MA: Addison-Wesley, 1996), pp. 93–9.

16 James Q. Wilson, "Gentleman, Politician, Scholar."

17 Theodor Herzl, The Jewish State (London: Henry Pordes, 1993), p. 26.

18 Stefan Halper and Jonathan Clarke, *America Alone: The Neoconservatives and the Global Order* (Cambridge: Cambridge University Press, 2004), p. 46.

19 Jeane Kirkpatrick, "Dictatorships and Double Standards," *Commentary*, November 1979, repr. in Gerson (ed.), *The Essential Neoconservative Reader*, pp. 163–89, specifically p. 188.

20 Ibid., p. 182.

21 James Mann, *Rise of the Vulcans: The History of Bush's War Cabinet* (New York:Viking 2004), p. 94.

22 Ibid., p. 121.

23 Jeane Kirkpatrick, "Neoconservatism as a Response to the Counterculture" in Stelzer (ed.), *Neoconservatism*, p. 239.

24 Ibid., p. 236.

25 Ibid., p. 236.

26 Allan Bloom, *The Closing of the American Mind* (New York: Simon and Schuster, 1987), p. 326.

27 Kirkpatrick, "Neoconservatism as a Response to the Counterculture," p. 240.

28 Quoted in Gerson, *The Neoconservative Vision*, p. 176.

Endnotes

29 Norman Podhoretz, "The Future Danger," *Commentary*, April 1981.

30 David Frum, *The Right Man* (London: Weidenfeld & Nicolson, 2003), p. 243.

31 Mann, *Rise of the Vulcans*, p. 145.

32 Bloom, *The Closing of the American Mind*, pp. 141–2.

33 Leo Strauss, *On Tyranny* (Chicago: University of Chicago Press, 2000), p. 23.

34 Francis Fukuyama, *The End of History and the Last Man* (London: Penguin, 1992), p. 280.

35 Quoted in Stelzer (ed.), *Neoconservatism*, p. 10.

36 See Kirkpatrick's contribution to "How Has the United States Met its Major Challenges since 1945?" *Commentary*, November 1985.

37 See Fukuyama, *The End of History and the Last Man*, p. 281–2 and notes 4–6 of Chapter 26, "Toward a Pacific Union," p. 385.

38 Irving Kristol, "The Emergence of Two Republican Parties" in *Neoconservatism*, p. 357.

39 Quoted in Gerson, *The Neoconservative Vision*, p. 166.

40 Jacob Weisberg, "The Cult of Leo Strauss," *Newsweek*, 3 August 1987.

41 Irving Kristol, "A conservative welfare state," *Wall Street Journal*, 14 June 1993.

42 Brigitte Berger and Peter Berger, "Our conservatism and theirs," *Commentary*, October 1986.

43 Francis Fukuyama, "A reply to my critics," *National Interest*, Autumn 1989.

44 Francis Wheen, *How Mumbo-Jumbo Conquered the World* (London: Fourth Estate, 2004), p.76.

45 See for instance Joel Achenbach, "The clash," *Washington Post*, 16 December 2001.

46 Fukuyama, *The End of History*, p. 303; see especially pp. 303–7.

47 Fukuyama, "A reply to my critics."

48 Francis Fukuyama, "The End of History?," *National Interest*, Summer 1989.

49 Fukuyama, *The End of History*, p. xii.

50 "Responses to Fukuyama," *National Interest*, Summer 1989.

51 Ibid.

52 Ibid.

53 Fukuyama, *The End of History*, p. 70.

54 Wheen, *How Mumbo-Jumbo Conquered the World*, pp. 66–71. Incidentally, since Wheen is keen to highlight the punctuational curiosities of both Huntington and Fukuyama's work, as well as criticizing the didacticism

of both, it is interesting to note that Wheen crucially misquotes Fukuyama on p. 67 of his book, turning Fukuyama's "We may be witnessing"
into the rather less humble "What we are witnessing."

55 Philip Bobbitt, "Bobbitt on Bobbitt," *Open Democracy*, 4 November
2002. For Fukuyama on the resurgence of nationalism, see *The End of
History*, pp. 266–75; on Islamic resurgence see pp. 235–6.

56 Samuel Huntington, *The Clash of Civilizations and the Remaking of World
Order* (London: Free Press, 2002), p. 31.

57 Ibid., p. 31.

58 Allan Bloom, in "Responses to Fukuyama," *National Interest*, Summer
1989.

59 Fukuyama, *The End of History*, p. 16.

60 Joshua Muravchik, "Patrick J. Buchanan and the Jews," *Commentary*, January 1991; Gerson, *The Neoconservative Vision*, pp. 315–16.

61 See Dennis Ross quoted in Mann, *Rise of the Vulcans*, p. 190. Also see
interview with Paul Wolfowitz by Radek Sikorski, *Prospect*, 1 December
2004 and American Enterprise Institute, 16 November 2004.

62 William Kristol and Robert Kagan, "Introduction: National Interest and
Global Responsibility" in Kagan and Kristol (ed.), *Present Dangers: Crisis
and Opportunity in American Foreign and Defense Policy* (San Francisco:
Encounter, 2000), p. 19.

63 Margaret Thatcher, "New Threats for Old," from a lecture delivered in
Fulton, Missouri, 9 March 1996, repr. in Stelzer (ed.), *Neoconservatism*, p.
94.

64 Mann, *Rise of the Vulcans*, p. 81. The Pentagon Study was declassified in
2003.

65 Paul Wolfowitz, "Victory Came Too Easily," *National Interest*, Spring
1994.

66 Jay Winik, "The Neoconservative Construction," *Foreign Policy*, Winter
1988/9.

67 Kristol, *Neoconservatism*, p. 40.

68 Ibid., p.xi.

69 Norman Podhoretz, "Neoconservatism: A Eulogy."

70 AEI Bradley Lecture Series, published 15 January 1996.

71 Ibid.

72 Charles Krauthammer, "Universal Dominion: Toward a Unipolar
World," *National Interest*, Winter 1989/90.

73 Charles Krauthammer, "The Unipolar Moment," *Foreign Affairs*, Winter
1990/1.

74 Richard Perle, 2001 interview with Brendan Simms in Simms, *Unfinest*

Endnotes

Hour: Britain and the Destruction of Bosnia (London: Allen Lane, 2001), p. 339.

75 Joshua Muravchik, "Conservatives for Clinton," *New Republic*, November 1992.

76 Quoted in Fred Barnes, "Neocons for Clinton: They're Back!," *New Republic*, 7 March 1992.

77 Joshua Muravchik in Stelzer (ed.), *Neoconservatism*, p. 254. Also "Lament of a Clinton Supporter," *Commentary*, August 1993.

78 Quoted in Simms, *Unfinest Hour*, p. 54.

79 "What the West must do in Bosnia," *Wall Street Journal*, 2 September 1993.

80 Halper and Clarke, *America Alone*, p. 90.

81 Letter to the President on Milosevic, 20 September 1998, Project for the New American Century.

82 Interview in *Independent*, 23 September 2004.

83 Norman Podhoretz, "Strange Bedfellows: A Guide to the New Foreign Policy Debates," *Commentary*, December 1999.

84 Robert Kagan, *Paradise and Power* (London, Atlantic Books, 2003), p. 42.

85 Ibid., p. 25.

86 Lawrence F. Kaplan and William Kristol, *The War over Iraq: Saddam's Tyranny and America's Mission* (San Francisco: Encounter, 2003), p. 120.

87 Kagan, *Paradise and Power*, p. 46.

88 See David Frum and Richard Perle on Major Pierre-Henri Bunel's leaking of target information in *An End to Evil* (New York: Random House, 2003), pp. 237–8 and note.

89 Michael Ignatieff, *Virtual War* (New York: Picador, 2001), p. 164. See also Lawrence Freedman, "The Revolution in Strategic Affairs," Adelphi Paper 31, International Institute for Strategic Studies, 1998.

90 Ignatieff, Virtual War, p. 151.

91 Comments of Governor George W. Bush, Memorandum to Opinion Leaders from Gary Schmitt, Project for the New American Century, 7 May 1999.

92 Tony Blair, "Doctrine of the International Community," speech delivered in Chicago, 24 April 1999, repr. Stelzer (ed.), *Neoconservatism*, p. 107.

93 See Brendan Simms, "Bush's ideas men" (review of Halper and Clarke's America Alone), *Sunday Times*, 11 July 2004.

94 Kagan, *Paradise and Power*, p. 51.

95 Statement of Principles, Project for the New American Century, 3 June 1997. Available through www.newamericancentury.org

96 Kagan and Kristol, *Present Dangers*, p. 9.

Endnotes

97   Ibid., p. 21.

98   Ibid., p. 20.

99   Ibid., p. 16.

100 Ibid, p. 13.

101 Ibid., p. 110.

102 Project for the New American Century, Open Letter to President Clinton, 26 January 1998.

103 Ibid., p. 316.

104 Ibid., p. 310.

105 Ibid., p. 314.

106 Ibid., p. 318.

107 Ibid., pp. 322–23.

108 Ibid., pp. 333–34.

109 Ibid., p. 320.

110 Mann, *Rise of the Vulcans*, p. 316.

111 Fukuyama, *The End of History*, pp. 4–5.

112 Kagan and Kristol, *Present Dangers*, p. 8–9

113 Halper and Clarke, *America Alone*, p. 139.

114 Mann, *Rise of the Vulcans*, pp. 313–14.

115 Ibid., pp. 298–9.

116 Kagan, *Paradise and Power*, p. 85.

117 Norman Podhoretz, "World War IV: How It Started, What It Means, and Why We Have to Win," *Commentary*, September 2004.

118 Rumsfeld comment of 8 October 2001. Quoted by Paul Wolfowitz in his Speech to the Committee on the Present Danger and the Foundation for the Defense of Democracies, Mayflower Hotel, Washington, DC, Wednesday, 29 September 2004.

119 Quoted in Byron York, "Clinton Has No Clothes: What 9/11 Revealed About the Ex-president," *National Review*, 17 December 2001.

120 Secretary Rumsfeld with US Troops at Bagram Airfield, Afghanistan, 16 December 2001. Transcript via Defense Department website.

121 Bob Woodward, *Plan of Attack* (London: Simon & Schuster, 2004), p. 281.

122 Kagan, *Paradise and Power*, p. 28.

123 Norman Podhoretz, 'World War IV."

124 President Bush's Acceptance Speech to the Republican National Convention, 2 September 2004.

125 Mark Steyn, "The Right Side of History," *Spectator*, 5 March 2005.

126 Cited in Jeffrey Gedmin, "The Prospect for Neoconservatism in Germany" in Stelzer (ed.), *Neoconservatism*, p. 291.

Endnotes

127 Robert Fisk, "We are being set up for a war against Saddam," *Independent*, 4 December 2002.

128 Michael Gove, "The deadly Mail," *Spectator*, 17 April 2004.

129 Halper and Clarke, *America Alone*, p. 181.

130 Quoted in "Bush nominates weapons expert as envoy to U.N.," *New York Times*, 8 March 2005.

CHAPTER THREE

1 "Conclave begins with day of ritual," *Washington Post*, 19 April 2005.

2 Francis Fukuyama, *The End of History and the Last Man* (London: Penguin, 1992), p. 332.

3 "Relativism" in Leo Strauss, *The Rebirth of Classical Political Rationalism, Essays and Lectures by Leo Strauss* (Chicago: University of Chicago Press, 1989), p. 17.

4 See Allan Bloom, "Reply to Fukuyama," *National Interest*, Summer 1989; and Fukuyama, *The End of History*, p. 278.

5 Marianne Talbot in *Sunday Times*, 24 July 1994. Cited in Melanie Phillips, *All Must Have Prizes* (London: Little, Brown, 1996), p. 221.

6 For further discussion of these and other issues, see Mark Steyn, "Expensive Illiterates: Victimhood & Education," *The New Criterion*, January 2004.

7 Arthur M. Schlesinger, Jr., *The Disuniting of America* (New York: Norton, rev. ed., 1992), p. 43.

8 "Lottery denies Samaritans 'for neglecting minorities,'" *The Times*, 10 February 2005.

9 "Refuge for homeless may lose grant for saying mealtime grace," *Daily Telegraph*, 3 May 2005.

10 Fukuyama, *The End of History*, p. 332.

11 Leo Strauss, *The City and Man* (Chicago: University of Chicago Press, 1964), p. 1.

12 Mark Steyn, "The Slyer Virus: The West's Anti-westernism," *The New Criterion*, February 2002.

13 Amy Gutmann, "Democratic Citizenship" in Matha C. Nussbaum et al., *For Love of Country: Debating the Limits of Patriotism* (Boston: Beacon Press, 1996), pp. 68–9.

14 See, for instance, Ali's account of one of his television performances in *The Clash of Fundamentalisms* (London: Verso, 2002), p. 293n.

15 See Noam Chomsky, "Reply to Hitchens," *The Nation Online*, 1 October 2001. Christopher Hitchens, "A Rejoinder to Noam Chomsky," *The*

Nation Online, 15 October 2001, repr. *Love, Poverty and War: Journeys and Essays* (New York: Nation Books, 2004), pp. 421–7.

16 Hitchens, "A Rejoinder to Noam Chomsky."

17 See transcript of speech at ww.zmag.org/GlobalWatch/chomskymit.htm

18 David Horowitz and Ronald Radosh, "Noam Chomsky's Jjihad against America," *Frontpage Magazine*, 19 December 2001.

19 "Noam Chomsky: You Ask the Questions," *Independent*, 4 December 2003.

20 Mark Steyn, "Democrats Down a Hole," *National Review*, 31 December 2003.

21 Hitchens, "A Rejoinder to Noam Chomsky."

22 Arundhati Roy, *The Ordinary Person's Guide to Empire* (London: Flamingo, 2004), p. 47.

23 Ibid. pp. 33–4.

24 Arundhati Roy, "Come September," *Guardian*, 26 September 2002, repr. *The Ordinary Person's Guide to Empire*, p. 33.

25 Roy, *The Ordinary Person's Guide to Empire*, p. 76.

26 Benjamin Netanyahu, *Fighting Terrorism: How Democracies Can Defeat Domestic and International Terrorism* (New York: Farrar Straus Giroux, 1995), p. 82.

27 Roy, *The Ordinary Person's Guide to Empire*, pp. 26–7.

28 Netanyahu, *Fighting Terrorism*, p. 128.

29 See David Horowitz, *Unholy Alliance: Radical Islam and the American Left* (Washington: Regnery, 2004), p. 11.

30 Eric Foner in "11 September," *London Review of Books*, 4 October 2001.

31 Horowitz, *Unholy Alliance*, p. 32.

32 See *Guardian* Letters, 1 October 2002.

33 Response to Anthony Browne's 11 August 2004 *Times* piece "This sinister brotherhood." Anonymous of MAB, "MAB responds to vile attack," MAB online, 12 August 2004.

34 Horowitz, *Unholy Alliance*, p. 32.

35 Mary Wakefield, "I don't lie. Whoops, there I go again," *Daily Telegraph*, 9 January 2004.

36 "Philosophers and Kings," *Economist*, 19 June 2003.

37 Geoffrey Wheatcroft, "Blair still took us to war on a lie," *Guardian*, 5 March 2005.

38 Anthony Glees and Philip H. J. Davies, *Spinning the Spies: Intelligence, Open Government and the Hutton Inquiry* (London: Social Affairs Unit, 2004), p. 91.

Endnotes

39 Joshua Muravchik, "Conservatives for Clinton," *New Republic*, November 1992.

40 Peter Stothard, *30 Days: A Month at the Heart of Blair's War* (London: HarperCollins, 2003), p. 42.

41 See Peter J. Boyer, "The Believer," *New Yorker*, 1 November 2004.

42 See William Shawcross, *Allies: The United States, Britain, Europe and the War in Iraq* (London: Atlantic Books, 2003), p. 29.

43 Saddam Hussein in January 2000, celebrating the anniversary of the Iraqi armed forces. Quoted on the title page of "Regime Finance and Procurement," Vol. I of the Comprehensive Report of the Special Advisor to the DCI on Iraq's wmd, 30 September 2004.

44 Rodger W. Claire, *Raid on the Sun: Inside Israel's Secret Campaign that Denied Saddam the Bomb* (New York: Broadway Books, 2004), p. 40.

45 Ibid., p. 240.

46 *Review of Intelligence into Weapons of Mass Destruction*, Chaired by Lord Butler, 14 July 2004, paragraph 499, p. 123.

47 Jeffrey Goldberg, "The great terror," *New Yorker*, 25 March 2002.

48 Shawcross, *Allies*, p. 103.

49 See *Frankfurter Allgemeine Sonntagszeitung*, 16 February 2003.

50 "Ministers play down threat of smallpox attack," *Deutsche Welle*, 19 February 2003.

51 "The Germans and smallpox," Andrew Sullivan blog, online, 18 February 2003.

52 Lawrence F. Kaplan and Wiliam Kristol, *The War Over Iraq: Saddam's Tyranny and America's Mission* (San Francisco: Encounter, 2003), p. 92.

53 John Pilger, "Blair is a coward," *Mirror*, 29 January 2003.

54 Toby Harnden, "Hoping for the worst," *Spectator*, 15 May 2004.

55 Ibid.

56 Tariq Ali, "Re-colonizing Iraq," *New Left Review*, May/June 2003.

57 BBC *Newsnight*, interview with John Harris, 18 January 2005.

58 Naomi Klein, "Bring Najaf to New York," *Nation*, 13 September 2004.

59 Ward Churchill, " 'Some people push back': On the justice of roosting chickens," online, 11 September 2001.

60 Donald Rumsfeld, "The price of freedom in Iraq," *New York Times*, 19 March 2004.

61 Robert Fisk, "An illegal and immoral war, betrayed by images that reveal our racism," *Independent*, 7 May 2004.

62 Katha Pollitt, "Show & Tell in Abu Ghraib," *The Nation*, 24 May 2004.

63 Maureen Dowd, "Shocking and Awful," *New York Times*, 6 May 2004.

Endnotes

64 Mary Ann Sieghart, "The case for the war undermined," *The Times*, 13 May 2004.

65 Mark Steyn, "This is one armchair warmonger still fighting," *Daily Telegraph*, 30 May 2004.

66 Speech by President George W. Bush at United States Army War College, Pennsylvania, 24 May 2004.

67 President Bush, speech to the American Enterprise Institute, 26 February 2003.

68 See Mahdi Obeidi and Kurt Pitzer, *The Bomb in my Garden* (Hoboken, N.J.: John Wiley & Sons, 2004), *passim*.

69 Mahdi Obeidi, "Saddam, the bomb, and me," *New York Times*, 6 October 2004.

70 CNN, 26 June 2003.

71 See Comprehensive Report of the Special Advisor to the DCI on Iraq's WMD, 30 September 2004 (Duelfer Report), Vol. I, pp. 119–22, 274–6. Early findings, as with the interim testimony of David Kay, summarized in David E. Sanger and Thom Shanker, "A region inflamed," *New York Times*, 1 December 2003.

72 See John Lloyd, *What the Media Are Doing to Our Politics*, p. 209.

73 Oriana Fallaci, *A Man* (New York: Simon & Schuster, 1980), p. 256; *The Rage and the Pride* (New York: Rizzoli, 2002), p. 176.

74 Roger Scruton on Tom Nairn in *England: An Elegy* (London: Chatto & Windus, 2000), p. 254.

75 Terry Eagleton, "A different way of death," *Guardian*, 26 January 2005.

76 Richard Gott, "The prime minister is a war criminal," *Guardian*, 26 April 2005.

77 Roy, *The Ordinary Person's Guide to Empire*, p. 84.

78 Yasmin Alibhai-Brown, *Evening Standard*, 29 June 2004.

79 Michael Moore, "Heads up . . . from Michael Moore," michaelmoore.com, 14 April 2004.

80 Pip Hinman interview with John Pilger, "Truth and lies in the 'war on terror,' *Green Left Weekly*, 28 January 2004.

81 *Amnesty International Report 2005*, foreword by Irene Khan, Secretary General of Amnesty International.

82 Comments during an interview with Howard Dean on WOAI Radio, San Antonio, 5 December 2005.

Endnotes

CHAPTER FOUR

1 Tony Blair, "Doctrine of the international community," from a speech delivered at the Economic Club of Chicago, 24 April 1999, repr. Irwin Stelzer (ed.), *Neoconservatism* (London: Atlantic Books, 2004), p. 113.

2 Irwin Stelzer (ed.), *Neoconservatism* (London: Atlantic Books, 2004), p. 20.

3 See "CIA May Need Decade To Rebuild Clandestine Service," Reuters, 1 January 2006.

4 Robert Skidelsky, *The World After Communism* (London: Macmillan, 1995), p. xiii.

5 See especially Owen Harries, "The Australia Connection" in Christopher DeMuth and William Kristol (eds), *The Neoconservative Imagination: Essays in Honor of Irving Kristol* (Washington: The AEI Press, 1995), pp. 35 ff, esp. p. 42.

6 Francis Fukuyama, *The End of History* (London: Penguin, 1992), p. 307.

7 Irving Kristol, "Thoughts on Reading About a Summer-Camp Covered with Garbage," *New York Times Magazine*, 17 November 1974.

8 Richard John Neuhaus, "Combat ready," *National Review*, 2 May 1994.

9 T. S. Eliot, Choruses from "The Rock," VI.

10 For further discussion of this matter, the author recommends Caroline Cox and John Marks, *The "West," Islam and Islamism* (London: Civitas, 2003) and Robert Spencer, *Islam Unveiled* (San Francisco: Encounter Books, 2002).

11 Leo Strauss, *Natural Right and History* (Chicago: University of Chicago Press, 1999), p. 5.

12 Johann Hari, "Smells like teen spirit?" *Independent*, 7 March 2003.

13 See especially Melanie Phillips, *All Must Have Prizes* (London: Little Brown, 1996), *passim* and Allan Bloom, *passim*.

14 Irving Kristol, "Republican virtue v. servile institutions," *The Alternative: An American Spectator*, February 1975.

15 Saul Bellow, *Ravelstein* (London: Viking, 2000), p. 19.

16 Leo Strauss, *Liberalism: Ancient and Modern* (New York: Basic Books, 1968), p. 5.

17 Robert H. Bork, "Culture and Kristol" in DeMuth and Kristol (eds), *The Neoconservative Imagination*, p. 135.

18 Adam Wolfson, "Conservatives and Neoconservatives" in Stelzer (ed.), *Neoconservatism*, p. 217.

19 See discussion of this in Roger Scruton's *Conservative Thinkers: Essays from "The Salisbury Review"* (London: Claridge Press, 1988), pp. 8–9.

20 Irving Kristol, "A conservative welfare state," *Wall Street Journal*, 14 June 1993, repr. Stelzer (ed.), Neoconservatism, p. 147.

Endnotes

21 Gertrude Himmelfarb, *Poverty and Compassion: The Moral Imagination of the Late Victorians* (New York: Vintage Books, 1991), p. 6.

22 Fukuyama, *The End of History*, p. 296.

23 See for instance in the UK, James Bartholomew, *The Welfare State We're In* (London: Politico's, 2004), *passim*.

24 James Q. Wilson and George L. Kelling, "Broken windows" in Stelzer (ed.), *Neoconservatism*, pp. 154ff.

25 Michelle Malkin, *In Defense of Internment* (Washington: Regnery, 2004), p. xxii.

26 Peter Brimelow, *Alien Nation: Common Sense about America's Immigration Disaster* (New York: HarperPerennial, 1996), p. 241.

27 Samuel P. Huntington, *Who Are We?* (London: Free Press, 2004), p.226.

28 Ibid, p. 239.

29 Ibid, p. 318.

30 Samuel P. Huntington, *Who Are We?* (London: Free Press, 2004), p. 171.

31 Irving Kristol, "The Tragedy of Multiculturalism" in Kristol, *Neoconservatism: The Autobiography of an Idea* (Chicago: Elephant Paperbacks, 1999), p. 52.

32 See especially on the matter of population growth Anthony Browne, *Do We Need Mass Immigration?* (London: Civitas, 2002), pp. 37–47.

33 "Vote for EU constitution or risk new Holocaust, says Brussels," *Daily Telegraph*, 9 May 2005.

34 See also George F. Will, "The Slow Undoing: The Assault on, and Underestimation of, Nationality" in Stelzer (ed.), *Neoconservatism*, pp. 129ff.

35 Allan Bloom, *The Closing of the American Mind* (New York: Simon and Schuster, 1987), pp. 320–1.

36 Roger Scruton, *The Need for Nations* (London: Civitas, 2004), p. 16.

37 See "German ambassador's VE Day message: the war ended 60 years ago—get over it," *Sunday Telegraph*, 8 May 2005.

38 Matthias Matussek, "My personal VE day," *Open Democracy*, 6 May 2005.

39 Leo Strauss, *Natural Right*, p. 2.

40 Will, "The Slow Undoing," p. 133.

41 See, for example, *Sunday Times*, News in Brief, 22 May 2005.

42 David Frum and Richard Perle, *An End to Evil* (New York: Random House, 2003), p. 266.

43 Reinhold Niebuhr was commenting on the League of Nations' failure to punish Japan for its invasion of Manchuria, *Moral Man in Immoral Society: A Study in Ethics and Politics* (New York: Scribner's, 1932), p. 110.

44 Statement by the Action Council for Peace in the Balkans, quoted in Ste

Endnotes

fan Halper and Jonathan Clarke, *America Alone: The Neoconservatives and the Global Order* (Cambridge: Cambridge University Press, 2004), p. 93.

45 Robert Cooper, *The Breaking of Nations* (London: Atlantic, 2003), p. 58.

46 Mark Steyn, "Let's quit the U.N.," *Spectator*, 8 February 2003.

47 Scruton, *The Need for Nations*, p. 9.

48 The disgusting piece was by one Rohan Hayasekera, who continued to defend his piece in spite (or perhaps because) of protest and notice not afforded to *Index* for many years.

49 Joshua Muravchik quoted in interview, 1994, with Mark Gerson, in Gerson, *The Neoconservative Vision* (Lanham, MD: Madison Books, 1997), p. 106.

50 See "Beyond the barbarians at the gate." Timothy Garton-Ash interviewed by Dominic Hilton, *open Democracy*, 24 February 2005.

51 Frum and Perle, *An End to Evil*, p. 250.

52 Condoleezza Rice, "The President's National Security Strategy," from a lecture in New York, 1 October 2002, repr. Stelzer (ed.), *Neoconservatism*, p. 83.

53 Frum and Perle, *An End to Evil*, p. 252.

54 Michael Gove, "The Very British Roots of Neoconservatism and Its Lessons for British Conservatives" in Stelzer (ed.), *Neoconservatism*, p. 274 and *passim*.

55 See Rafsanjani's Al-Quds Day sermon at Tehran University on 14 December 2001, MEMRI Special Dispatch Series No. 325, 3 January 2002; Ahmadinejad's comments at Tehran conference, MEMRI Special Dispatch Series No. 1013, 28 October 2005.

56 Re Iran's capabilities, see especially "Iran's Strategic Weapons Programmes: A Net Assessment," The International Institute for Strategic Studies, London, 2005.

57 Transatlantic Trends 2003, www.transatlantictrends.org

58 Alasdair Palmer, "This is al-Qa'eda Rule 18: 'You must claim you were tortured,'" *Daily Telegraph*, 30 January 2005.

59 See, for instance, the leading article "Terror endures," *The Times* (London), 5 August 2004.

60 Bernard-Henri Lévy, *Who Killed Daniel Pearl?* (London: Duckworth, 2003), p. 243.

61 "Al-Qa'eda terror trio linked to London School of 'Extremists,'" *Daily Telegraph*, 27 January 2002.

62 See Sir John Stevens interviewed by John Kampfner, *New Statesman*, 2 August 2004.

Endnotes

63 See Tariq Ali, "The price of occupation," *Guardian*, 8 July 2005 and Dilpazier Aslam, "We rock the boat," *Guardian*, 13 July 2005.

64 Frum and Perle, *An End to Evil*, p. 35.

65 Niall Ferguson, "The 'E' word," *Wall Street Journal*, 6 June 2003.

66 See Norman Podhoretz, "World War IV: How It Started, What It Means, and Why We Have to Win," *Commentary*, September 2004; and "The war against World War IV," *Commentary*, February 2005.

67 Tony Blankley, *The West's Last Chance* (Washington: Regnery), p. 185.

68 Stefan Halper and Jonathan Clarke, *America Alone: The Neo-Conservatives and the Global Order* (Cambridge: Cambridge UP, 2004), p. 313.

69 Paul Wolfowitz, "Support our troops," *Wall Street Journal*, 2 September 2003.

70 David Ignatius, "Beirut's Berlin Wall," *Washington Post*, 23 February 2005.

71 Irving Kristol, "On Conservatism and Capitalism" in Kristol, *Neoconservatism*, p. 233.

72 Fukuyama, *The End of History*, p. 265.

73 Fukuyama, *The End of History*, p. 330.

74 See, for instance, Robert Kagan, *Paradise and Power* (London, Atlantic Books, 2003), p. 81.

75 See also David Horowitz, *Unholy Alliance: Radical Islam and the American Left* (Washington: Regnery, 2004), *passim*.

76 President Bush's inaugural address, 20 January 2005. Full text on the White House website.

77 Tony Blair, "Doctrine of the international community," speech given in Chicago, 24 April 1999, repr. Stelzer (ed.), *Neoconservatism*, pp. 112–13.

78 Tony Blair, speech to the US Congress, 18 July 2003. Full text on the Downing Street website.

79 See, for instance, Halper and Clarke, *America Alone*, p. 338. Francis Fukuyama, "After Neoconservatism," *New York Times*, 19 February 2006.

INDEX

Index

Index

A NOTE ON THE TYPE

Neoconservatism has been set in Monotype Garamond, a French Renaissance type with a noble heritage extending back to the types cut by Francesco Griffo for Aldus Manutius in the late 1400s. Chosen by Stanley Morison as one of the first types to be revived by the Monotype Corporation, the roman was modeled after the types cut by Robert Estienne by Claude Garamond in Paris in the sixteenth century. At the time of the Monotype revival, Garamond had already become quite fashionable, appearing in a variety of guises in the catalogues of most of the major typefoundries – though the success of those types depended heavily on the specimen followed in the recutting. § *Claude Garamond is known to have cut only two italic types, neither of them as accomplished as his romans. For this reason, the italic currently paired with Garamond is based on the types of Robert Granjon, one of the first French punchcutters to abandon the Italian preference for roman capitals with italic lowercase. As a pair, the two types harmonize elegantly, amply displaying the "sparkle" so prized by typographers.*

DESIGN & COMPOSITION BY CARL W. SCARBROUGH